P9-AGS-958

From Jazz to Swing

Jazz History, Culture, and Criticism Series

William J. Kenney III, *Editor*

Books in this series

Jazz in Mind: Essays of the History and Meanings of Jazz,
edited by Reginald T. Buckner and Steven Weiland, 1991

*From Jazz to Swing: African-American Jazz Musicians
and Their Music, 1890-1935*
by Thomas J. Hennessey, 1994

From Jazz to Swing

African-American Jazz Musicians and Their Music, 1890 - 1935

Thomas J. Hennessey

Wayne State University Press   Detroit

Riverside Community College
Library
4800 Magnolia Avenue
Riverside, CA 92506

ML 3508 .H46 1994

Hennessey, Thomas J., 1945-

From jazz to swing

Copyright © 1994 by Wayne State University Press,
Detroit, Michigan 48201. All rights are reserved.
No part of this book may be reproduced without formal permission.
Manufactured in the United States of America.
98 97 96 95   5 4 3 2

Library of Congress Cataloging-in-Publication Data

Hennessey, Thomas J., 1945–
From jazz to swing : African-American jazz musicians and
their music, 1890–1935 / Thomas J. Hennessey.
p.   cm. — (Jazz history, culture, and criticism series)
Includes bibliographical references and index.
ISBN 0-8143-2178-X. — ISBN 0-8143-2179-8 (pbk.)
1. Jazz—History and criticism.   2. Jazz musicians—United States.   I. Title.   II. Series.
ML3508.H46   1994
781.65'0973—dc20   93-33865

DESIGNER
Mary Krzewinski

Contents

Preface 9   Acknowledgments 13

1

Raising the Curtain on Jazz   15

Territory Jazz Roots: 1890–1914   *16*
New Orleans   *20*
Chicago   *21*
New York City   *24*
Conclusion   *27*

2

Jazz Goes on Record 1914-1923   28

The Great Migration and New Entertainment Forms   *28*
Rise of the Dance Hall   *30*
The Impact of the Phonograph   *32*
New Orleans   *34*
Chicago   *36*
New York City   *41*
Conclusion   *48*

3

Territory Bands 1914-1923   49

East Coast   *49*
Southeast   *51*
Midwest   *54*
Northwest   *56*
West Coast   *58*
Southwest   *60*
Conclusion   *65*

CONTENTS

4

Chicago Sounds 1923-1929   67

Theater Bands   *70*
Ballrooms and Dancing Classes   *71*
Cabarets   *73*
Recording Sessions and Innovations   *76*
Conclusion   *80*

New York Scores 1923-1929   82

New York Trends   *84*
Fletcher Henderson and His Orchestra   *87*
Other New York Dance Jobs   *95*
New York Cabaret Bands   *98*
Conclusion   *101*

Territory Scuffles 1923-1929   103

East Coast   *104*
Southeast   *105*
Midwest   *109*
Northwest   *113*
West Coast   *114*
Southwest   *116*
Conclusion   *120*

7

The Rise of the National Bands 1929-1935   122

Duke Ellington and Irving Mills   *123*
Changing Business Conditions   *127*
Radio   *131*

Contents

Racism and Segregation in the Depression   *132*
The Impact of National Bands   *134*
Band Business Pyramid   *135*
The Emergence of the Swing Style   *136*
Conclusion   *138*

The Impact of the National Bands   140

New York: Home of National Bands   *140*
East Coast   *146*
Chicago   *147*
Midwest   *148*
Southeast   *149*
Northwest   *150*
West Coast   *151*
Southwest   *151*
Conclusion   *155*

Notes 157   Bibliography 199   Index 207

Preface

The history of jazz has often been told in isolation from the history of the American and particularly the African-American people. This needs to be changed. As a uniquely American music, jazz fits into the American heritage. This book presents the story of the black musicians who shaped the early years of jazz. It looks at them as musicians as well as members of the African-American and American communities.

The early periods of jazz, from its origins in the 1890s to the beginning of the Swing Era in 1935, saw enormous change in America. The impact of those changes on African-American jazz musicians helped to shape their music. This book traces that interaction.

Between 1890 and 1935, the United States changed from a rural, handmade, homemade culture to an urban, mass-produced, mass-consumed culture. Jazz as an art form and entertainment medium was a product of this shift. In this same period, the rise of disfranchisement and segregation increased the discrimination facing African-Americans. At the same time, economic factors during World War I and the 1920s reduced opportunities for small farmers and farm workers but increased industrial jobs. These factors created the Great Migration from the rural South to the urban North. This movement changed race relations and African-American culture. Jazz and jazz musicians were part of this change.

Their participation In the shared experiences of many Americans enabled African-American jazz musicians to produce an art that entertained mass audiences. Still, the lives of black jazz musicians were not typical of the average American or black American. These differences may have shaped the music even more than their similarities.

As artists, these musicians had perceptions and, more importantly, a medium for expression missing in many Americans. They were unique among African-Americans since music was one of the few fields in which racial stereotypes and prejudice did not hinder black achievement. Like

9

all African-Americans in this period, they faced discrimination, but they did not have doors slammed completely in their faces.

This may in fact be the key to understanding one of the basic realities of the development of jazz. From within the perspective of the African-American community of 1890–1935, jazz was less a revolution against the values of mainstream America and more a way to "make it" into the mainstream. It was one of the very limited ways in which an African-American could receive recognition and economic success. Jazz was also one of the ways in which African-American culture had a direct impact on the larger society.

The history of jazz as a whole can be briefly divided into three periods. The first, 1890–1935, saw the development of the music from a variety of sources into a unified entertainment music for a mass audience. This movement was capped in the second period, the Swing Era of 1935–1945, in which jazz was *the* American popular music form. In the modern period, from 1945 to the present, jazz has evolved into a variety of art and popular music forms.

This book focuses on the first period and describes the process by which this music was created from within the life experiences of the artists. I have focused on African-American jazz musicians because jazz had its roots in the African-American community and culture. This history provides some insights into the place of African-Americans in a changing American society. Jazz is both an art form and a business product. I have placed jazz in those contexts.

I have divided the 1890–1935 period into four stages. During the 1890–1914 pre-history phase, the music developed out of the local experiences of musicians around the country. They experimented with African- and European-American musical traditions to create a new entertainment form. The results varied in the territories, New Orleans, Chicago, and New York, but shared common threads.

Between 1914 and 1923, the new music received a name, jazz, and a medium, the phonograph record. This increased the ability to document and study jazz. This period also saw the growth of the Great Migration and its transformation of African-American culture. Jazz clearly became a saleable commodity, but limited recordings by black artists restricted the role of black media models, leaving local musicians and audiences to develop their own versions of jazz. Local cultural traditions and business conditions created a wide variety of styles.

Between 1923 and 1929, large numbers of black jazz bands were recorded. These recordings showed the developing regional styles. However, as the decade went on, the New York sound of a group of young black musicians led by Fletcher Henderson and Don Redman began to dominate. These men and their counterparts around the country shared many of the experiences of the Black Renaissance of the 1920s. They had trained artistic skills which they used for personal expression and to satisfy a mass audience. Their success and the operation of the music business turned jazz into a mass-produced cultural commodity.

After 1929, the national nature of the band business and the pressures of the depression squeezed most regional styles out of existence. The rise of white gatekeepers in radio, records, business management, booking, and publicity increasingly limited the freedom of action of the black musicians. At the same time, this structure and their own talent created enormous opportunities for success for a few black musicians and entertainers such as Duke Ellington, Louis Armstrong, and Cab Calloway. To cash in on their popularity, they began national tours, which took away audiences and musical freedoms from the regional bands. By 1935, swing had become a national popular music and a learnable style. It was dominated by white bands beginning with Benny Goodman's Palomar ballroom appearances in the summer of 1935, the official beginning of the Swing era.

The transformation of jazz from a primarily local music rooted in black folk traditions to the tightly managed product of a national industry controlled by white businessmen and aimed at a predominantly white mass market paralleled the changing nature of American society. It also showed many of the problems facing African-Americans as the Great Migration brought them into an urban setting at precisely the time that the city became a dominant force in American life. The ability of the black jazz musicians to catch the spirit of that move created a music which was at the core of American popular culture in the Swing Era.

The demands of the national music industry helped to establish the professional, educated, middle-class oriented musician as the dominant figure in the black national bands and therefore on the jazz scene. Self-discipline, punctuality, good appearance, and reliability were as important as musical ability. Musical standards also shifted with more emphasis on reading and ensemble playing for most players while solo abilities were required only for certain key performers. The swing style was complex, using written arrangements which demanded full technical control by the musician of his instrument. The African-Americans who fit these demands experienced economic and artistic success.

Their accomplishments were muted by constant awareness of the limits placed on African-American achievement in American society by not only the legal segregation of the Southern states but also the systematic discrimination in the North and West. Also, their very commercial

11

success with white audiences challenged these men to define the musical boundaries of jazz in African-American and European-American terms. Their work kept them in frequent contact with whites, often on some terms of equality, while their daily lives were marked by discrimination. The ambivalent nature of this experience shaped the music and lives of black musicians in the movement from jazz to swing.

Acknowledgments

Any author builds up a great many debts over the process of completing a project. When the project takes as long to reach print as this one, those debts are enormous. I am afraid that I may miss many important contributors but let me at least try to reach most. I emphasize that the sole responsibility for the ultimate product in its strengths and particularly its weaknesses are mine. Many people have contributed over the years by both strengthening my views and directing me away from pitfalls.

This work began as a dissertation directed by George Fredrickson with strong support from Howard Becker and Sterling Stuckey. The original germ of the idea was developed in a seminar with Christopher Lasch who encouraged me that popular culture *was* worth studying.

The basic research was done at the Institute of Jazz Studies at Rutgers University-Newark whose staff was very accommodating. Charles Nanry, Richard Seidel, Dan Morgenstern, and others provided a variety of aid. The Chicago Public Library collections of the *Chicago Defender* and Works Progress Administration files were also very important resources. The libraries of Fayetteville State University, Northwestern University, University of California-Berkeley, Columbia University, Antioch College, and Cumberland County, North Carolina, helped in various ways.

A grant from the National Endowment for the Humanities directed by Gunther Schuller allowed me to study at New England Conservatory of Music where Jaki Byard's rehearsals confirmed some thoughts about the dynamics of big bands. Other NEH grants allowed me to participate in seminars led by Chadwick Hansen and Bonnie Wade. They and the other participants gave me interesting feedback on my project. John Varnum's stories of the lives of professional musicians in Montana and Elaine Pruitt's research into country musicians broadened my picture of the territory world. Olly Wilson and Scott DeVeaux were very understanding to a historian stomping around in their turf.

ACKNOWLEDGMENTS

My colleagues at Fayetteville State have been supportive in many ways. Special thanks go to Bob Collins, Joe Ross, Eric Moore, Garett Davis, George Barnes, who *was there* in so many ways, and all of my coworkers at WFSS. Ray Codrington, Malachi Sharpe, Wayne Waylette, Richard Jones, and the late Tom Gavin, illustrated much about the lives of territory jazz musicians by living that life.

I only met Walter C. Allen once, but his work on Fletcher Henderson was an invaluable guide and resource. I would like to thank two groups of people whom I have only met on paper but without whom this work in its present form would have been impossible. Dave Peyton, Walter Barnes, Sylvester Russell, Ragtime Billy Tucker and all of the entertainment correspondents of the *Chicago Defender* from 1910 through 1935 left a unique record of the African-American experience of that era. Also, the jazz writers of the 1930s–1960s caught that period through their interviews and memories. The two key men here were George Hoefer and Marshall Stearns whose columns and collections became the foundation of the irreplaceable Institute of Jazz Studies.

The key figures in the final stages of seeing this project into print were Lewis Erenburg, William Kenney, Mary Gillis, Lynn Trease, and Kendal Gladish. Each brought special skills to the task and I am thankful to them all. Finally, my family has lived with this project much longer than they or I expected: my mother, Florence, who lived to see it finished; and father, Noel; sister, Elizabeth; and mother-in-law, Mary Lees; all of whom did not. My sisters, brothers, and in-laws encouraged in various ways. And last, and certainly not least, I thank my wife, Mary Kay; daughters, Sarah and Eleanor; and son, Joseph.

1

Raising the Curtain on Jazz

J AZZ is a uniquely American music that comes from a special period in American history. This book will look at this music and its time to see what they can tell us about each other.

In 1890, only 35 percent of the population in the United States was urban. America was still a nation of farms and small towns, of handmade products and homemade music. Black Americans were concentrated in the sharecropping farms and towns of the rural South. By 1935, more than 56 percent of Americans lived in urban areas, and mass-produced culture dominated their lives. Life was more complex and segmented. Mass media and specialization in jobs increased greatly.

Black Americans were very much a part of that trend: moving in increasing numbers from farms to cities and from the South to the North in the "Great Migration"; changing from sharecropping to service and industrial jobs in the city; and exchanging the isolation of the farm and the security of the small town for the opportunities and problems of the urban ghetto.[1] Black jazz musicians experienced all of this, and out of it created an entertainment art that captured the spirit of the age.

Jazz began out of the complex black musical life of the late 1880s to 1914. While rooted in the oral folk music tradition of the black community, the music that would become known as jazz after 1914 began as various forms of entertainment music before recordings or the term jazz itself existed to give the form a special definition. It is important to see the birth of jazz in the musical and social life of this period.

FROM JAZZ TO SWING

In 1890, most black Americans lived in the rural areas and small towns of the South. That is not surprising since most Americans in 1890 still lived on farms or in small towns and 90 percent of black Americans had lived in the South since the colonial period. As late as 1900 the largest black urban communities were in the cities of the South like New Orleans (78,000–27 percent), Baltimore (79,000–16 percent), and Washington, D.C. (87,000–31 percent). Communities in the North such as New York (61,000–2 percent), Philadelphia (63,000–5 percent), and Chicago (30,000–2 percent) were smaller in both pure numbers and percentages of blacks in the total urban population.[2]

This chapter looks first at the general background out of which jazz emerged and then at specific factors in three urban centers, New York, Chicago, and New Orleans, which shaped black music in these areas in distinctive ways.

Territory Jazz Roots: 1890–1914

The small and medium-sized communities where most black Americans lived in 1890 were later called the "territories" by jazz musicians. The musical and social life of these territories produced many of the performers and the bulk of the audience for jazz. The strongest musical traditions in the territories in 1890 were folk music, the spirituals of the black church, and the vocal tradition rooted in the work song that was developing into the blues. These African-American musical forms showed strong African folk roots, including: (1) the call-and-response form; (2) bent, blues notes that went off the European scale; (3) emphasis on solos and collective improvisation; (4) a rough, personal vocal tone; (5) strong, complex rhythm; and (6) oral rather than written transmission. These forces were a strong part of the background of jazz, but they were vocal forms of music.

As instrumentalists, the young musicians who would play jazz were more directly influenced by brass bands, pianists, and small groups playing for theaters and dances. Even in this period, these traditions reflected European musical norms: (1) structured, composed pieces; (2) the European scale; (3) grouping instruments together in sections; (4) "legitimate" tone and phrasing; and (5) written transmission, which required reading skills for performance. The interaction of these two very different traditions shaped the history of jazz. That interaction came from choices made by African-American musicians in the social, economic, and cultural context of the 1880–1935 period.

16

The strongest instrumental traditions in the rural and small town areas of this time were the local amateur and touring professional brass bands. The dazzle of these bands filled the memories of young future jazzmen. Many of their fathers played with local amateur bands, which had important roles in their black communities at funerals, church affairs, street shows, and parades. Their membership was segregated and they often played exclusively within the black community. They were frequently sponsored by lodges such as the Knights of Pythias or simply represented the community.[3]

Local bands could be found in places as diverse as Evergreen, Alabama; Savannah, Georgia; Charleston, West Virginia; St. Louis, Missouri; Omaha, Nebraska; Columbus, Ohio; Baltimore, Maryland; and Buxton, Iowa.[4] Many of these communities also sponsored "kid" bands that gave young musicians their first performing experiences. A 1917 Knights of Pythias convention had kid bands from St. Louis, Philadelphia, and Birmingham, Alabama.[5] Sy Oliver (Zanesville, Ohio), Gene Sedric (St. Louis), and George Washington (Jacksonville, Florida) were jazzmen who played in K of P bands as youths.[6] These fraternal groups and informal outfits organized by local music teachers were particularly important in this early period when instrumental music training and performance groups were rarely available in the public schools.

The musical road opened by these local groups was widened by touring brass bands bringing entertainment to the smallest hamlets and rural areas. Colleges such as Tuskegee Institute and orphanages such as the Waifs' Home of New Orleans, where Louis Armstrong began his career, or the Jenkins Orphanage of Charleston, South Carolina often had large bands that toured to raise money.[7] The Eighth Illinois National Guard had a well-known adult band as did the four black army regiments.[8] Much more important were the circus, carnival, and tent shows, which were the only real professional entertainment that could reach out to the rural folk of nineteenth century America. In the South, tent shows were often all-black minstrel entertainments playing mainly to black audiences. The smallest of these and their cousin, the medicine show, might have only folk performers on banjos, fiddles, and jugs playing blues and ragtime.[9] However, many black tent shows featured brass bands. Moreover, black brass bands often accompanied white circuses, carnivals, and even Wild West shows such as the *101 Ranch*. In these shows, the black bands were usually attached to a black sideshow or annex called a "jig tent."

The black musicians in these brass bands were busy professionals. The shows toured for months at a time: minstrel and tent shows in the South from Florida all the way to Texas, and circuses and Wild West shows throughout the country. They were very influential on the musicians of the small black communities in Ohio, Indiana, and Nebraska. Men like Red Perkins and Garvin Bushell had vivid memories of the life and sound of these bands.

These bands demanded a complex repertoire: marches in the parade to signal the show's arrival in town; marches and overtures in concerts on the midway; and overtures, instrumental ragtime, and popular music to back up the sideshow acts. Often, after-hours, they were playing ragtime and blues for local dances. These bands were large, often including eleven to twenty-four pieces based on the military band model. A typical line-up included three to five each of trumpets, trombones, and clarinets, a baritone and a bass horn, and often one or two flutes and alto horns plus a snare and bass drum team.[10] The sound of the bands varied widely. While the blues was strong in shows such as the Rabbit Foot Minstrels where Ma Rainey held forth, Garvin Bushell remembers the circus bands as "instrumental ragtime . . . a lot of notes without the blues feel or quarter-tone pitch."[11]

Unfortunately, the sound of these brass bands may only be imagined. While white brass bands like John Philip Sousa's recorded frequently from the 1890s forward, no recordings were made by black bands at that time. However, three sets of later records suggest the spectrum of sounds. The 1918–19 recordings of Jim Europe's 369th Infantry band and Ford Dabney's band display marches and instrumental ragtime in written arrangements. While there is more rhythmic looseness and personal tonal variation than in the Sousa recordings, the groups clearly belong to the same tradition. This indicates the touring bands had strong elements of classical training in their backgrounds. New Orleans tradition recordings of the 1920s and 1940s show a mixture of written arrangements and improvisation that would become typical of jazz. It is unclear how much this was unique to New Orleans or shared by other communities where readers tried to carry along colleagues who were playing by ear. Finally Fred Ramsay's field recordings of the 1940s show a rural folk tradition with horns used almost as percussion instruments, which has clear roots in African musical tradition. This model represents many small town ensembles of this period including some heard by future jazzmen.[12]

The growing cities were developing two new indoor environments for music, vaudeville motion picture theaters and the intimate atmosphere of the cabaret, dance hall, and sporting house scene. The motion picture had been invented in the late nineteenth century, and by 1903, picture theaters began to appear all across the country. Managers usually used pianists or small groups to play background music for the silent films and mood music in between. While sheet music was often provided, the moods were standard enough that ear musicians could usually fit things in. Count Basie is one of many jazzmen who began his career as a theater pianist.[13]

The vaudeville theater was a new example of the mass entertainment forms springing up in the growing American cities. Albert McLean argues that vaudeville was a means for the "new folk," confused masses of urban immigrants, to deal with the pressures of urbanization by both finding their own roles in the city and maintaining links with their ethnic traditions.[14] Black entertainers had some access to vaudeville from its beginnings, but their roles increased from 1900 to 1914. Black touring shows like the Black Patti Troubadours and Smart Set companies began to play some theaters. Vaudeville theaters catering to primarily black audiences grew in Southern cities such as Atlanta, Memphis, and Winston-Salem and in the growing black neighborhoods of New York, Chicago, Detroit, and Philadelphia. In 1912, former tent show comedian Sherman Dudley started organizing these theaters into a black vaudeville circuit. By 1921, several small chains had merged into the Theater Owner's Booking Association (TOBA) circuit which lasted into the depression era.[15] Each theater had a pianist and often a small three- to five-piece pit band to accompany the touring acts. Often these were non-reading musicians who would "work something out" with each week's performers. These circuits brought live black entertainment to a growing black audience and provided jobs to local black musicians.[16]

Other entertainment forms also helped to ease the loneliness and provide amusement to McLean's "new folk." The sporting house, the saloon which could become a nightclub or cabaret, and the public dance hall emerged in this period to provide single people opportunities to meet without the benefit of traditional introductions. In the lower class neighborhoods of the new cities, red-light districts, bars, and dance halls were accepted as necessary evils.[17]

Out of this environment emerged ragtime, the first black mass media entertainment music. Ragtime is actually three different things: a syncopated on-the-beat style of playing music, a specific form of music composition based on the march structure, and a popular music craze that swept America in the 1890s. The playing style and repertoire influenced the brass bands, but ragtime was primarily piano music that could be reproduced by sheet music and piano rolls. Its key significance to the development of jazz was its pioneering of the mass media. Scott Joplin and other ragtime performers could distribute their music as sheet music or in piano rolls, and stimulate further interest in hearing live performances. This model would be mirrored by the phonograph record's impact on jazz. By 1900, ragtime pianists could be heard around the country in theaters, clubs, and sporting houses, and regional differences between Westerners

19

such as Scott Joplin and James Scott and the East Coast school of Eubie Blake and Luckey Roberts were developing.[18]

This spectrum of brass bands, theater jobs, and ragtime provided a complex musical background for the black musicians who were creating jazz in the 1890–1914 period. The elements in that mix shifted from region to region. Three places are worth special study because of the unique nature of their mixtures: New Orleans, Chicago, and New York.

New Orleans

In 1890, the largest black urban community in the United States lived in New Orleans. It is not surprising that the social, cultural, and musical changes being felt in the country were very strong here. In addition, New Orleans had several unique factors: (1) the "downtown" black Creole population with its strong ties to French culture, (2) the strong African elements of Congo Square, (3) the blues-rooted "uptown" style of rural migrants from the Mississippi Delta, and (4) the strong, early impact of legal segregation reflected by the Louisiana-based 1896 U.S. Supreme Court decision of *Plessy v. Ferguson*. The key factor was simply the size of New Orleans that allowed it to support many competing brass bands instead of just one or two community groups. Also, the presence of more musical groups led to discoveries of new ways to use them such as advertising for stores. Similarly, the opportunities in the indoor music area were also wider with a very active dance scene and the sporting houses of Storyville. Still, most New Orleans musicians had day jobs. They could not make their livings just from music.

What is striking about New Orleans in this period is how much it was like the territories. The size and instrumentation of the Onward, Excelsior, and other brass bands were similar to those of the territory groups. The New Orleans bands, particularly the Creoles, often used standard published arrangements which were available around the country, although New Orleans bands would often go beyond the published arrangements.[19] Music historian William J. Schafer says, "Musicians trained in this tradition approached music in a complicated way: they were prepared to read straight arrangements, to rely on head arrangements of standard tunes in the repertoire, and to improvise on new tunes."[20]

This was particularly true after 1900 as the reading tradition Creoles and ear-playing, blues-based rural blacks were combined by job opportunities and the force of the new segregation laws which squeezed the Creoles from their special traditional place between the black and white worlds of New Orleans and moved them more clearly into the black community. As

Joseph Robichaux remembers, "The fellows from Downtown were soon playin' the blues like the musicians from Uptown who, then in turn, started learnin' to read."[21]

This merger of styles and traditions was also occurring in the dance field as the bands of younger men like Oscar Celestin and Armand Piron began to challenge Joseph Robichaux for the Creole and white society dances. While they remained reading bands playing stock arrangements they began to include more of the blues-flavored slow drags in their repertoire for the younger dancers. Meanwhile in the uptown cabarets, bands were adding reading musicians who could help them keep up with the latest published popular tunes, showing the early impact of mass media on the strong folk tradition in uptown jazz. In Storyville, the pianists like Jelly Roll Morton kept a local flavor in the music and developed original tunes but also included popular hits.[22]

By 1914, in New Orleans as in the territories the music that would become known as jazz was a spectrum of brass bands, pianists, and bands playing for dancing. While the styles were merging, the spectrum was still wide, ranging from the classically-influenced readers in the society dance bands through the adaptable pianists and band members to the folk-rooted blues players of uptown. New Orleans musicians by 1914 clearly had musical roots but they were also flexible and open to change. While a few New Orleans men had toured with tent shows, circuses, or vaudeville, the style was still local before 1914.

Chicago

Chicago was representative of the Northern cities that would become home to black Southerners in the period of the Great Migration starting in 1914. It was a rapidly growing city built on industry, mass merchandising, public transit, and a construction boom. It was very much a part of the new mass urban culture at the turn of the century. In fact, as America's second largest city, a major railroad center, and the home of major direct-mail firms like Sears and Roebuck and Montgomery Ward, it helped to extend that culture.

Certain unique characteristics about Chicago shaped its history and the development of jazz there. As a transport center, Chicago began to pull in black migrants even before the official beginning of the Great Migration. In 1890, there were only 14,271 blacks in Chicago—just a little more than 1 percent of the total population. By 1900, the black population had doubled to 30,150—almost 2 percent of the total. Between

1900 and 1910, the black population jumped to 44,103, passing Nashville, Louisville, St. Louis, and Charleston, South Carolina.[23]

The physical and institutional ghetto also began to grow early in Chicago, predating the Great Migration. By the turn of the century, the bulk of the black population was already concentrated in a narrow band along State Street on the near South Side. Here, black churches, stores, clubs, and other institutions grew, well-documented by the black newspaper, the *Chicago Defender*.[24]

The social structure of black Chicago was complex even at the turn of the century. Economic and social differences set off the elite establishment of doctors, lawyers, and businessmen from the growing mass of working people. Perhaps even more important for cultural analysis was the difference, pointed out by St. Clair Drake, between the "respectables" and "shadies." These distinctions applied not to how much money one made but rather how one made and spent it. Shadies often were involved in illegal activities, and their social lives involved conspicuous consumption and hedonism. Respectables worked in legal and socially acceptable jobs, saved and invested their money, and contributed to churches and social organizations. They emphasized decorum and appearance or "front."[25] "When upper-class and middle-class people speak of 'advancing the race,' what they really mean is creating conditions under which lower-class traits will eventually disappear."[26]

These views and conflicts strongly affected the role of black jazz musicians in Chicago because they were on the line between these two worlds. On the one hand they were the most numerous black professional group. On the other hand, their profession was not considered as respectable as others since it often required work in a shady environment. This tension was very clear to Chicago musicians, and many of their concerns from 1890 to 1935 focused on their status.[27]

In 1890, Chicago's black musicians were clearly tied to the respectable establishment's institutions and emphasis on appearances and traditions. Those institutions, the black lodges, churches, and the Eighth Illinois National Guard Regiment, provided most of the job opportunities for musicians. The major events were church choir concerts, classical music recitals, brass band concerts, and lodge dances. The fact that musical news was on the same page as society news in the *Chicago Defender* illustrates its place in the community. Music for these events was provided by the brass bands of the Eighth Regiment, the Knights of Pythias, and Elks and by society dance orchestras led by George Boarman, Garfield Wilson, Will Dorsey, and others. The dance repertoire included waltzes, schottisches, and two-steps as late as 1910.[28]

Music education had a high priority, and the reading of traditional European notation was stressed. Many performing musicians were also music teachers. Their advertisements were quite prominant in the *Chicago Defender*, and their students' recitals were well covered. It was a musical world very similar to that of the New Orleans Creoles. One difference was the emphasis on professionalism. As early as 1900, 256 black Chicagoans (including forty-nine females) listed their occupations as musicians. A black American could make a living as a musician in Chicago—something that was still rare then even in New Orleans.[29]

Musicians approached their work as a business and insisted on professional dedication. In 1902, members of the Eighth Illinois band led by Alex Arment, a Creole, organized the all-black Local 208 of the American Federation of Musicians. They sought to set pay scales, check on working conditions, enforce standards for membership, and require membership for job opportunities, forcing non-member or delinquent musicians off jobs. This action set a professional climate for music in Chicago. Musicians and employers knew where to look to arrange jobs and what the standards were. This became more important as the range of musical jobs grew.[30]

After 1900, the new forms of the theater and cabaret became more important. In 1905, Robert T. Motts, a very successful shady controlling much of the South Side's gambling, opened up the Pekin Inn in the black neighborhood, offering not only a beer garden and cabaret but also one of the first black-owned theaters in the United States. Its musical and dramatic fare was very popular, and it soon had competition from two other neighborhood theaters in the black community, the Grand and the Monogram. All had small pit bands to play for vaudeville acts or silent films. The musicians in these bands became a very important factor in the musical life of black Chicago, and they all had strong roots to the respectable community.

In 1910–1912, these pit bands included three active music teachers, Charles Elgar, Erskine Tate, and Wilbur Sweatman, and three active composers or arrangers, Dave Peyton, Will Dorsey, and George Reeves. Elgar was from New Orleans, and Tate from Memphis. Sweatman, born in Missouri, was a minstrel show veteran who had toured much of the country before settling in Chicago. Peyton was born in Louisiana but raised and schooled in Chicago and considered himself a Chicagoan. They were professional reading musicians, with training either in the South or at Chicago's black Coleridge Taylor School of Music or white American Conservatory. They were all active members of Local 208, and Elgar served as its president for many years. They were aware of the national music world. Eventually Sweatman, Elgar, and Dorsey all worked in New York.[31]

Once again, historians are forced to guess at the sound of these extremely influential groups. They left behind no recordings and only very vague descriptions of their performances. The bands were all small, often trios with a violin or clarinet or cornet, piano, and drums. An exception was Dave Peyton's thirty- to forty-piece Grand Theater symphony orchestra. This group with a twenty-seven piece string section was put together for five special concerts in the 1914–1916 period. The programs for this group were filled with light classics such as the "William Tell" and "Poet and Peasant" overtures and with the compositions of black popular composers such as Will Vodery's "Carolina Fox-Trot" and W.C. Handy's "Memphis Blues." This indicates that Peyton, who helped set standards for the pit bands, was strongly influenced by traditional European classical music and written notation.[32]

The theater bands were not the only new influence in Chicago. From 1905 to 1914, cabarets, sporting houses, and dancing schools grew. The cabarets and sporting houses had the strongest folk elements with nameless players who influenced the blues and boogie-woogie players of the 1920s. The earliest New Orleans influence was evident with pianists like Jelly Roll Morton and Tony Jackson, the composer of "Pretty Baby," both of whom came to Chicago in the 1910–1914 period. They were often accompanying female blues singers like Lucille Hegamin, Ada "Brick-top" Smith, and Mattie Hite.[33]

The dancing schools were events held in rented private ballrooms. They were very popular, particularly after the fall of 1911, but the nature of the music at the dancing schools is very unclear. Some dances used the established society bands like George Boarman's and Garfield Wilson's but new groups like Clarence Miller's Peerless Orchestra also played. The bands may have resembled Jim Europe's developments in New York or they may have had stronger influences from the blues sounds of the rent party folk traditions.[34]

What emerges by 1914 is the picture of a very busy black musical life in Chicago with a wide variety of job opportunities, an established professional structure and attitude, and an apparent variety of styles.

New York City

New York City also had several distinctive factors in the 1890–1914 period. First, as the center of the American entertainment industry it included the headquarters of major music publishing houses and vaudeville chains, and the Broadway stage. Second, the rapidly growing black community was scattered in several small neighborhoods including the Tenderloin (7th Avenue and 34th Street) and San Juan Hill (Columbus Circle).[35] There was no central location for a cohesive black neighborhood and entertainment center. These two factors created a situation in which the dominant black musicians in New York City before 1914 were professional reading and writing musicians working for mainly white audiences.

As early as 1910, New York City had a larger black population than New Orleans and more than twice the number of black people in Chicago. Also, as the heart of the national entertainment industry, it had a special place in the world of the black musician. Both of these factors shaped how black music developed in New York. The large population meant that some musicians were native New Yorkers with a different feel for a colder, faster-paced, multi-ethnic city. Other musicians, because of the migration pattern along the East Coast railroads and boat lines, hailed from the Carolinas, Maryland, Virginia, Georgia, and Florida, where the folk music traditions had closer contacts with white models and ragtime was stronger than the blues.[36]

The entertainment business in New York in the Gay Nineties meant sheet music publishing, vaudeville, and above all the Broadway theater, so it is not surprising that the city attracted reading and writing musicians and composers like Will Marion Cook from Washington, D.C., J. Tim Brymn from North Carolina, and J. Rosamond Johnson from Florida. With writer-lyricists like James Weldon Johnson, Paul Laurence Dunbar, and Bob Cole, and performers like Bert Williams and George Walker, these men established a very active black presence in the Broadway theater. Cook's *Clorindy* (1898), which opened the cycle, and *In Dahomy* (1902), which was the first black musical hosted by a major Broadway theater, presented written black popular entertainment music aimed at a white audience, and remained models for many black musicians such as Dave Peyton.

Large pit orchestras played for these shows using typical European instrumentation and written arrangements. The tunes included overtures, ballads, comedy tunes, and instrumental ragtime. They were written out by the composer, who expected them to be played accordingly. Composers considered sheet sales an important part of their income. While these black composers brought individual style to their work it was clearly in the Euro-American popular song tradition. The music was judged by the norms of European musical analysis and criticism and frequently praised on these standards.

Still, this music could also move into the folk tradition. The music was often based on folk melodies and when these shows toured the country after their Broadway success, the tunes could be learned by ear by territory musicians. These shows challenged territory and Chicago theater musicians to develop their reading skills and shape up to higher standards. Several Chicagoans in fact moved to New York for a crack at the Broadway and publishing scene there.

Will Marion Cook, J. Rosamond Johnson, J. Tim Brymn, and the other musicians in this school shared classical musical training and an acceptance of the norms of this style. Cook was a product of Oberlin College and three years of study in Europe, while Johnson received instruction at the New England Conservatory and Brymn at the National Conservatory. They remained active in New York into the early 1920s, and their influence helped to strengthen the written and arranged style of black popular music there.[37]

By 1910, black shows were off Broadway although black entertainers like Bert Williams and black musicians like Ford Dabney continued to work for white promoters like Florenz Ziegfeld. The center of action for black musicians had shifted: "the majority . . . play and sing in the leading hotels and cafes . . . for the Smart Set."[38] These cabaret musicians formed the Clef Club to secure better jobs for black musicians, maintain high standards of musicianship, and generate artistic recognition for black musicians and black music. The Clef Club was a central agency for booking black musicians who were getting weak representation in the New York musician's union. It sponsored a series of quarterly concerts from 1910 to 1914 in which orchestras of 100 to 145 men played programs of light classics, rags, and spirituals.

The leader of the Clef Club was a young man from Mobile, Alabama, by way of Washington, D.C., named James Reese Europe. He had written several songs for black shows and led small groups playing instrumental ragtime and light mood music at cabarets, hotels, and society dances.[39] In several newspaper interviews, he set out his standards for judging black music: "We play the music as it is written, only that we accent strongly . . . the notes which originally would be without accent. I have to call a daily rehearsal of my band to prevent the musicians from adding to their music more than I wish them to . . . and I have to be continually on the lookout to cut out the results of my musicians' originality."[40] While Europe saw some distinct black music characteristics, particularly in rhythm, he stressed the role of the written arrangement and exact performance over spontaneous improvisation.[41]

Europe had problems getting these concepts across in his daily work. Eubie Blake, a member of the Europe band before World War I, stressed that this was a very well-rehearsed, reading band playing special and stock written arrangements. However, these skills were hidden from the rich, white patrons of the bands to fit the racial stereotypes of the period. Europe's Society Orchestra players did not bring music stands to their jobs. When a request was made, Europe would say that he "would try to work something out with the boys" and then have a whispered discussion with the band either about where to eat afterwards or how they were "puttin' on ole massa" again. The band would then launch into a complex written arrangement of the song they had worked on long and hard in rehearsals.[42]

White patrons were a greater part of the audience for black musicians in New York than anywhere else. Even cabaret pianists such as Luckey Roberts, Eubie Blake, Willie "The Lion" Smith, James P. Johnson, and Willie Gant were often playing for white patrons as well as blacks. These pianists were all East Coast men from New York City (Gant), New Jersey (Johnson and Smith), Philadelphia (Roberts), and Baltimore (Blake). Their East Coast ragtime style had limited connection to the blues and more connections to white popular and folk music.[43] By 1914, black music in New York City was very strongly influenced by the European reading tradition and the professional entertainment world and only weakly influenced by black folk traditions.

Conclusion

By 1914, black popular music was thriving in most of the United States, and its styles clearly varied from country to city, and from North to South. Its actual composition in various regions is unclear because of the lack of recorded evidence and confusion in the written evidence. Still, certain shared elements clearly set the stage for the emergence and shape of jazz: (1) the tension between the traditional entertainment forms of the brass band and tent show and the new forms of the theater, dance hall, and cabaret; (2) the roots of musicians in small towns even with their willingness to move to cities for work; and (3) the tension between the folk tradition of improvisation and learning by ear and the emphasis of many professional musicians on reading music.

2

Jazz Goes on Record 1914–1923

BETWEEN 1914 and 1923 two events made it much easier to track the history of jazz. First, the word jazz began to be used to describe a musical form. Second, recordings of jazz and black popular music appeared, which documented these sounds and styles. These two events occurred in the context of several important movements that were affecting the direction of jazz and American popular music. These were: (1) the Great Migration of blacks from the rural South to the urban North, (2) changes in the role of social dancing as entertainment and social interaction, (3) the growth of vaudeville and movie theaters as forms of mass entertainment, and (4) the emergence of the phonograph as a home entertainment medium. These movements were felt nationally but their impact differed from region to region. This chapter will briefly introduce each of these themes before focusing on their impact and the development of jazz in New Orleans, Chicago, and New York.

The Great Migration and New Entertainment Forms

With the beginning of World War I in August 1914 European nations stopped emigration in order to boost their war efforts. Soon the naval war in the Atlantic Ocean made the crossing hazardous. At the same time, the war increased the need for industrial workers to fill orders for goods from the fighting nations. African-Americans from the Southern states helped fill this demand for workers. Companies sent recruiting agents into the

South and even chartered whole trains to bring workers to the North. These industrial jobs promised economic progress at a time when farm jobs were declining due to mechanization. Also, social and political conditions for African-Americans in the South were worsening as segregation laws and discrimination tightened.

These factors created one of the major internal movements of people in American history. Between 1914 and 1920 more than half a million black Americans moved from the rural South to the urban North. Black populations and neighborhoods in Northern cities skyrocketed. In 1920, three of the four largest black urban populations were now in the North: New York (152,467), Philadelphia (134,229), and Chicago (109,458); while New Orleans (100,930) had dropped to sixth. Black populations in Cleveland (34,451), Detroit (40,838), Pittsburgh (37,725), Cincinnati (30,079), and St. Louis (69,854) were all expanding rapidly.[1]

The migration consisted of three distinct movements following the railroad lines. African-Americans from Virginia, the Carolinas, Georgia, and Florida moved up the Seaboard and Atlantic Coast railroads to the cities stretching from Washington, D.C., to Boston. The largest number settled in New York City. Those from the Deep South (Mississippi, Alabama, and Louisiana) and border states (Kentucky and Tennessee) moved to the Midwest cities of Cleveland, Cincinnati, Detroit, St. Louis, and, most importantly, Chicago. Migrants from the Southwest including Louisiana, Arkansas, Texas, Oklahoma, and Missouri moved into cities in their own region, particularly to Kansas City and Dallas, or moved out to the West Coast, mainly to Los Angeles.[2] This division is important because it means that the black communities of New York, Chicago, Kansas City, and Los Angeles had significant cultural and economic differences based in part on the different sources of their populations.

Economics played a major role in the Great Migration but politics and social conditions were also significant. Between 1898 and 1910 most blacks in the South lost the right to vote as white-controlled state legislatures wrote disfranchisement into their constitutions after the Supreme Court's 1898 *Williams v. Mississippi* decision.[3] Denied political power, African-Americans now saw segregation laws formally define them as inferior in education, public facilities, and other areas of life. Escape from the tightening walls of segregation was a strong motive for many black migrants.[4] Also, family ties and images of a more active social life pulled increasing numbers of people to urban areas. Letters from migrants to their families stressed dreams of a better life in the city. The *Chicago Defender* published such letters to encourage migration.[5]

The *Chicago Defender*'s entertainment pages promoted migration in a very different way. The motion pictures, vaudeville shows, and dance halls which it advertised and reviewed showed the wider variety of cultural activity available in the city. Urban cultural and economical appeals led many African-Americans in the South to move from country to city. Black populations in Birmingham, Richmond, Atlanta, Memphis, Houston, and Dallas all grew rapidly in this period.

The rapid growth of the black populations in the urban North and the social tensions and economic opportunities they created were a key part of the experience from which black jazz musicians created music in the 1914–1923 period. That their experiences and music matched the growing mass audience of the 1920s helps explain the enormous popularity of jazz in the Roaring Twenties. In the 1920s, the average American was someone from the country who had moved to the city for a job and was adjusting to a new social environment. Jazz spoke to this generation because it reflected the same forces.

Black musicians from all parts of the South, not just New Orleans, were part of this migration. Some like Fletcher Henderson came for other jobs and moved into music, but others like Louis Armstrong followed their audiences or specific musical job offers. Increasingly, the new social life and entertainment world of the city made it easier for musicians to give up their day jobs and make a full-time living from their music. Vaudeville, the motion picture theater, the nightclub, and the dance hall provided the bulk of the new jobs for black musicians.

Black vaudeville expanded dramatically in this period. S. H. Dudley's chain of theaters went through several changes until it emerged as the TOBA circuit. Vaudeville pit bands provided regular work for regional musicians. Others such as The Creole Band became touring acts on TOBA and white circuits. The rapid growth of motion picture theaters after 1914 demanded pit bands to accompany the silent films and play concerts between shows.[6]

Rise of the Dance Hall

Dance halls were another growing institution that drew patrons from the "new folk" of the cities. Increasing numbers of single individuals of both sexes were in the cities with some spending money and leisure time but limited traditional connections for meeting people. They were on their own without family chaperones and church, school, or community dances for structured meeting places. They fueled the enormous growth of the dance hall and cabaret in this period. The social changes of urbanization brought about a significant change in the attitude towards social dancing in America, and this opened tremendous new opportunities for black jazz musicians.[7]

As late as the 1880s, in the ethnic neighborhoods of the cities as well as in rural America, dancing, when it was acceptable at all, was a very formal arrangement closely regulated by the ties of church, school, community, and family. Whether the cotillions of society or the barn dances of rural folk, social dancing was a way for men and women to meet each other under close family and community supervision. "Communities of people of various ages congregate to give expression to their desire for fun, romance, and a little art in strictly social ways; governed by the habits and traditions and . . . older or more responsible members of their own racial, religious, and neighborhood groups. The dance . . . is a . . . community of interest and responsibilities."[8]

While this kind of dance would continue through the 1920s, increasing numbers of urban singles without family or community ties needed another outlet, and commercial dance halls developed to provide this. Dance halls started to appear in working class neighborhoods around the turn of the century and by 1920, New York City alone had 476 of them. "These . . . types are business institutions in form and fact. There is little or no pretence of social control or of intent to regard personal or group relations; there is merely recognition of a want for a dance place . . . and a commercial answer for that want."[9] The patrons were seen as "girls who have no other opportunity for social contact"[10] and "the man without country or a home, without much hope of introduction to a lady, or perhaps with too great bashfulness to seek one."[11] In the closed or taxi dance hall where men could hire women to dance with them, "The women employed appear . . . to be hard-working and honest; a minority have the earmarks of the hardened prostitute."[12] In fact, many early dance halls began as extensions of saloons or sporting houses. This connection kept social dancing unacceptable at the turn of the century.[13]

This changed around 1914 with the emergence of the ballroom dance team of Vernon and Irene Castle. The Castles took the dances of the working class dance halls, refined them, joined them to the philosophy of the Progressive Era, and popularized social dancing among the middle and upper classes.[14] They were accompanied by the black band of James Reese Europe. While black musicians had played for white dancers before this, the enormous visibility of the Castles and Jim Europe had a profound impact on the opportunities for black musicians, opening doors perhaps even more directly than Teddy Wilson's appearance with Benny Goodman twenty years later. White location managers noted the acceptance of this package. Black bands increasingly found that they could get jobs playing for white dancers even in the segregated South. As a result of the visibility given by his association with the Castles, Jim Europe was able to challenge W. C. Handy as the most well-known black musician in the United States. Europe's Society Orchestra was the first black band to make a national reputation playing music for a white dancing audience.[15] From 1914 on, this activity became a key part of the black jazz musician's world and shaped the sound and style of jazz.

A writer to the *Chicago Defender* in 1918, probably a member of Europe's band, reflected on Vernon Castle's importance.

> Born in England, he was not contaminated with the rotten prejudices which are a part of many American performers. . . . He was one of the first big dancing acts to use one of our bands. Being routed over many weeks, he contracted for James Reese Europe's Syncopated Band, fifteen strong and wonderful musicians, and they were with him until his contracts ran out playing every bit of music for the great Castle and his talented wife, known as the premier dancers of the world.[16]

The Impact of the Phonograph

Jim Europe's band was also one of the first black groups to record. The use of the phonograph was the last major element of change in this period. In dealing with the role of the phonograph on the development of jazz we must distinguish between its historical importance and its impact within its own time. First, the phonograph record makes the study of jazz history after 1914 clearer since it captures individual performances for analysis. Jazz recordings became historical documents on which the study of the music is often based. As such they have significant limits. Many important artists and styles were not often recorded, leaving holes in our view of the jazz world. Moreover, recordings which freeze the improviser at one moment in time may give a distorted view of actual nightly performances.

Secondly, records had a direct impact on black jazz musicians and their music. They (1) enlarged the audience for the music, (2) made it easier for musicians to learn from each other, (3) imposed technical limits on the music, and (4) introduced another layer of gatekeepers, the record companies, between the musicians and their audience.

Jazz and the phonograph made a perfect match of medium and message. The improvisation and tonal variations that were at the core of jazz performances could not be captured on sheet music, the main form of music distribution before 1914. A few piano performances could be marketed on piano rolls but the player-pianos often could not recreate the variations in tone, attack, and rhythm that make a jazz performance unique. This limited the jazz audience to those who could hear the music live. Records, even primitive ones, could catch many of the elements that sheet music missed. With the phonograph, the listeners could take the entire performance home to enjoy. This increased the reach of jazz beyond live audiences.

The phonograph record also made it easier for musicians to learn jazz without direct contact with each other. The hand-cranked phonograph could be slowed down below normal speed and repeated to provide a private master class. The following story of how Frank Trumbauer learned his tonal style from the records of popular performer Rudy Weidoeft shows how the new technology revealed personal secrets. "Frankie [Trumbauer] . . . went to him [Wiedoeft] to learn that remarkable staccato but he [Wiedoeft] . . . refused to teach it to him [Trumbauer]. . . . Frankie told me that he went out and bought a whole lot of Wiedoeft's records and he would slow them down until . . . one record . . . showed him how."[17] Fear of losing their personal styles kept Freddie Keppard and others from recording in this early period.[18]

The technological weaknesses of the equipment affected the music. The acoustic processes of the pre-1926 period were very limited in picking up the high and low end of the sound spectrum or large variations in volume. This made it very difficult to record a full trap drum set, or a string bass. Also, the guitar used as a rhythm instrument was often too soft to be heard over the ensemble. As a result of these limitations, some bands limited drum use and began to use the banjo and tuba rather than the guitar and string bass on recordings before 1926. This carried over to live performances as well. The use of the tuba over the string bass was particularly important since it encouraged the two-beat sound because of breath patterns. Also, the size and speed of the 78 rpm single limited records to just over three minutes. This set a specific model for popular music of three-minute performances, which often meant two to three choruses of thirty-two-bar songs.[19]

Finally, the record companies imposed limits on the musicians. They all wanted the widest possible audience, which prior to 1920 was clearly white. The Columbia and Victor companies controlled most of the market and stuck to what was already selling: popular vocals, comic monologues, brass band selections, and classical music for prestige. Virtually no black artists or jazz performers were recorded before December 1913. The

James Reese Europe recordings of this date provided a breakthrough for a few black entertainers who might appeal to white audiences. Bert Williams, vaudeville musician Wilbur Sweatman, and theater band leader Ford Dabney were among the early black recording artists.

It was not until 1920 and the collaboration of Mamie Smith and Perry Bradford on "Crazy Blues" that records by black artists aimed at a black audience became acceptable in the recording industry. The financial success of this record showed the companies that there was a market for black music. This coincided with the expiration of the Columbia-Victor monopoly of phonograph patents in 1919, opening the field to smaller companies willing to take more risks with musical styles. Bradford, Smith, and other jazz and blues artists were economically appealing to record companies because they wrote their own material, saving the companies royalty payments. This led some companies to emphasize the recording of original tunes rather than popular standards, which made some musicians' recordings unrepresentative of their live performances.[20]

From 1914 to 1923, the relationship between recordings and black music is complex. Many black styles were simply not recorded. At the same time, the bulk of the recorded examples of popular dance music and even of jazz were from white bands such as the Original Dixieland Jazz Band and Ladd's Black Aces, a New York white group that included Jimmy Durante. This increased the potential for white impact on black musicians.[21]

These four basic elements, the Great Migration, the increase in theater jobs, the development of social dancing, and the rise of the phonograph shaped the lives of black musicians around the country in this period, but the mixture varied in different locations.

New Orleans

In New Orleans, the major element in the 1914–1923 period was the Great Migration. Social dancing was already well established in New Orleans before 1914. Theater jobs were less important here than in other areas, and no recordings were made in the Crescent City until the mid-1920s.

The New Orleans migration followed the pattern of the larger black exodus; (1) it went in three directions; (2) it was fueled by job opportunities; and (3) it split on generational and personal lines. Most attention in jazz history has focused on the large group of New Orleans men including King Oliver, Jelly Roll Morton, and Louis Armstrong who moved to Chicago, some by way of St. Louis. However, this was not the sole direction of the New Orleans exodus. Some players toured around the country with vaudeville or tent shows. Others including Will Johnson, Wade Whaley, and Kid Ory moved to Los Angeles where they had a major impact on the development of jazz on the West Coast.[22]

The new opportunities in vaudeville and playing for dancing around the country fit the skills of many New Orleans men. The tours of The Creole Band and the records of the white Original Dixieland Jazz Band built an identification of jazz and New Orleans. This increased national demand for New Orleans jazzmen. Memories indicate that the impact of segregation was worsening in this period particularly for the "Creoles of color" who were losing their special place in New Orleans life to the statewide Jim Crow laws passed after *Plessy v. Ferguson* and the 1898 state disfranchisement constitution. All of this minimizes the role of the closing of the Storyville district in November 1917 stressed by Collier and earlier writers.[23] Freddie Keppard, Wade Whaley, Bill Johnson, Nenny Coycault, and others had left before 1917. Moreover, there does not seem to have been a significant drop in work in New Orleans for musicians as a result of the closing of Storyville. John Robichaux's Lyric Theater band and Armand Piron's dance orchestra and other groups continued to be very active.[24]

What did make a difference in the migration was age. Young, ambitious men out to succeed away from home made up the core of the black musical migration. The majority of New Orleans musicians who left the city in 1914 and after were thirty years old or less. Many of those between twenty-five and thirty such as Freddie Keppard, Richard M. Jones, Kid Ory, and Jelly Roll Morton who had reputations in New Orleans left for better opportunities, usually as band leaders. The sidemen who built their reputations outside of New Orleans like Louis Armstrong, Jimmie Noone, and Natty Dominique were generally under twenty-five in 1915. Noone was only twenty, and Armstrong, who left much later, was only fifteen.

The older established players and those with conservative personalities who might feel uncomfortable outside their hometown did not leave. John Robichaux and most men forty-five to fifty-five years old in 1915 remained. Very few men between the ages of thirty and forty-five left. Among them, Frankie Dusen, Manuel Perez, and Lorenzo Tio, Jr., returned to New Orleans quickly as did some sidemen in their upper twenties like Peter Bocage, Buddy Petit, and Manuel Manetta.[25]

This generation gap suggests several conclusions. First of all, it may signal a decline in music in New Orleans itself since the young innovators were leaving town. Second, it means that the migrants were not totally committed to an unchanging tradition rooted in the 1880s since many of them were not alive or listening to music before 1900. Third, the migrants viewed music as a money-making profession since it was often paying jobs in music which led them to leave. This implies a willingness to change to fit the demands of audience and employers.

This raises the unanswerable question of whether recordings such as those made by Kid Ory in Los Angeles in 1922 and by King Oliver's Chicago-based band in 1923 were really representative of the music of black New Orleans in the 1912–23 period. The answer seems to be that we will never know. Yet with the major migration and the slowing of creativity in New Orleans itself, this city could not remain a major center in the development of the music but would become just one of many territory hubs.

Chicago

New Orleans migrants were part of Chicago's very active black musical life in the 1914–1923 period. The black population of Chicago exploded during the Great Migration from 44,103 to 109,458. The black population in Chicago was half the size of that in New Orleans at the beginning of this period. By 1920 Chicago's blacks outnumbered New Orleans' blacks by 9,000.[26] Job possibilities for black musicians in Chicago were much greater. While the number of locations increased, the basic pattern of theaters, cabarets, and dance halls remained the same. The importance of established figures like Dave Peyton and Charles Elgar, and institutions like Local 208 remained, but new leaders like Charles "Doc" Cooke, Erskine Tate, Manuel Perez, Freddie Keppard, and Joe "King" Oliver emerged.

The population growth helped stimulate theater jobs for musicians. New bands joined the established pre-1914 groups or replaced them. By January 1915, Will H. Dorsey, Joe Jordan, and Wilbur Sweatman of the first wave of Chicago theater bands had all moved to New York. At the same time the four pit bands of 1912 had grown to seven groups of five pieces or less in black South Side theaters. They included "Professor" Ed Bailey's States' Theater orchestra of violin, cornet, clarinet, piano, and drums. By 1919, Bailey and his two chief competitors, Clarence Jones's Owl Theater orchestra and Erskine Tate's Vendome Theater group, had expanded to eight pieces. Jones had two violins and a cornet, trombone, clarinet, pianist-leader, cello-string bass, and drums. None of these musicians had any New Orleans background and only Tate's clarinetist "Buster" Bailey would have a significant career in jazz. They represent the spectrum of black music at the time. They came from Memphis,

36

Louisville, Cincinnati, Detroit, and small towns like Rockford, Illinois, and Logansport, Indiana. They brought formal musical training, some dance experience, and work with circus, minstrel, and other brass bands. All were readers doing concert, vaudeville, and film scores. They stressed written arrangements and section work with little emphasis at this point on improvised solos.[27]

Early in 1915, the vaudeville circuit brought Chicago its first strong taste of a black New Orleans jazz band when The Creole Band played the Grand Theater. Tony Langston's review shows that Chicago wasn't quite sure what to make of this music, "an aggregation of comedy musicians. . . . The members of the band know how to extract the most weird effects from their various instruments and are assisted by a character comedian of good voice. The act was a novel one and went well."[28] This shows that the sound of New Orleans jazz was something new in Chicago in 1915 and not entirely appreciated except as comedy. This was a two-week vaudeville stint to a black theater. The band did not become a regular part of the Chicago scene.[29]

It is unclear when the first black New Orleans jazz bands actually settled in Chicago. The *Chicago Defender* showed pianists like Tony Jackson and Jelly Roll Morton and blues singers dominating the cabaret scene between 1914 and 1918.[30] The first mention of a New Orleans jazz band in a Chicago job and one of the first uses of the word jazz came in February 1918 when Manuel Perez's Creole Orchestra opened at the Pekin Dancing Pavilion. From that point on, New Orleans men such as Perez, Freddie Keppard, and by 1919 Joe Oliver were clearly very important at the Deluxe Cafe, Royal Gardens, and other South Side cabarets. There were actually only enough New Orleans musicians for two and a half bands, but by doubling up jobs they completely dominated the cabaret scene by late 1918.[31] Their success attracted more men, which in turn lead to some tension with Local 208. That tension combined with shifting tastes, a new anti-cabaret law, some homesickness, and perhaps fear and disillusionment with the North after the Chicago race riot of the summer of 1919 led some New Orleans men to return home by early 1920. Others including King Oliver's band moved to other areas such as the West Coast by 1921.[32]

While the establishment bands dominated the theater jobs, and the New Orleans bands took over the cabaret jobs after February 1918, the dancing scene was less clear. Some New Orleans bands were playing for dancing but the dominant leader here was a migrant from Detroit, Charles "Doc" Cooke. In the summer of 1918 he had four different bands that were mixtures of Detroit and Chicago establishment players. At the same time, Charles Elgar, a New Orleans Creole, had a band of mainly Chicago men playing for mostly white dances. By 1923, both Cooke and Elgar were leading big bands that included violin, two cornets, trombone, alto and tenor sax, which both doubled clarinet, piano, banjo, tuba, and drums. Both bands seem to have relied primarily on written arrangements with little improvisation.[33]

What did these Chicago bands of 1914–1923 sound like? This is one area where the phonograph industry lets down the historian. None of the black Chicago bands recorded before 1923. Do their later recordings accurately represent the earlier period? The answer is unclear for four reasons. First, the bands themselves may have been changing before they recorded. Second, the records may not reflect the live performances of the groups. Third, the demands of the recordings themselves may change the sounds of the bands. Finally, the influence of some records may change the style of other bands. All of these questions are particularly important in looking at the 1923 recordings of King Oliver's Creole Jazz Band.

These classic recordings are enormously important in jazz history. They represent the first widely available recordings by a black New Orleans jazz band and have been heavily studied, but the key question of whether they are representative of the sound of the New Orleans-in-Chicago bands of 1918–1923 has never been clearly answered.

Despite the tendency to view King Oliver as part of an unchanging New Orleans tradition, it seems that his style and sound grew and changed throughout his career. Edmond Souchon remembered,

> By the time Oliver was playing at the Tulane gymnasium, he had acquired a technique that was much more smooth . . . his band was adapting itself to the white dances more and more. At Big 25 [in Storyville] it was hard-hitting rough and ready, full of fire and drive. He subdued this to please the different patrons at the gym dances, . . . By the time Oliver had reached Chicago and the peak of his popularity, his sound was not the same. It was a different band, a different and more polished Oliver, an Oliver who had completely lost his New Orleans sound.[34]

It is unclear if Souchon is talking about 1923 or later, exaggerating, or simply emphasizing tone qualities that would be less obvious to people outside the New Orleans tradition, but he does show an Oliver open to change. Warren "Baby" Dodds, the drummer on the 1923 recordings, emphasized the band's job and environment as a source of change. "The people came to dance. One couldn't help but dance to that band. . . . It was a dance band that liked to play anything. . . . We worked to make music and we played music to make people like it."[35]

John Lincoln Collier points out that the technology of these early recordings makes them very unreliable sources for elements such as musical keys and tone quality.[36] Also, Johnny St. Cyr's guitar and Dodds's drums are often faintly heard, and Bill Johnson's string bass was left out of the sessions because the recording equipment could not pick it up. This was part of the technological emphasis that would see the more recordable banjo and tuba dominate the 1920s rhythm sections.[37]

Finally, there is the question of how completely the 1923 Oliver band itself reflected the total New Orleans-in-Chicago tradition. Most of the men in the band, including Oliver and Louis Armstrong on cornets, Johnson, Baby Dodds and his clarinetist brother Johnny, were from the blues-tinged uptown New Orleans tradition. St. Cyr and Honore Dutrey, reading cello parts on his trombone, were Creoles, while pianist Lil Hardin was from Memphis. Only Armstrong was a recent arrival from New Orleans; the rest had been away from the Crescent City for several years.

Despite all of these cautions, it is clear that while the individual sound of the band is distinct, its overall approach to music is representative of a well-established tradition. The music of the Oliver band as shown in recordings like"Alligator Hop" was essentially ensemble music with each instrument given a specific task and range in a highly structured format. The cornets usually took the lead with the clarinet above and trombone below the lead. Unlike later jazz, there was very little space for individual instruments to solo, only occasional stop-time "breaks" where one player would be on his own. In some cases, this came from memorized written arrangements but in others it was collective improvisation from an established, shared tradition. Also, the rhythmic lope or swing of the music and the "dirty" or vocalized tone of the instruments were part of a tradition that went beyond the Oliver band itself. The memories and reviews of the time show that in these elements, the Oliver Creole Jazz Band recordings of 1923 represent the live tradition of the New Orleans-in-Chicago cabaret bands of 1918–23.[38]

It is as the product of a shared tradition among the musicians that much of early jazz is viewed as folk music. Still, this jazz tradition was one of professional performers not amateurs and thus moves away from the usual definitions of folk music. Moreover, after the recordings, King Oliver's music and its traditions became a product of the mass-produced culture, which could be frozen, sampled, and studied through the phonograph. The recordings multiplied the impact that Oliver and other New Orleans-in-Chicago bands made through live performances. Some of the black establishment men resisted any influence from the New Orleans style. Others, including younger black Chicagoans like Cecil Irwin, learned elements of tone and style but not the entire tradition. Similarly, white dance band musicians like trumpeter Louis Panico of the Isham Jones band came to hear Oliver to learn tricks that could be used in their professional styles, which also became mass-produced products. Elements of Oliver's muted cornet work emerged as Panico's "laughing" cornet in the Jones band's version of "Wang Wang Blues," which was admired by the young black blues singer Jimmy Rushing.[39]

In the mid-twenties, the interchange of black and white musical ideas was taken to another level by the young white high school students known collectively as the Chicagoans or the Austin High Gang: Jimmy McPartland, Bud Freeman, Eddie Condon, Frank Teschemacher, and many others. Many of these kids were listening to Oliver and other black New Orleans bands and to the white New Orleans Rhythm Kings. The Chicagoans tried to borrow the entire musical language of these bands. This is the first time that jazz emerged as a consciously learned style to be picked up by individuals who had not shared the personal experiences that had created the music. The Chicagoans were consciously choosing to express themselves in a different music, partly in revolt against the values of white middle-class America as they saw it.

They could do this in Chicago in 1918–28 because they had access to the music as a live tradition before it became a product of the mass culture. They could not only learn from the records as did others around the country, but they could also attend live performances which were limited to Chicago. It is to the Chicagoans and related figures such as Bix Beiderbecke that most of the images of jazz as a revolt against the values of white middle-class America can be traced, and for these musicians, those images hold true.[40]

The importance of the King Oliver Creole Jazz Band of 1923 in the history of jazz is much larger when viewed from the present than it was in Chicago in 1923. The theater bands of Erskine Tate and Clarence Jones, the dance bands of Doc Cooke and Charles Elgar, and the cabaret bands of Oliver, Perez, and Keppard were viewed as successful jazz groups in Chicago in 1923. Oliver, despite his records, might not be considered even first among equals.

Even in the cabaret area, Oliver's style had successful competition in Chicago in 1923. It was not Oliver but trumpeter Jimmy Wade and pianist Clarence M. Jones who opened the downtown Loop area to black bands. By 1923, the bands of these two leaders were alternating at the Moulin Rouge. Both groups consisted of violin, trumpet, trombone, clarinet, alto sax, piano, tuba, and drums. It is very hard to determine the sound of these other Chicago bands in the 1914–23 period. The cautions mentioned in discussing Oliver's records apply even more to the Chicago establishment because they made very few recordings, mostly later in the 1920s. Since they come after both the Oliver and early Fletcher Henderson recordings of 1923, these later sides may have been influenced by those black pioneers. Allowing for all that, Jimmy Wade's "Someday Sweetheart," Erskine Tate's "Cutie's Blues," and Doc Cooke's "So This Is Venice," show that these bands were going in very different directions than the polyphony of Oliver's Creole Jazz Band. All used more traditional European harmonies both in written arrangements and in worked up sections. Even the rhythmic swing and tonal qualities of these bands, while influenced by Oliver and others, were not the same.[41] New Orleans elements were a major part of the sound of Chicago in 1923, but the Midwest metropolis had merged and combined traditions to create a rainbow of sounds that was uniquely its own.

New York City

The situation in New York City between 1914 and 1923 was both similar to and different than that in Chicago. Clearly, the Great Migration also led to an enormous increase of the black population. By 1920, with more than 150,000 black residents, New York City had the largest black population in the country. Most of the blacks were still coming from the Southeast, particularly the Carolinas. Black musicians from New Orleans had very little presence in New York before 1923.

By 1914, Harlem was emerging as the magnet for the black community in New York City, providing the social cohesion and institutions that had been missing earlier. In fact, Harlem was becoming a magnet for black artists and intellectuals nationally as the explosion of talent that would be known as the Harlem Renaissance began to occur. Class and style distinctions in the black community similar to those in Chicago emerged.[42]

New York continued to dominate the entertainment world. Developments in social dancing, vaudeville, theater, cabaret, and phonograph recording were all highly visible in New York. The result was a black musical spectrum somewhat different than Chicago's. Large society orchestras playing for white and black private dances and ballrooms continued their reign. After 1917, World War I created a vogue for large military brass bands. Large theater orchestras reappeared on Broadway in 1921 but black theaters did not have prominent orchestras like Chicago's establishment. Various musical ensembles reached white and black audiences as vaudeville acts. In Harlem itself, small five-piece cabaret bands were developing, often mixing New York men with migrants from the Southeast including Jenkins orphanage alumni. These groups often backed up female blues singers. Some black bands were playing white cabarets outside Harlem in competition with a white New Orleans group, the Original Dixieland Jazz Band (ODJB). The ODJB's records and cabaret success in New York after 1917 established jazz as a name for a range of popular music forms. In some Harlem cabarets and private parties in flats, parlor or stride pianists performed regularly.

Due to the concentration of the phonograph industry in New York, most of these styles are represented on record. Recordings before 1920 occurred almost exclusively in New York. This reverses the Chicago problem. With so much black music recorded in New York between 1914 and 1923, the questions for scholars become: (1) was this music unique to New York?, (2) was it important to live performances there?, and (3) was it simply a creation of the record industry?

As indicated in the discussion of the rise of the dance hall, James Reese Europe's Society Orchestra, accompanying Vernon and Irene Castle and playing society dances, was the dominant black band in New York in 1914. They made the first black popular music dance records released that same year. The *Chicago Defender* headlined "Perpetuate Europe Music on Victor Records" and saw Europe's position as "the darling of white society" as "an advancement for the race."[43] The recordings are a valid sample of the tangos and fox trots that Europe played. The sound is clearly stiff instrumental ragtime. Several of the tunes like "Too Much Mustard" and Wilbur Sweatman's "Down Home Rag" are formal rags and are played through repeatedly with little variation. The string instrumentation was much larger and heavier than in King Oliver or the Original Dixieland Jazz Band. Europe used two violins, cornet, clarinet, trombone, piano, five banjo-mandolins, cello, string bass, and drums. The key players were Cricket Smith, cornet; Edgar Campbell, clarinet; and Buddy Gilmore, drums. Gilmore is remembered as one of the first drummers to use the modern trap set.

The sound was full but it left little space for individual musicians to stand out. As stressed in chapter one, Jim Europe believed in written scores and worked hard to limit improvising by his musicians. The result is a very steady, repetitive music that provided a good basis for dancing. Still, it does not have the variety and freshness of Oliver's music. Remember that Europe was playing primarily for a white dancing audience, and he seems to have consciously sought a sound that would fit into the

American popular music tradition. How well he succeeded can be seen by comparing his version of "Down Home Rag" with that of the Six Brown Brothers, a white vaudeville group. Although Jim Europe's version is taken at a much quicker tempo, both show the same stiff rhythm that would fit white dancers but would be far from the African-American folk tradition. Between 1914 and 1917 Jim Europe's instrumental ragtime was the dominant dancing sound in New York. His reign ended only when Europe and much of his band left town for war service with the fighting 369th by October 1917.[44]

The gap he left was filled at first by similar bands, including one led by pianist Ford Dabney, which opened in the pit of Florenz Ziegfeld's *Midnight Frolics* revue in late 1916. Dabney kept that job for eight years and between 1916 and 1920 made over forty-five records for the Aeolian label. Based on these recordings, it is evident that Dabney also played the music as written and discouraged individual improvisation. The rhythm was stiff and on the beat. The repertoire was larger since Dabney was a show as well as dance band and played more popular tunes and even some blues. Several of his key players like Cricket Smith and Edgar Campbell and Dabney himself were veterans of Jim Europe's bands.[45]

The end of World War I brought James Reese Europe's 369th Hell-fighters band and other military bands home. The Hellfighters had been the toast of France and England with their jazz and personality, and Jim Europe expected to continue the group as a professional performing band in the tradition of John Philip Souza. They recorded thirty-nine sides for Pathe in March and April of 1919. The selections show a wide repertoire of choral works, spirituals, overtures, marches, and popular tunes including Shelton Brooks's "Darktown Strutters' Ball," W. C. Handy's "St. Louis Blues," and the Original Dixieland Jazz Band's "Clarinet Marmalade." Europe had a complete entertainment package with his own singers, dancers, composers, and arrangers such as Eubie Blake, Noble Sissle, Eugene Mikell, and Creighton Thompson. The huge band included more than thirty pieces, and Europe still stressed playing the music as written. At the same time he announced that he was playing and defining jazz.[46]

Europe was stabbed to death by one of his drummers while on tour in Boston in May of 1919, but large brass bands or orchestras playing for theater concerts and dances continued to be very important in New York. Will Marion Cook, J. Tim Brymn, Deacon Johnson, Ford Dabney, and Happy Rhone all led groups of this type. Rhone, Will Vodery, Allie Ross, Gus Creagh, and Duncan Myers dominated both black and white society dances with large orchestras that included string sections playing written arrangements of waltzes and popular songs. Several of these leaders were composers who earned more from their compositions than from their band jobs.[47]

Another black musician reaping rewards in Tin Pan Alley from 1914 to 1923 was composer-bandleader W.C. Handy. This veteran of Mahara's Minstrels had led a successful touring brass band based in Memphis for years. He brought this group to New York and recorded several sides between 1918 and 1922, clearly in the brass band tradition. His move to New York and his recordings were primarily aimed at selling his arranged, composed versions of the folk blues. His partner Harry H. Pace had convinced Handy to let him open an office of their music publishing firm in New York City and Handy soon followed. Handy's primary success in New York between 1918 and 1923 was as a composer rather than a performer. He and other blues composers created a craze in the sheet music field between 1914 and 1920, repeating the earlier success of the theater composers.[48]

Two Hellfighters alumni, lyricist-singer Noble Sissle, and composer-pianist Eubie Blake, created more opportunities for large reading black bands when they brought black musicals back to Broadway. Their show *Shuffle Along* opened on May 23, 1921, setting a pattern of black musicals for the white Broadway audience that would last into the depression. Although Blake was in the East Coast ragtime piano school, the score was written and strictly played in the manner of earlier black Broadway composers. The pit band included violin, viola, cello, flute, two trumpets, trombone, clarinet, c-melody sax, piano, string bass, and drums. William Grant Still and Hall Johnson, whose later careers were primarily in the classical world, played in the *Shuffle Along* pit band. Broadway pit bands were another opportunity for black composers and reading rather than improvising musicians.[49]

The first real challenge to the reading school was the 1917 arrival in New York of the Original Dixieland Jazz Band. This white group had left New Orleans in 1916. Early in 1917, they brought the word jazz and their version of the New Orleans sound into Reisenweber's cabaret in Manhattan and were a smash hit. They recorded two sides for Columbia in January and two more for Victor in February, and the records were very successful. Here was a serious alternative to Jim Europe and the other black sounds of New York, admired by even some black musicians.

The ODJB was only a five-piece group: Nick LaRocca, cornet; Larry Shields, clarinet; Eddie Edwards, trombone; Henry Ragas, piano; and Tony Sbarbaro, drums. They used the same ensemble format of cornet lead, clarinet high, and trombone low shown in the Oliver recordings. They were basically ear players, playing a syncopated but on-the-beat ragtime with no blues notes but with "freak effects" such as the animal sounds on their first hit "Livery Stable Blues," which fit the "animal dances" of the period. The breaks were pale versions of the muted cornet work of black musicians like Freddie Keppard and King Oliver. The band shared some elements with black New Orleans groups like The Creole Band and the New Orleans-in-Chicago cabaret bands. The ODJB's great success in New York may have come because they had no black New Orleans competition there.[50]

On the other hand, in the year of the East St. Louis race riot that killed forty African-Americans, being white may have been the ODJB's ace in the hole. It eased their dealings with white managers and recording executives. While Keppard may have been offered a chance to record and turned it down, LaRocca certainly wasn't hurt in talking to Victor Records because of his skin color. Being in New York also gave the ODJD a much better opportunity to record. The companies were not yet recording away from their home base in New York. That was why Europe and Dabney were so widely recorded while equally fine groups elsewhere in the country were not. Finally the ODJB, unlike the Creole Band, was playing primarily for white dancers.

The tone and rhythm of the ODJB defined for many listeners the new sound called jazz. Although it is unclear how new the music of the ODJB was, it clearly had a new name. While the root of the term is very unclear, its continuous use for a music form starts with the ODJB recordings.[51] At first, "jazz" had no clear musical meaning. After March 1917, all of the black bands previously mentioned and many white groups would claim to be playing jazz and there would be no clear rules to deny their claims.

One of the black performers who took advantage of this confusion was vaudevillian Wilbur Sweatman. He recorded frequently from 1916 to 1921 and after March 1917 often used the title Jazz Band or even Original Jazz Band for his group. The records are rare but descriptions emphasize his novelty playing. His main vaudeville calling card was playing three clarinets simultaneously. The band's repertoire was heavy with popular songs. The group was small and included primarily reading brass band veterans.[52]

While some black sounds were on record between 1917 and 1923, they seem to have had limited availability and impact. The most accessible recorded examples of jazz in New York between 1917 and 1923 were from white groups like Ladd's Black Aces and Earl Fuller's Famous Jazz Band who took their lead from the ODJB. The Aces' pianist Jimmy Durante was typical of New York area musicians who played in the ensemble style of ODJB with "legitimate" tone, no blues notes, and a stiff on the beat rhythm. They simply continued the notion of the jazz band as a small, five-piece group with a front line of cornet, clarinet, and trombone.[53]

At the same time larger eight- to ten-piece white dance bands such as Art Hickman's and Paul Whiteman's began to call their music jazz as well. These groups of violin, one or two cornets, trombone, one or two clarinets and saxophones, piano, string bass, guitar, and drums, playing written arrangements of popular tunes, were clearly in the society dance mode. In person and on record, jazz encompassed a confusing spectrum of music.[54]

In August of 1920, Mamie Smith, a black cabaret singer, recorded "Crazy Blues," by black composer Perry Bradford, who arranged the session for Okeh records. While neither the song nor the singer were purely in the folk blues tradition, they were close enough for the song to sell very well in Northern black neighborhoods. This success led other white companies to record black female blues singers often with a three- to five-piece band. This pattern became common in the cabarets as well.[55]

Prior to 1919, the cabarets in New York as in Chicago had featured pianists, often in the Eastern ragtime style called stride developed by James P. Johnson, Luckey Roberts, and others. These pianists now combined with a mixture of brass band men like Johnny Dunn of Handy's Band, circus-influenced Garvin Bushell, and Jenkins Orphanage alumni Gus and Buddy Aiken. Joined by youngsters developing their style like New Yorker Bubber Miley and Missourian Coleman Hawkins, they created music to back up the blues singers. This style is well represented on recordings but the blues, unlike other jazz recordings, stressed singing. The bands were often very much in the background. The sound was still stiff, usually on the beat. Improvisation and blues notes were starting to appear more, particularly when a stride pianist was present. Wandering New Orleans original Sidney Bechet also brought his distinctive and influential sound to the cabaret scene and blues records briefly between tours in Europe.[56]

The blues recording boom provided a new and unique job opportunity for New York black musicians and helped to draw some men to New York. Clarence Williams, the junior partner in the Williams-Piron Music Company of New Orleans, moved first to Chicago and then to New York to promote the interests of the firm and himself. He was a smart businessman, a smooth-talking promoter, a composer comfortable in a variety of styles, and a pianist-vocalist who could adapt to solo and band accompanying. He made his first recordings under his own name for Okeh in 1921 and by 1923 had become musical or artists and repertoire (A & R) director for that label's race or black series. In that job he had a strong impact on the recording of black music throughout the 1920s.[57]

Fletcher Henderson, another figure who would have an enormous impact on the course of jazz, also arrived in New York at this time through a similar route. A school principal's son from Georgia, he came to New York in 1920 to pursue an education and career in chemistry. Instead he joined Pace-Handy as a song plugger. Harry Pace left the firm to start his own Black Swan Record Company and hired Henderson as musical director. This usually meant providing or arranging accompaniments for blues singers such as Ethel Waters who were the core of the label. Miss Waters complained that Henderson was not comfortable in the blues tradition and ordered him to listen to James P. Johnson piano rolls. Henderson developed his own style and more importantly a core of young black players who could work in the studio. Henderson and his men recorded very frequently in the 1921–1923 period. They were clearly developing a new style as they went along, drawing on all of the sources that existed in the New York spectrum up to that time. It was a style that would try to merge the looseness and improvisation of the blues and the ODJB with the discipline and structure of the brass band and Jim Europe schools.[58]

Although the development of that style will be discussed in detail in chapter five, here are a few key points about the Henderson recordings before the band began its first cabaret job. First, the band was going in several directions at once, reflecting the many sounds around it. However, there was very little polyphony and collective improvisation. Also the Orleans style was not strongly influencing these players even in 1923. It is not clear if these developments were unique to the Henderson studio gang or whether they reflected larger trends in New York. The Oliver Creole Jazz Band sides are the products of a well-developed tradition, while Henderson sides of 1921–23 represent just the first stumbling steps in the process of developing a new black popular music style.

In early 1923, jazz in New York was essentially anything a person said it was. Black musicians in New York had a wide range of jobs and an abundance of music models, all referred to as jazz. The brass bands, society dance orchestras, Broadway pit bands, cabaret bands, and stride pianists were all equally accepted as the sound of jazz in New York at that time. The record industry gave New York musicians another type of job opportunity, and it documented the city's sound. Still, recordings did not yet dominate the national scene. The lack of one clear jazz sound meant that while New York was an interesting part of the jazz spectrum in 1923, it did not define the music.

FROM JAZZ TO SWING

Conclusion

Between 1914 and 1923 the Great Migration, the rise of new jobs in cabarets and theaters, and the emergence of the phonograph as a home entertainment medium, all helped to transform the black music that was now calling itself jazz. That transformation varied in the three major black musical centers. New Orleans lost local musicians to the national musical world. The sound of the Crescent City was carried to much of the country and was changed in the process, while musical opportunities within New Orleans declined slightly. A strong New Orleans infusion in Chicago added to a rapidly growing musical scene of cabaret and theater jobs and created a wide spectrum of musics. Part of this spectrum was documented at the end of the period with the King Oliver Creole Jazz Band recordings of 1923, which represent a snapshot late in the development of the New Orleans tradition.

In New York, black New Orleans music had little impact before 1923. Here, the most active growth of the black music scene was dominated by classically-trained musicians such as James Reese Europe and Fletcher Henderson. The growth of jobs for black musicians in New York included more opportunities to play for white audiences in dance and theater settings than in Chicago. The resulting differences in black jazz in this period can be heard in the extensive recordings of Europe, Henderson, and Ford Dabney made between 1914 and 1923. Prior to 1923, New York jazz is more available on record than any other style. This changes with the Oliver recordings.

Between 1914 and 1923, New Orleans exported musicians while Chicago synthesized jazz styles and New York developed the national structure of the black entertainment world of the future. Still, the bulk of the black audience and much of the black musical community were not in these three major centers before 1923. We must look to the territories to complete the picture of black musical life of this period to fully understand the developments in the rest of the 1920s and 1930s.

3

Territory Bands 1914–1923

WHILE New Orleans, Chicago, and New York tend to be the centers of attention, it is important to remember that the bulk of black Americans in this period still lived in the "territories," rural areas and rapidly growing cities that made up the rest of America. In the territories, where city and country met most directly, the conflict of cultures that helped create jazz and the jazz age of the 1920s was most keenly felt. Black territory jazzmen were key to creating expressions of the new feeling that made this music important.

These areas experienced the same social and entertainment changes as the major centers. The Great Migration, the rise of motion pictures, vaudeville, the phonograph, and particularly the revolution in social dancing affected the territories. The term jazz gained currency, and it was even more difficult to ascertain its exact meaning because no territory bands recorded until 1923. Still, it is possible to get a good idea of the changes that were occurring and to see the emergence of six distinct territories: East Coast, Southeast, Midwest, Northwest, Southwest, and West Coast, each with a somewhat different cultural and musical life.

East Coast

The East Coast territory included the New England and Middle Atlantic states and reached as far south as Washington, D.C. It was an area of cities with only a few smaller towns. There was more emphasis on the new urban entertainment of vaudeville, movies, and dance halls, and less interest in brass bands and circuses. By 1920, it included four of the United States' five largest black urban centers: Philadelphia, Baltimore, Washington, D.C., and of course New York City. New York City always dominated the musical life of this territory, providing musicians for outlying jobs and drawing in the best local musicians.

The dominant sound in this territory in this period was the school of ragtime known as stride piano. James P. Johnson, Luckey Roberts, and Eubie Blake, all of whom had gone on to New York, had their roots here. A new crop of players including Duke Ellington, Count Basie, and Claude Hopkins soon followed. In 1914, the stride piano was heard in vaudeville and movie theaters, cabarets, dance halls, and sporting houses. As a resort town, Atlantic City in particular brought New York and local players together in its cabarets and other locations. By the end of the period small bands were in many of these locations.[1]

While stride had a strong hold on the area other styles were heard, but they were usually imported. The New York orchestras of James Reese Europe, Will Marion Cook, and Ford Dabney, all originally from Washington, D.C., played the Howard Theater in D.C. and some society dances but local dance bands remained much smaller.[2]

The black vaudeville theaters of Washington, D.C., Baltimore, and Philadelphia brought in the best of the touring shows like S.H. Dudley's Smart Set, the Black Patti Troupe, and the Whitman sisters. The jazz bands of Will Marion Cook and Wilbur Sweatman played on both black and white vaudeville circuits in this region. The touring groups enjoyed playing in this area since the crowds were responsive. Groups could play a whole week at one theater instead of split weeks or one-nighters. In fact, playing the New York, Philadelphia, Baltimore, Washington, D.C., circuit became known as "going around the world."[3]

By 1917 the dance craze had arrived in the capital with dance halls and society dances providing opportunities to black musicians. Duke Ellington moved up from piano to leading a dance band for "Doc" Perry, and then to his own group, the core of which he would later take to New York. He competed with Meyer Davis by taking out the same size advertisement in the phone book.[4]

Philadelphia developed its own dance and theater bands by 1920.[5] The music seems to have been influenced by stride. The bands featured pianists and had an on-the-beat approach and an absence of blue notes. The style was similar to that shown by the early black New York blues accompanists, some of whom were from this area. Before 1923, stride piano was much more important than instrumental band jazz in the East Coast scene.

Southeast

The Southeastern territory, south of the Potomac and Ohio rivers and east of the Mississippi, had the largest black population of the entire United States, but it was spread out across many towns and rural areas. It was losing residents and influence as the Great Migration drew people away to the new black meccas in the North. Black opportunity in the Southeast was more obviously limited by segregation laws, but the strengths of community and folk tradition were stronger. Musically, the tent, minstrel, and circus bands were still active, and church music and the blues were a part of daily life for many musicians and much of their audience.

All of these influences shaped the music and lives of black jazz musicians in this area. This enormous territory had several urban centers with wide influence over the farms and small towns. These urban centers were New Orleans, Memphis, Louisville, Birmingham (Alabama), and Charleston, South Carolina. Atlanta became important later in the 1920s. In each of these areas, older musicians were adapting to new demands, and young musicians were developing new styles, both helping to form jazz.

The influence of New Orleans did not extend very far into the rest of the Southeast territory. With so many New Orleans men migrating away, opportunities available in the Crescent City were sufficient for those remaining. New Orleans bands and musicians rarely traveled far for work. Some bands played rural dances in Louisiana, and others worked in Mobile and along the Mississippi-Alabama Gulf Coast, but the New Orleans men could comfortably stay close to home.[6] The major exception was the work on the Mississippi riverboat excursions which took New Orleans players like Louis Armstrong, Pops Foster, and others out of the Southeast by basing them in St. Louis.

Musical jobs were not as plentiful in the other Southeastern hubs. In many ways the influence of Memphis, Louisville, Birmingham, and Charleston musicians was greater in the small towns of the Southeast because the musicians needed these towns for jobs and visited them often. These cities and the rest of the territory did not share the French-Spanish heritage and uptown Anglo-downtown Creole distinction of New Orleans, and thus New Orleans music may have seemed a bit alien in the rest of the territory.

Memphis was particularly important from the turn of the century to 1918. The open town run by "Mister" Ed Crump drew entertainers and musicians. The major black musical figure was W. C. Handy. This minstrel veteran and former music professor dominated the area not only with his blues compositions but also with his bands. He moved into the dance field in Memphis around 1910 beginning as the fourth best band and gradually becoming the top man, booking three different small bands of violin, cornet, trombone, clarinet, saxophone, string bass, and guitar. Band members were mostly reading men but they played the blues in the bars and riverboats of Memphis. In the rest of the territory, Handy was known for his twenty-five-piece brass band which toured extensively in the Southeast from 1912 until he left for New York in 1918.

Blues, like ragtime, involves three overlapping concepts. First, it is a specific musical form, usually twelve bars in groups of four with specific rules on chord progressions and movement. Second, it is a general approach to music favoring a rough tone and "blue" notes: slides, slurs, and tones between those of the European traditional scales. Finally, it was a popular music craze which flourished between 1900 and 1923 and was based to a large extent on the compositions of W. C. Handy. Handy's compositions came from his merger of the oral and written traditions. After a bad experience with the white publishing house handling his first big hit, "Memphis Blues," Handy had opened his own publishing house in Memphis with a partner, Harry Pace.[7]

By 1918, Memphis was losing many of its best musicians. Handy and his publishing partner Harry Pace moved their operation to New York, while Lil Hardin and Buster Bailey moved to Chicago. By May of 1919, Memphis-born Erskine Tate had brought several other Memphis players into his Vendome Theatre Orchestra in Chicago. Handy blames this exodus on the worsening of race relations during World War I. That may have had a definite impact, but the job opportunities in New York and Chicago were also major factors. While many good musicians remained in Memphis, it was less important to jazz in this territory after 1918.[8]

Louisville had a very active black musical life throughout this period. Brass bands were important here. The kid band of the Booker T. Washington Community Center brought together musicians from the middle and lower classes. Dickie Wells remembers, "Most of the younger guys in the brass band wanted to pull out and swing, but the older guys used to prefer to stay with the marches. . . . All we did was try to make a better arrangement than the next band had. We played as we felt, so some nights it was good, and some nights bad. There were no set solos."[9]

The Washington brass band, which included at various times Wells, vocalist Helen Humes, and trumpeters Buddy Lee and Jonah Jones, and the older Louisville Musical Club band including trumpeter George Mitchell and drummer John Wickliffe, played funerals, parades, and other events throughout Kentucky. They also spun off small jazz bands to play for dances. "The big band played in the day and the jazz band at night. . . . We would travel in a truck and play country fairs and the pay was three dollars and a half a week."[10]

By 1919, Stanley R. "Fess" Williams, Lockwood Lewis, and Howard Jordan all led small jazz bands playing for dances in and around Louisville. Lewis, a circus veteran, cashed in on the new fame of jazz with a small jazz vaudeville act in the winter of 1917–18. Later he led the Booker T. Washington brass band. His vaudeville style and entertaining skills made his dance band the most popular in the area.

Lewis strongly influenced Fess Williams, a twenty-five-year-old who in 1919 left the secure profession of teaching for the uncertainties of the life of a dance musician. For the next four years, his quintet of sax, trombone, piano, banjo, and drums toured Kentucky, Tennessee, Alabama, Indiana, Virginia, West Virginia, and South Carolina from its Louisville base, playing one-night dances in firehouses, armories, and tobacco barns. By the early 1920s, Williams's dazzling showmanship dominated the area although Lewis was stiff competition for local jobs. Williams still felt frustrated in this setting and disbanded to go to Chicago and later New York where he was successful.[11]

The tension between education and music as careers was resolved in the Birmingham area by N. Clark Smith and John "Fess" Whately who were both performers and music teachers. Major Smith had a brief career in the Southeast but with a lasting impact. As music professor and head of the brass band at Tuskegee Institute, he taught many future jazz musicians including Fess Williams. Smith also toured the band to raise money for the school and recruit future students. He left Tuskegee in the early 1920s, eventually moving to Chicago where he led a boys band for the *Chicago Defender* and influenced a whole new generation of young musicians.[12]

Fess Whately, a native of Alabama, became the dominant black music teacher in the state. He started teaching at Birmingham's Industrial High School in 1917 and organized the first public school band in the area. His society dance band was the most important early territory band in Alabama. Very little is known about the actual style or sound of this band but it was clearly respected in the area, and Whately proved that one could be both performer and teacher in the territories.[13]

In Charleston, South Carolina, the dominant black institution was the Jenkins Orphanage. By the turn of the century, it was training its children to play brass band music and using their touring bands to raise money. Many graduates became professional musicians. They left segregated Charleston in large numbers, often leaving with the vaudeville and tent shows that swung through town. They often ended up in New York where some like the Aiken and Benford brothers became key players in the early bands of this period. Their stiff on-the-beat rhythm and "legitimate" tone were early influences on Eastern jazz style.[14]

The touring vaudeville and tent shows with their brass bands and blues singers playing for primarily black audiences were an extremely important part of the picture in the Southeast in this period. The bulk of the developing TOBA black vaudeville circuit was in this territory, providing work for touring musicians and small pit bands, which were also playing for silent films. In the Southeast, particularly in the smaller towns, often the bands could not read and theaters simply had pianists rather than groups.[15]

The picture in the Southeast in this period was mixed. Lots of people from different backgrounds were playing jazz but what that meant was not clear. The New Orleans sound did not dominate the territory though musicians were still very active in the city itself. The older brass band sound of the tent shows, the Jenkins Orphanage, and the Handy band was important, but many brass band men like Lockwood Lewis were trying new things. Younger musicians like Fess Williams and Fess Whately were shaping music specifically for dancing. The dance bands included only three to five pieces, because jobs were limited and pay was very low. In many smaller locations, musicians played by ear and the blues were probably strongest in the Mississippi through Tennessee area. In the most rural areas, the country blues men with their guitars and vocals dominated while other areas heard the improvised instruments of jug bands.[16] Southeastern jazzmen usually had less contact with white audiences and musicians than their colleagues in other areas.

Midwest

The Midwestern territory included Ohio, Indiana, Illinois, Michigan, West Virginia, and western parts of Pennsylvania and New York state. It included not only big cities such as Cleveland, Detroit, and Pittsburgh with sizeable and rapidly growing black populations, but also medium-sized cities like Buffalo, and small communities with small black populations. Perhaps surprisingly, many of the jazz musicians of this area came from small towns like Evansville and Crawfordsville, Indiana, and Ripley, Xenia, and particularly, Springfield, Ohio.

In this environment, middle class values and frequent contacts with whites were more common than in the Southeast. The result was a style with a smoother sound and more emphasis on reading music. Throughout the swing era, Midwestern sidemen would be known for their pure tone and reading abilities.

While circuses and vaudeville shows continued to tour this area, the major development of 1914–23 was the enormous growth in the number of bands playing for dances. In Detroit, the large society orchestra style was important. By 1917, "there were at least four orchestras of 12 or more players working steady engagements in Detroit."[17] These included the large band that "Doc" Cooke brought to Chicago in 1918 and the Leroy Smith orchestra that arrived in New York in 1921 to be the first band at Connie's Inn.[18] "The Smith band was essentially a show band. He being of the old school, always insisted on playing what was written, having been taught himself by European musicians. When he started playing, the older musicians with whom he worked were just as rigid as to reading, intonation etc., and they all frowned upon improvisation and 'getting off'."[19] The Smith group included two violins and the reedmen doubled on cello, oboe, and bassoon. Their classical leanings made them very successful with white society dances in Detroit. Smith may have been experimenting with "symphonic jazz" even before Paul Whiteman. Smith's 1928 "St. Louis Blues" record was clearly in that category.[20]

In the rest of the territory, the dance bands were smaller, made up of three to seven pieces. The most popular band in Columbus, Ohio, early in this period looked like a trimmed down version of the Leroy Smith group. Charlie Parker's Popular Players, consisting of violin, flute, bassoon, cello, and piano, was playing sedate tea music at fashionable white hotels as early as 1912. By 1917, a jazz influence was being felt with the addition of a clarinet, banjo, and drums plus a saxophonist and trombonist both doubling on trumpets. In 1918, Parker's pianist Sammy Stewart formed his own seven-piece Singing Syncopators with an emphasis on showmanship and competed with Parker for the next three years. Stewart's band spent 1922 in Toledo and then moved to Detroit and expanded to ten men, picking up several Parker alumni. In March 1923, Stewart took this band into the Entertainer's Cafe on Chicago's South Side to become an important part of that jazz story.[21]

In Indianapolis, small dance bands founded by brass band musicians were very popular, playing for white hotel dances as well as for clubs in the black entertainment district.[22] Cleveland had several small trios and quintets playing for dancing particularly in the black community by 1919 and also benefitted from touring vaudeville groups such as J. Rosamond

Johnson's, which played at a white theater in 1919. Besides Sammy Stewart, the most interesting band in Toledo was a 1921 group that included James P. Johnson, June Clark, and Jimmy Harrison who had been stranded by touring bands. Joe Smith played with small groups in the Cincinnati area at this time.[23]

Interestingly, the territory's biggest impact on jazz in the 1920s came from Springfield, Ohio, a town of 60,000, which produced two whole national impact bands and a host of sidemen. The triangle of Springfield, Xenia, and Wilberforce had been an important area for black Americans since the pre-Civil War establishment of Wilberforce College, one of the first black schools in the United States. By 1910, the black community and its institutions were well established. Around 1920, two small bands were competing for dance jobs here, the Synco Jazz Band led by former circus drummer Bill McKinney, and a group led by two young brothers, Cecil and Lloyd Scott. McKinney lured away two of the Scotts's men and his new Synco Septette became the dominant group in the area touring Indiana, Kentucky, Michigan, Virginia, and West Virginia.[24]

The McKinney and Scott groups were small and stressed showmanship and novelty tunes in the vaudeville tradition of the Creole band and the ODJB. Synco trombonist Claude Jones remembers, "It was a show. There was dancing, singing, everything in it. And comedy too."[25] McKinney danced around his drums while Jones played his slide with his foot, but Jones emphasizes that the band could also play good music. Jones and pianist Todd Rhodes both had college music training and admired reedman Milton Senior who according to Jones was the real musical leader of the band. McKinney had showmanship and business sense. The Scotts continued to compete and learn from McKinney. Both groups would later have national impact, the Synco group as McKinney's Cotton Pickers and the Scott group as Cecil Scott's Bright Boys.[26]

Northwest

The Northwest jazz territory included Minnesota, Wisconsin, Iowa, North Dakota, South Dakota, Nebraska, and Colorado. "Several things characterized this territory: bitterly cold, icy, and snowy winters, tiny towns, the complete absence of Negro population except for in the few bigger towns in the area, and a corny and backward musical taste among the population . . . miserably bad roads in most area."[27] This was not a major stop for the Great Migration and the black population remained small throughout the period. Nevertheless, this area had a very active and unique black musical life. The small-town and rural folk traditions and small number of blacks created a situation where black music was accepted as another ethnic tradition and valued as a rarity. Black entertainers often had to be imported into the territory and because of its isolation often went on to the Southwest or Chicago later.

Black minstrel and circus show bands had toured the area since the late 1800s. Both W. C. Handy and Wilbur Sweatman toured here with Mahara's Minstrels. Sweatman stopped off in Minneapolis long enough to make some extremely rare cylinder recordings for a furniture shop, which are actually among the earliest records of black music.[28] The Western Vaudeville Managers Association (WVMA) and Pantages vaudeville circuits brought the New Orleans sound of the Creole band through this area occasionally between 1914 and 1918.[29]

Maceo Pinkard, who later composed "Sweet Georgia Brown" and "Sugar," dropped off the vaudeville circuit to lead a "saxophone band" playing dances, theater, and hotel work in the Omaha area during the 1916–1917 season.[30] This put him in the city that would be the most important in the territory. Omaha had an established black community. Its musical tradition was represented by Dan Desdunes's thirty-piece brass band, well known locally and nationally at lodge conventions and other events.[31]

In 1921, one of the territory's rare home-grown musicians, Frank "Red" Perkins, led a dance band in Omaha. Born in Iowa in 1890, Perkins toured with a minstrel show in the territory from 1910 to 1915. In 1919, he was a nightclub musician in Fort Dodge, Iowa, enjoying the prosperity created by mustering out servicemen. The white owner of the club moved it to Des Moines, imported a large show with thirty dancers and chorus girls and comedians, and encouraged drummer Perkins to organize and lead a quartet of trumpet, trombone, piano. Prohibition closed the club, and Perkins's band began touring the territory in vaudeville and then with a carnival playing dances on the side. Perkins built a reputation as a trumpeter comparable in the territory to Mamie Smith's trumpeter Johnny Dunn, the first black recording trumpet star. This touring took Perkins to Omaha where from 1921 to 1923 he led a five-piece cabaret group including future Fletcher Henderson trombonist Charlie Green. They traveled to dances in small towns in a 1916 Ford.[32]

Although not as well documented, similar patterns were being followed elsewhere in this territory between 1914 and 1923. George Weaver led a dance band in St. Paul and Milwaukee. Jack Moore's group played Milwaukee from 1919 to 1920. Milwaukee often imported bands from Chicago. Charles Elgar's band played there as early as 1918. John Wickliffe, a classically-trained musician from Louisville, led a group of violin, cornet, trombone, clarinet, sax, piano, banjo, and drums at a Milwaukee cabaret and hotel from 1917 to 1920. Like the Parker group in Columbus it seems to have been more of a society orchestra playing afternoon teas, though it may have played rougher for evening dances. The hottest group in Milwaukee before 1924 probably belonged to Everett "Happy" Robbins, an Oklahoma born pianist-entertainer whose forte was improvising verses about members of the audience. He had played with Bob Shoffner, Ed Vinson, and other New Orleans musicians in Chicago and toured with Mamie Smith's Jazz Hounds. He led a five- or six-piece cabaret band in Milwaukee from 1921 to 1923 that apparently had a hot New Orleans style sound.[33]

While musicians would still need to be imported, by 1923 the Twin Cities, Omaha, and Milwaukee all had strong bands that would also play dances in the small towns and rural areas. Where bands could not be afforded, entertainers like pianist-vocalist Jimmy Rushing were available to play dance music for the youngsters in competition with polka or string bands for the older generation.[34]

West Coast

The West Coast territory stretched from California east to the Rockies through Nevada, Oregon, Washington, Arizona, and New Mexico. The jazz scene here was shaped by four factors. First, the territory was geographically isolated from the rest of the country. This meant it was often slower to respond to things happening elsewhere and its developments had no impact outside its own borders. Second, most activity was centered in a few cities, Los Angeles, the San Francisco Bay area, and Portland, Oregon.[35] Third, although the black population grew rapidly in Los Angeles, it was rather small and the music business was easily and informally organized. Finally, most jazz musicians, like many people in this area, were migrants from somewhere else. The result was a unique musical style that was a complex blend of influences from other regions.

Many blacks on the West Coast came from the Southwest and New Orleans. In fact, given the much smaller musical community, the percentage of New Orleans men and their impact on the music was probably greater on the West Coast than in Chicago between 1910 and 1924. Lawrence Gushee has traced the beginning of this influence back at least to 1908 with the arrival of Bill Johnson and what would become the roots of The Creole Band. Johnson and several other New Orleans men were working in Los Angeles and the Bay area between 1908 and 1913. By April 1914, The Creole Band was fully organized in Los Angeles.

58

There, it got the vaudeville offer that would keep it on tour until 1918. Those tours would often bring the band to the West Coast, so its influence remained.[36]

As The Creole Band was leaving, the Great Migration and the entertainment business brought more black musicians to the area. Johnny and Reb Spikes came to the West Coast from Oklahoma with a minstrel show in 1915. They settled in the area and worked in Seattle, the San Francisco Bay area, and Los Angeles. In 1919, they opened the Spikes Brothers Music Store in Watts. This area was already developing as the major black neighborhood in Los Angeles, and the store soon became the musician's hangout and unofficial union hall. The Spikes brothers took advantage of the situation by serving as bookers for up to eight bands made up mainly of men hanging around the store.[37]

The Black and Tan orchestra, a Texas brass band, toured to the West Coast with a tent show in 1918 and was reformed by trombonist Henry Southard into a small jazz band to play cabarets and dances, which were the major jobs for all of these bands. The band in 1918 included Paul Howard, a teenaged reedman from Ohio who had recently moved West with his family, and New Orleans cornetist Ernest "Nenny" Coycault.[38] In 1922, Texas-born pianist Sonny Clay, who had played with both Spikes and Kid Ory, formed his own band in Los Angeles, and touring show veteran Curtis Mosby started a six-piece group in the Bay area.[39]

Trombonist Edward "Kid" Ory and other New Orleans men were flocking to the West Coast in 1919–22. Ory moved for his health and by November 1919 had organized a band including several Crescent City men. They played long cabaret jobs in both Los Angeles and the Bay area. The band included at different times Mutt Carey, Ed Garland, and Pops Foster. King Oliver brought his band to San Francisco in June 1921 and played there and in Los Angeles until returning to Chicago in the spring of 1922. Jelly Roll Morton led a band in San Francisco in 1919.[40]

The West Coast is one of the few territories with recorded examples for this period. The Spikes brothers caught on to the record boom and arranged to have records made in 1922 by Kid Ory's band on their own label. Sonny Clay's band also recorded for the Spikes in 1922 or 1923. There were very limited numbers of copies and they had no influence outside the West Coast, but they do show the unique sounds of this territory at this time.[41]

The Ory sides are New Orleans style jazz with collective ensembles by a front line of cornet, trombone, and clarinet. Ory's tailgate trombone is featured on the tune "Ory's Creole Trombone" and shows some similarities to brass band trombone tricks such as "Slidus Trombonus." The ensemble style with each of the three front-line instruments in a specific role is very clear on "Society Blues," which consists almost completely of ensemble work. Their similarities to the 1923 King Oliver Creole Jazz Band records helps confirm that both groups were representative of a larger New Orleans tradition. Also, the different emphases on ensemble and solo between this version and the 1927 Louis Armstrong Hot Five record of "Ory's Creole Trombone" show how Armstrong was moving away from that tradition to more solo space.[42] The Clay sides, by contrast, while featuring good lead cornet work by Nenny Coycault, another New Orleans player, show a reed section playing harmony chords leaning in the direction of the big band arranged jazz that Don Redman and Fletcher Henderson were developing in New York at the time. This is particularly intriguing if the Clay sides were recorded before he heard any of Henderson's records.[43]

The West Coast in this period showed a very active musical life with a strong New Orleans tradition competing with styles brought from other parts of the country. They mixed together in the cabarets and dance halls of this area. The fascinating glimpses of the music on the Ory and Clay recordings makes even clearer how much was lost by the lack of similar recordings elsewhere.

Southwest

The Southwest territory included Louisiana, Arkansas, Texas, Oklahoma, and Missouri. While there was activity in much of the territory, interest has focused on the Missouri cities of St. Louis and Kansas City. Before 1923 St. Louis was key, but Kansas City increased in importance in the 1920s. This area was unique in several ways. The Great Migration involved people who stayed within the territory, moving from rural to urban areas in the same state or to St. Louis and Kansas City. This movement within the area may explain the stronger connection of jazz and blues in this region.

St. Louis plays a key role in the 1914–1923 expansion of jazz nationally because of the decision, made around 1917 by the white Streckfus brothers of St. Louis, to hire a black band to play on their boats on tours up and down the Mississippi River.[44] There had been black music on the river before, both in St. Louis and New Orleans, on excursion boats that went out every evening for four-hour cruises. For years, these local boats were just floating dance halls tightly bound to the musical life of New Orleans or St. Louis.[45] The Streckfus "tramp boat" idea extended the reach of black bands up and down the river connecting New Orleans,

St. Louis, and St. Paul and bringing together in certain ways the Southeast, Midwest, Northwest, and Southwest territories.

Fate Marable, a light-skinned black from Paducah, Kentucky, who had been playing on the river for ten years, mostly with white groups, was chosen by the Streckfus brothers to organize their new black band. He put one together in Paducah, and it toured the Ohio, Missouri, and upper Mississippi River trips in 1917–1918 but did not go down the river to New Orleans. In 1918, Marable organized a band in New Orleans that toured up to St. Louis. From that time into the mid-1920s, New Orleans and St. Louis men blended styles on the riverboats up the Mississippi and its tributaries.

The Streckfuses clearly wanted a dance band, and Marable's early bands were heavy with reading Creole musicians like Peter Bocage, Manuel Perez, and Davey Jones.[46] However, Marable also included young jazz players like Warren "Baby" Dodds, George "Pops" Foster, and, in the 1919–1921 period, Louis Armstrong in his first job outside of New Orleans. These hirings were both musical and business compromises. The Streckfuses liked sweet dance music and so did much of their audience, but there was also demand for the new hot music and the boat owners were in business to make a profit.[47]

Perhaps even more importantly, while pay on the boats was good, working and living conditions made it hard to hold older reading players on the job. Employment on the boats meant accepting room and board, which was almost like being in jail. The musicians were not allowed to go ashore at the various towns or mix with the passengers. The season was long and it meant separation from families or loved ones. Like the migration itself, the "tramp" boats got the younger men with fewer social ties. This is particularly true after the "Red Summer" of 1919 when the black hands on the boats were targets of racial violence.[48]

All of the memories of the riverboats stress that the Streckfus brothers were the real bosses, hiring, firing, choosing leaders, setting tempos, and selecting music. They wanted reading bands playing popular dance music.[49] Johnny St. Cyr remembers,

> This was strictly a reading band, no hot solos. . . . Now the music we played—how the band sounded—this would be more like a swing band than the New Orleans type jazz band . . . We just played the arrangements as they were, we never changed them. . . . The old recordings I've heard that sounded much like we did was the old Fletcher Henderson recording of 'Mandy, Make Up Your Mind.' The ensemble parts of this

number sound about like we did, we had no hot solos. Any solos would be written out.[50]

The riverboats seem to have been quite a musical melting pot with stylistic changes and learning moving in several directions. Some New Orleans men like Armstrong, Dodds, and Foster were adding new rhythms and tones to the music, while the Creoles and St. Louis men were stretching the reading skills and fitting the jazz sound into an arranged format. As the decade turned, the sounds blended and more and more St. Louis men were featured on the boats. By 1920 local trumpeters like Dewey Jackson, Ed Allen, and Charlie Creath were taking over the leadership of the riverboat bands and were even more popular than the New Orleans players.[51] Creath, a Missouri-born circus band veteran who came to St. Louis after World War I, was very influential. "He played with a rhythmic swing that just made you feel like dancing, and he had a piercing, brilliant tone that seemed to touch your soul. . . . Charlie used to swing the lead in such a way that he never got too far away from the melody."[52]

The riverboat stars influenced a whole raft of younger trumpeters such as Louis Metcalf, Irving "Mouse" Randolph, Joe Thomas, Leonard "Ham" Davis, and R.Q. Dickerson who were growing up in St. Louis at the time. They supplemented the riverboat influence with lessons from men like Professor P. B. Lankford, the conductor of the Odd Fellows Band. They learned to read as well as improvise.[53] While the brass men were advancing, it was the St. Louis reedmen who began to beat out New Orleans players for jobs. When Ed Allen was chosen in 1923 to lead a mixed New Orleans-St. Louis group that would go down river, the brass and rhythm sections were split, but the whole reed section was from St. Louis. This reflected the growing importance of the saxophone in dance bands and its absence in the New Orleans tradition.

Before 1923, the models for the saxophone were mostly white vaudeville performers like the Six Brown Brothers or the dance band and pop music players like Rudy Wiedoeft. Blacks like Jerome Don Pasquall and young whites like Frankie Trumbauer were picking up tones and style from the recordings of these performers. By the early 1920s, St. Louis had developed a good core of sax players like Gene Sedric, Bert Bailey, Norm Mason, Walter "Foots" Thomas, and Pasquall. Few became famous jazz soloists but they were solid section men for the big bands of the 1920s and 1930s.[54]

The riverboats were controlled by white managers with the musicians playing for dancing white audiences. The Streckfus brothers set the conditions. "We played orchestrations, bought in complete form. . . . We played waltzes, tangos, reels, polkas. We had fourteen dances to play in an evening. You played a whole number and two encores. On Friday nights we'd play three choruses as an encore. . . . If Fate didn't get the fourteen numbers in by 11 P.M. he had to pay a fine."[55] The Streckfuses seem to have asked for the addition of saxes to get the fuller orchestrations and to bring the black bands closer in style to the white dance bands. Saxes also may have provided a louder sound for the dance floor size.

On the riverboats, white management exerted tremendous pressure on the New Orleans players to accommodate the audience, management, and stylistic demands of popular dance music. The New Orleans and St. Louis men adapted. The result was the merger of the written arrangements of popular dance music with the rhythm, feel, and tone of the New Orleans tradition. This independent emergence of another type of big band arranged jazz parallels the development of new styles by Doc Cooke and Charles Elgar in Chicago and Fletcher Henderson and Don Redman in New York.

In the rest of the Southwest, jazz was evolving more slowly in this early period. In the small towns, the brass band and touring show traditions still reigned supreme but some new things were brewing. Some medicine shows in the area apparently carried jazz bands. "A medicine show used to have four or five pieces: trombone, clarinet, trumpet, and a drummer, every man blowing for himself as loud as he could blow to attract a crowd for the doctor."[56] Small bands playing for dances also grew. Gene Coy had one around Amarillo perhaps as early as 1918 and soon was moving throughout the area looking for dances to play. By 1923, Alphonso Trent in Oklahoma and Gene Crooke in Helena, Arkansas, also had small dance bands going.[57]

Along the Central Track, Dallas's equivalent of Chicago's Stroll, honky-tonks, speakeasies, and after-hours spots were mixed with barber shops, rooming houses, and rib joints. Here a mixture of bluesmen, boogie-woogie pianists, and small jazz combos provided an intense musical education to young jazzmen. Some like reedman Buster Smith came from the surrounding farms, lured by the better pay of music over day labor. Others were part of the black middle class. Booker T. Washington's daughter, Mrs. P. Washington Pittman, was teaching music in the early 1920s in Dallas, and many of her middle class pupils found themselves drawn to the action on the Central Track. By 1922, Buster Smith was playing in a trio led by a barrelhouse style pianist, and the young pupils were learning different lessons.[58]

In Kansas City, the movement was generally from ragtime piano to small combos. Around 1918, pianist Bennie Moten led a trio with a vocalist and drummer. Soon after World War I, drummer-pianist Paul

Banks started a six-piece band. He was influenced by theater bands he had seen while on a vaudeville tour. Walter Brown was also leading a six-piece band in Kansas City at that time. Soon, both Moten and the brother-sister team of George E. and Julia Lee had expanded their trios to sextets, while Jesse Stone was using Kansas City as a base for playing dances in rural areas and small towns in Kansas and Missouri. By 1923, Bennie Moten's group seems to have emerged as the leading band in the area.[59]

This was the beginning of the key Southwestern jazz tradition. Moten recorded two instrumentals and six blues accompaniments in 1923 and five instrumentals in 1924. While it is very difficult to make sweeping generalizations on such a limited sample, these recordings do give some insight into the emerging Southwestern style. Half of the Moten recordings were twelve-bar blues—much more than in any other band of the period. This instrumental blues tradition seems to be a Southwestern specialty. One source of this tradition was the close rural heritage of many of the players. Also, in the Southwest unlike in the Southeast, the guitar-vocal blues tradition had strong early roots in the cities. Finally, in these smaller black communities, the blues found acceptance from all segments of the community, unlike in Chicago where the "respectable" versus "shady" split kept blues a lower class music.[60]

The attempt to develop a band blues style led the Southwestern bands to a unique invention, the riff, "a melodic idea stated in forceful rhythmic terms and usually contained in the first two bars. The simpler the germ idea the better, as long as it had rhythmic force."[61] The riff was repeated often throughout the piece which built on the riff. "Elephant's Wobble," one of the Moten 1923 instrumentals, was the first recorded example of this Southwestern riff style, and it is striking. Still, it and the other Moten tunes are very stiff in rhythm and predictable in form. This may reflect the youth of the musicians and their style.

Moten's approach merged out of several different traditions. The instrumentation and polyphonic ensemble sound came from the New Orleans tradition, but the Moten band seems uncomfortable with it, as if wearing borrowed clothes. Moten uses solos more than the Oliver band of 1923 or the ODJB, and again this may be due to uneasiness with the ensemble tradition. The solos show other elements as well. Sam Tall's strongly featured banjo is from the medicine and minstrel show traditions. Thamon Hayes's trombone and Woodie Walder's clarinet reflect the vaudeville novelty effects of Wilbur Sweatman or the Six Brown Brothers as well as the recordings of the ODJB. Moten was still primarily a ragtime pianist, which shows in his solos. The clear star of the band, partly by default, was cornetist Lamar Weight. Both Ross Russell and Gunther Schuller see strong traces of King Oliver, probably from records, in Wright's early playing.[62]

These records show that the new jazz style in Kansas City was a mixture of influences: ragtime piano, the New Orleans tradition, vaudeville novelty effects, tent show music, and the local blues tradition. The special blend of those elements was not unique to the musical and social life of that city. Similar developments were apparent in Texas, Arkansas, and Oklahoma. At the same time, St. Louis was moving in a somewhat different musical direction. One key distinction here may be that the St. Louis bands were the only ones in the Southwest before 1923 to be playing for mostly white audiences. This fact, as well as more direct contact with players from New Orleans and locations outside of this territory, may account for these differences.

Conclusion

The music situation in the territories changed rapidly in the 1914–1923 period. The term jazz quickly came into use to describe all black entertainment music as well as some white models. Tent-show, circus, and vaudeville bands continued to provide entertainment often calling music "jazz" that had been "rag" a year before. The number of local kids groups grew as public schools and colleges added bands. Most importantly many small bands grew up to play for dancing, some only in individual cities, others traveling widely in rural and small town areas. Recordings provided a few models for these players to follow, and for a very few, chances to make their own marks on the music.

The result was the emergence of a wide range of regional styles combining local musical and social influences in a way that reflected the lives of the local musicians and suited the needs of local audiences. In all the regions, black musicians were combining African-American and Euro-American musical styles into a hybrid music that could entertain both black and white audiences.

They all worked in an entertainment world that was still very loose and informal. Most bands got their own jobs by contacting location owners. A few groups like the black local in St. Louis and the Spikes brothers operations in Los Angeles served as middlemen, but most contacts were direct and informal. Even the vaudeville tours that involved chain managers were booked directly by bands involved. A band signed up with a chain manager and then worked through the chain for a set period of time. Bands usually did their own publicity and arranged their own travel. No real attempt was made to connect recordings and public appearances.

This informality helped to maintain the local nature of the music business and the music itself. This informality and rooting of the music in local regional lifestyles helped to keep a folk music element in early jazz. It also maintained regional variations that contributed to the background of the young players moving into jazz around the nation.

Chicago Sounds 1923–1929

O N the evening of June 12, 1926, thousands of Chicagoans, mostly black, flocked into the Coliseum at 15th and Wabash for a gala evening sponsored jointly by Okeh Records and the black Local 208 of the American Federation of Musicians. The event was heavily publicized in the black community; the *Chicago Defender* even printed a special insert on the event for its Chicago edition.[1] The event showed the wide range of personalities, musical directions, and performance situations in Chicago's black music scene in the 1920s. It affirmed the strength of black institutions such as the *Chicago Defender* and Local 208. It also confirmed the growing impact of outside forces like the record industry on Chicago's black musicians.

The runaway stars of the evening, Louis Armstrong and his Hot Five, were not a regular live working unit. They made up the first super group, a creation of the Okeh company that existed only in the recording studio and on wax. They had only recorded ten sides at this time but would later record almost forty more.[2] Their success at the Okeh ball was an indication of the eventual victory of Chicago recordings of the 1920s over the actual live sounds of the period.

The period 1923–1929 is the heart of the "jazz age" of the Roaring Twenties. Those years witnessed the acceptance of jazz as America's popular music and its distribution through the growing mass media, particularly records and the radio. This process involved a further narrowing of the definition of jazz by eliminating ragtime, brass bands, and some earlier pre-jazz forms. A variety of jazz styles remained. This chapter and the following two will look at the different results of this process in Chicago, New York, and the territories. In each location, musicians selected and modified elements from recorded models to fit the strengths of local performers, the demands of local performance situations, and the tastes of local audiences. This was fitting since those same three elements created the recorded models.

By 1923 Chicago had two distinctly different black musical traditions: (1) the black establishment of classically-influenced theater bands such as Erskine Tate's and (2) the New Orleans-in-Chicago cabaret bands such as King Oliver's Creole Jazz Band. Despite the success of Oliver's 1923 recordings, the New Orleans collectively improvised sound did not become the clearly dominant live sound in black Chicago in the 1920s, and the two strains did not merge to produce a synthesis. There are several reasons for this. One may be age. Important Chicago leaders were older than similar figures in New York or the territories. Of major Chicago figures in 1923, Dave Peyton, Charles Elgar, Jelly Roll Morton, and King Oliver were all thirty-eight, while Sammy Stewart, Johnny Dodds, Kid Ory, and others were also in their thirties. The major exception was the twenty-three-year-old Louis Armstrong, the most adaptable and successful of all. By contrast, in New York Fletcher Henderson was twenty-six; and Don Redman, twenty-three. Many territory men like Speed Webb, seventeen; Bennie Moten, twenty-nine; Walter Page, twenty-three; were even younger.[3] This meant the Chicago leaders were more entrenched in their styles and perhaps less flexible. Also, the rough-edged personalities of Morton, Peyton, and Oliver made compromise difficult.

Still, there were deeper reasons for this musical split. The entertainment business and social environment of Chicago in the 1920s provided each group with strong support for its position and made synthesis unnecessary or difficult. The community was sharply divided on class and racial lines. Despite the bi-racial coalition forged by Mayor "Big Bill" Thompson and the increasing role of black politicians such as Oscar DePriest, the scars of the race riot of 1919 still lingered. Violence and disrespect for the law increased as Al Capone and his competitors thrived on filling needs made illegal by Prohibition.[4]

The Great Migration dramatically increased the size of the black community and heightened tensions between its "respectable" and "shady" elements. The impact of black institutions such as the *Chicago Defender* and Local 208 strengthened while contact between the races lessened in many ways.[5] With these conflicts, Chicago in the 1920s produced some marvelous jazz and explored themes that would be very important in the future of jazz. At the same time, it failed to fit the mainstream development of jazz as a readily accessible entertainment music and by the end of the decade had lost its leadership position to New York.

The social cleavages in the African-American community and tensions between the white and black communities restricted job opportunities available to black bands in Chicago. Despite the best efforts of Local 208, black bands almost never played in white theaters and had limited access to white ballrooms because of the pressure of the white A.F.M. local and its aggressive leader James C. Petrillo as well as the racism of managers and audiences.[6] There were no Chicago versions of the New York Broadway orchestras. This left four types of jobs: ballrooms, black theaters, cabarets, and recordings. Each type had very different audience demands, working conditions, and musical styles.

The establishment bands completely ruled black theater work and were very strong in the ballrooms, while the New Orleans men had the bulk of both the cabaret and recording work. The theaters and some dances suited the respectable elements in the black community while the ballrooms attracted working class white ethnics. The music and the values of the establishment musicians satisfied these groups.[7] Dave Peyton, the leading publicist for the establishment in his *Chicago Defender* column, painted a picture of the hard-working, well-dressed, sober, and reliable musician that hit a responsive chord with those blacks and ethnics who appreciated the importance of maintaining "front" to be respectable.[8]

By contrast, the Chicago cabarets during Prohibition were clearly the realm of the shadies. As early as July 10, 1920, the *Chicago Defender* was asking for the police to close "notorious Second ward cabarets . . . for the protection of the young men and young women of the community."[9] Virtually every club had mob connections and many on the South Side were directly tied to Al Capone's organization.[10] Normal occupational hazards in the lives of cabaret musicians like King Oliver included having clubs closed by Prohibition agents or blown up or burned down by rival gangsters.[11] This discouraged not only respectable blacks but many whites from coming to these clubs. Both black and white shadies seemed to appreciate the thrills of the collectively improvised New Orleans style. It also appealed to white professional musicians who could steal tricks and to the rebellious white teenagers, like the Chicagoans or Austin High Gang, who moved this style in new directions.[12]

The recording dates were special cases in which the musicians were responsible only to other professionals such as artist and repertoire (A&R) man Richard Jones and to the technical demands of the recording equipment. Moreover, this music could be aimed at a national rather than local audience. These unique conditions created great music that has lasted through time but is often unrepresentative of what was happening in many live performances.

Theater Bands

The motion picture and vaudeville pit bands of the black community were much more important in the Chicago black music scene of the 1920s than they were in New York. They were very well paid with job security and prestige. Black musicians had no access to white theater jobs in Chicago, so they worked in black theaters, unlike black New York musicians who could work on Broadway. While discrimination in Illinois theaters was illegal, prosecutions for civil rights violations were rare. The lack of certainty of treatment led many blacks to seek entertainment in their own neighborhoods, particularly after the race riot of 1919 revealed the depth of race hatred in Chicago. At the same time, the increasing size of the black community provided a large black audience for many South Side theaters.[13]

Theater bands drew much of their audience from the respectable elements in the black community and their leaders from classical music teachers. The number and size of theater bands continued to grow until late in the decade. By 1926, "Professor Erskine Tate's Symphony Orchestra" at the Vendome Theater had grown to fifteen pieces and included Louis Armstrong as a trumpet soloist. Tate's strongest competitor was Sammy Stewart's classically-oriented twelve-piece group from Ohio at the Metropolitan Theater. When the Regal Theater opened in February 1928, it featured a twenty-piece orchestra put together by Dave Peyton including men raided from Tate. Smaller theater bands included the septets of Jimmy Bell and Clarence Jones, Walter Dyett's quartet, and Lovie Austin's duo.[14]

All played background music for the silent films, often from scores sent for the films or standard books of mood pieces. Some accompanied touring vaudeville acts. The bigger bands also played concert sets between films. Tate and Stewart continued Peyton's tradition of operatic arias and overtures as well as popular tunes. The theater orchestras provided an outlet to those in the black community who wished to hear classical music played by black performers who were still blocked out of jobs with major symphony orchestras.[15]

In the 1920s, the presence of jazz soloists did increase, although precisely how much is unclear since their full repertoire was not recorded. The few popular numbers recorded such as Tate's "Stomp Off, Let's Go" show a big band ensemble style with fine solos by Louis Armstrong and pianist Teddy Weatherford. Stewart recorded a year after his Metropolitan heyday when he had been playing dances and cabarets. Still, his version of "Old Man River" may catch his theater style. Sounding much like a Broadway pit band, the complex written arrangement showcased the musicianship of the band. Clarence "Cosperous" Moore's violin was prominently featured both in a society style voiced with the reeds and in a countrified fiddle solo.[16] Armstrong's presence in the Tate band was rare for a black Chicagoan at this time since he was moonlighting from a less-respectable cabaret job.[17] Until the arrival of talking pictures in 1928–1929, theater musicians were among the most secure and respected in Chicago's black community.

Ballrooms and Dancing Classes

Chicago's dance music scene was also quite different from New York's. There were two very distinct types of dance jobs in Chicago until late 1927—jobs in ballrooms in white neighborhoods and informal dance gigs in the black community. Throughout the 1920s, the stiff resistance of the white local of the musicians' union and its tough president, James Petrillo, limited black access to white ballroom jobs. With dozens of ballrooms in Chicago, black bands never held more than five jobs at one time and were often limited to two. The key jobs were those at Paddy Harmon's Dreamland and Arcadia ballrooms. Harmon, a well-connected Irishman, could buck Petrillo and use black bands. Harmon liked a sweet sound, indicated by his invention of the Harmon mute to soften the sound of brass instruments.

For most of the 1920s, the bands of Charles Elgar and Charles "Doc" Cooke played Harmon's jobs. Both were big bands playing dance music in written arrangements. Elgar recorded rarely but his band was very well respected. Cooke made some big band sides, and his star sidemen including Freddie Keppard and Jimmie Noone recorded some fine small group, New Orleans-style improvised jazz as Cookie's Gingersnaps. Still, in the ballrooms for straight dance audiences of white ethnics, the Cooke band generally played close to white dance orchestra style while giving some solo space to Keppard and others. The 1924 Cooke recording of "The One I Love Belongs to Somebody Else" sounds like vintage Paul Whiteman. By 1928, Cooke and the white Coon-Sanders Nighthawks were influencing each other and swapping arrangements so that recordings like "Sluefoot" and "Brainstorm" are very similar except for the solos. Both Cooke and Elgar were moving towards the style that Fletcher Henderson and Don Redman would develop in New York, but the Chicagoans seem

71

less comfortable with this evolution and more wedded to older traditions than the New Yorkers.[18]

Jimmie Wade's ten-piece band was also creating a similar sound as shown by its few recordings. Although it was actually working in a white cabaret in the Loop, its working conditions and stylistic influences were closer to Elgar and Cooke than to black South Side cabaret bands. An even clearer indication that Wade was moving in the big band arranged style is that he was one of the few Chicago bands to make a successful jump to New York. In May 1926, Wade took his band into Manhattan's Club Alabam, which had earlier been home to Fletcher Henderson and Sam Wooding. The Wade band was successful on that job for about a year then broke up with some men going to Europe and others returning to hard times in Chicago.[19]

Black dancers in Chicago had little access to ballrooms. Until 1927, there was no public ballroom in the black community, and hostility from white crowds and managements discouraged black attendance at Harmon's and other white locations. Before the opening of the Chicago Savoy, black dances were private affairs. For the lower class, there were house rent parties with boogie-woogie pianists or blues guitarists. Here, the developments that led to the early city and urban blues excluded most jazzmen.[20] Instead, the many middle-class social clubs rented halls for group dances. Some black bandleaders rented halls, did the publicity, set admission prices, paid the debts, and hoped for profits from "dancing schools."

Apparently, most groups were small in the New Orleans collective ensemble style. Few of these bands recorded, but sides by Hightower's Night Hawks show a much looser sound than either the Chicago establishment or the Henderson style. Lottie Hightower, the pianist-leader of this group, had conservatory training, while her husband, trumpeter Willie Hightower, was a good New Orleans-style player who occasionally subbed for Louis Armstrong on his big band jobs. Willie Hightower is featured on Carroll Dickerson's records of "Missouri Squabble" and "Black Maria."

These dance schools tested the business abilities of the band leaders and reflected the informal nature of the band business in the 1920s. Louis Armstrong's brief stab at running a dancing school ended in financial failure, but Lottie Hightower's group was one of the most successful at this level.[21]

The dance scene changed drastically in November 1927 with the opening of the Chicago Savoy ballroom. This was the first important black ballroom in Chicago, and from the beginning it showed a preference for the developing national big band style represented by Fletcher Henderson over any established Chicago style. Charles Elgar lasted four months as the opening band and was replaced by the Carroll Dickerson orchestra, featuring Louis Armstrong and Earl Hines. Dickerson's orchestra was the Chicago band that was closest to the Henderson style. The Savoy's choice may reflect the New York ties of its management, the success of Henderson at Chicago's Stevens Hotel, or a shift to a new generation of dancers. For whatever reason, it was a clear move away from all of the previously established Chicago styles. The four sides made by the Dickerson orchestra while at the Savoy are firmly in the Fletcher Henderson-Don Redman big band arranged style.[22]

The Savoy brought in Henderson, McKinney's Cotton Pickers, and white theater bands for special engagements. Later house bands were younger eight- to ten-piece groups led by Jimmy Bell, Clarence Black, and Walter Barnes. These bands were not strongly identified with either the older establishment sound of Elgar and Cooke or the small, collective ensemble New Orleans sound. Barnes and similar bands led by Jerome Don Pasquall and Clifford King replaced Elgar and Cooke in the Harmon ballrooms as well.[23] By the end of the decade, Chicago's black dance music was beginning to fall in line with the big band arranged model emerging in New York, but the conflict between the establishment and New Orleans styles in Chicago delayed that development as it made some marvelous music.

Cabarets

Most major South Side clubs of the early 1920s like the Royal Gardens had predominantly black audiences with some whites mixed in, mainly entertainers, musicians, and mobsters. This may reflect the harsher racial climate in Chicago. The *Chicago Daily News* rejoiced over the closing of a South Side cabaret because, "there Negroes and whites of both sexes disported nightly all night long in nauseating revels. . . . So the insolent parade of black and tan immorality has been dispersed." This was reprinted by the *Chicago Defender*, which was shocked by the article's racism although it agreed that many cabarets should be closed, stressing that "lewdness and immorality were brought here but not by our race."[24]

The cabaret scene had been dominated by New Orleans style bands since at least February 1918. They continued to be important in the cabarets from 1923 to 1929, but some things were changing. First, the bands were growing in size. Almost as soon as King Oliver's Creole Jazz band stopped recording in 1924, cabaret bands began to expand beyond its eight-piece size and particularly beyond its four-piece front line of two cornets, clarinet, and trombone that was so important for collective ensembles with set ranges and roles for instruments. By 1926 there were still four eight-piece bands doing cabaret work in Chicago but they were competing with one twelve-piece and four ten-piece groups. The key was the rise of the saxophone as an accepted instrument in the cabaret band and the expansion in the reed section to three or four pieces, which increased the need for harmonies and written arrangements.[25]

A few bands continued live performances in the small group format, often in after-hours places or small cafes with white audiences. After leaving King Oliver in 1924, Johnny Dodds led a group at Kelly's Stables, a white North Side bar. This five-piece band featured Dodds and trumpet players like Natty Dominique and Freddie Keppard. The various recordings such as "Ballin' the Jack" (Chicago Footwarmers), and "Bucktown Stomp" (Johnny Dodds' Washboard Band), show collective ensembles still in full flower.[26] New Orleans clarinetist Jimmie Noone also led small groups at the Nest and Apex clubs. Jimmie Noone's Apex Club Orchestra, which is also well documented on record, created a unique variation on the collective ensemble by having the lead played by Joe Poston on alto sax or clarinet with Noone and pianist Earl Hines weaving lines around the lead.[27] As the decade went on, however, it became harder and harder to find a traditional New Orleans front line in a Chicago cabaret.

The career of King Oliver after 1923 shows the impact of instrumental and environmental changes on the cabaret bands. Even before the Oliver Creole Jazz Band era ended, Oliver had been experimenting with new sounds, bringing Stump Evans in on sax at times. In 1924, the band split up. Armstrong moved to Fletcher Henderson's band in New York. Oliver organized a new nine-piece band for the Lincoln Gardens but before he could open the cabaret burned, perhaps due to Prohibition-era gang warfare. Oliver found himself as a sideman in Dave Peyton's Plantation Cafe orchestra. Oliver took over that band and job in March 1925, staying for two years. His new band, the Dixie Syncopators, was a ten-piece group with a full sax section. Increasingly, as shown by its recordings, Oliver's band moved away from collective ensemble playing towards arranged section work and strings of solos. Even the rhythm shifted from Oliver's earlier sound as a banjo-tuba rhythm section replaced the guitar and string bass. The solos of this most New Orleans of the New Orleans-in-Chicago musician remained rooted in the Crescent City tradition, but his surroundings were changing. In the title of the first Dixie Syncopators record, he was in "Deep Henderson."[28]

What was happening? It appears that both management and audiences at the big Chicago cabarets wanted a larger sound, and Oliver aimed to please. He left Chicago in the summer of 1927 for New York and never regained the stature of his Chicago heyday.[29] By the end of Oliver's run at the Plantation, he was being challenged by bands of ten or more pieces led by Louis Armstrong, Dave Peyton, Doc Cheatham, and Hugh Swift. Both Swift and Peyton were on the radio. The one record by any of these working bands at this point, Louis Armstrong's May 1927 "Chicago Breakdown" (Columbia, release no. 36376) shows a ten-piece band quite removed from the Creole Jazz Band or even Armstrong's own Hot Five and Hot Seven records, moving in the Fletcher Henderson direction.[30]

From March 1927 on, theater bands led by Sammy Stewart and Clarence Jones joined the younger bands of Laurence Harrison, Alex Calamese, and Tiny Parham, with outside influences provided by the Missourians, to move Chicago's cabaret scene in new directions. Fletcher Henderson's younger brother Horace worked with Sammy Stewart's band in Chicago cabarets in 1928, which may account for the strong Henderson influence in Stewart's records of "Crazy Rhythm" and "'Cause I Feel Lowdown."[31]

Former Tate violinist Laurence Harrison fronted the Alabamians, a young band which opened at Chicago's Plantation Cafe in late 1927 and later moved into the Sunset. The floor show there included a young dancer and singer named Cab Calloway who became the front man for the band. Its competition nearby at the Dreamland Cafe was the Cotton Club Orchestra Inc., a St. Louis band which, prior to moving to Chicago, had been the house band at New York's Cotton Club before Duke Ellington.

It is unclear exactly what each band sounded like in 1927–28, but the 1925 and 1929 recordings of the Missourians and the 1929 sides of the Alabamians show sounds very different from the earlier Chicago styles. The early Cotton Club sides are in the New York cabaret style of Sam Woodling. By 1929, the Missourians had established a Southwestern identity in the Moten manner. The Alabamians suggest early Jimmie Lunceford with a stress on singing and section work. Both groups later had success as New York-based national bands. Their Chicago success showed the openness of the cabaret audiences to different styles by 1928.[32]

Several trends emerge for the active Chicago cabaret scene of this period. Employment continued to be uncertain because of the pressures of Prohibition. Changing tastes and working conditions required expansion and changed styles for most bands. All of this weakened the impact of improvised New Orleans jazz performed by small groups in this environment. By the end of the decade, young Chicagoans were providing music more in tune with developments elsewhere and much less unique than the 1923 sound of Chicago.

FROM JAZZ TO SWING
Recording Sessions and Innovations

Chicago in this period was producing some of the most important musical changes and most impressive phonograph records in the history of jazz. The musical achievements of the bands of Louis Armstrong and Jelly Roll Morton are superlative, but neither group was a live Chicago working unit. Louis Armstrong's Hot Five appeared in public only twice, at special Okeh Record Company galas. It was exclusively a recording band, and all of its members had long-term jobs in very different groups. Armstrong was in the big bands of Erskine Tate, Clarence Jones, and Carroll Dickerson. Kid Ory worked for Dave Peyton and Clarence Black, while the Dodds brothers had their own Kelly's Stables band.[33] Similarly, the personnel that recorded the Jelly Roll Morton Red Hot Peppers sides did not work together outside of the recording studio. George Mitchell worked for Vernon Roulette, Dave Peyton, and Doc Cooke. Darnell Howard and Barney Bigard were with King Oliver, while Omer Simeon played with Charles Elgar. Morton's regular performing groups usually worked as a Midwest territory band, which limited his actual impact on the Chicago scene.[34] Other recording groups such as Cookie's Gingersnaps were small groups out of bigger bands, while a few such as the Dodds brothers's band and Lottie Hightower's Night Hawks were regular working small groups.

There were striking differences between what was acceptable in the recording studio in Chicago and what worked in live jobs. Two questions arise: What created these differences? and How can we use the recorded output of Chicago in the 1920s to recapture the larger picture of live Chicago in that period? First, it is important to remember that the record industry, particularly the major companies like Columbia and Victor, were still headquartered in New York, but they no longer had a monopoly on the business. The success of Mamie Smith's blues sides and King Oliver's jazz sides, as well as early country and blues records, had helped stimulate the growth of many small record companies around the nation. Brunswick (Vocalion) and Paramount recorded extensively in Chicago but much "Chicago jazz" of the 1920s was in fact recorded in Richmond, Indiana, for Gennett and Port Washington, Wisconsin, for Paramount.

Also, many establishment bands with long location jobs that kept them busy every day rarely recorded because they had no time off. Smaller groups were easier to transport and record, particularly in the pre-electric days when all the instruments had to cluster around the recording horn. Paramount was recording numerous blues artists, and many of the jazz recordings were extra instrumentals by small groups booked to back singers. Finally, a key point is that most of the "Chicago jazz" records sold better in the rural and small-town South and in other cities than they sold in Chicago. The music fit the rural roots and shady communities of many places outside of Chicago.[35]

Still, this does not explain where the enormous artistic jumps of Hot Five and Red Hot Peppers came from. The full story may never be known. There is no clear agreement on why or how the Hot Five came into being. Its first session on November 12, 1925, occurred almost immediately upon Louis Armstrong's return to Chicago to play in his wife Lil's band at the Dreamland. Dave Peyton congratulated Lil's band on October 31, stating that, "Their rendition of jazz is pleasing, not that vulgar, mushy kind that invites immoral dancing."[36] On November 7, Peyton noted that Louis would return that week to the Dreamland from his work in New York with Fletcher Henderson's orchestra. The November 14 issue carried an advertisement for Lil's band featuring "The World's Greatest Cornetist, Louis Armstrong," while Peyton's November 21 review rhapsodized, "Louis Armstrong? Who is he? He is the jazz cornet king and he just got in from old New York. . . . He could be called King Louis because he is the king of them all."[37]

Armstrong had recorded frequently with Henderson. His last recordings in Chicago had been completed more than two years before with King Oliver. Who decided to combine him with some of the same players? The answer is unclear. His wife Lil may have had a hand in it. Richard M. Jones as A&R man for Okeh's race series was instrumental in setting up the first session, but it is not known if the session was his idea. The success of the first release in late 1925 (Okeh 8261), "Yes, I'm In The Barrel" and "Gut Bucket Blues," led to a second session in February 1926. This produced Armstrong's first serious hit "Heebie Jeebies" with its scat vocal, which quickly sold about 40,000 copies. This hit convinced Okeh to continue the series with the same pattern of small, informal sessions.[38] According to Kid Ory, the tunes were worked out casually either in the studio or a day or two before the recording date. He stressed that "The Okeh people left us alone, and didn't try to expert us."[39]

The company was wise to let the group work out its own approach. At first sight, the approach seems to be the culmination of the collective ensemble tradition of New Orleans jazz, seen earlier in the Kid Ory Sunshine sides and King Oliver's Creole band. In fact, Armstrong was firmly breaking with the earlier traditions by dramatically expanding the musical vocabulary for the soloist. In the process, he directed attention away from the ensemble. In the Oliver recordings and the earlier New Orleans jazz tradition, the focus was the ensemble sound occasionally varied with a break by an instrument. In the Armstrong Hot Fives, the focus was the solo with brief ensemble passages to tie things together.[40] The result is an approach consisting of a string of solos, which looks ahead to the directions taken by Charlie Parker, Dizzy Gillespie, and the modern jazz players who followed them from the early 1940s into the land of extended solos and minimum ensemble playing. The New Orleans tradition was also reworked, then becoming the Dixieland style with a very different string of solos.

Armstrong's stretched solos proved his own virtuosity and the art music potential of jazz. The dancing public was not quite ready to stop its feet long enough to sit back and listen, but Armstrong clearly had a strong impact on black musicians around the country from the release of the first Hot Five sides through the end of the 1920s. Trumpeters by the score were influenced by Armstrong's tone, swing, musical ideas, and emphasis on the solo. Others began to develop the range and command of their instruments to follow Armstrong's fireworks. Most other jazz players of the time, including his own band members, had quite a distance to go. Johnny Dodds on clarinet, Kid Ory on trombone, and particularly Lil Armstrong on piano, were all far behind Armstrong in his conception of how to solo, but they followed his lead. The ensembles became less and less a part of the Hot Five's sound.

The Hot Five records extended over twenty sessions from 1925 to 1928 and gradually blended with the larger Hot Seven sessions and later the Savoy Ballroom Five sessions which often included arranged passages from Alex Hill, Don Redman, and others. Remember that at this same time, Armstrong was playing regularly in Carroll Dickerson's big band, soloing from within a written arranged format. With this in mind, the role of the Armstrong recordings of 1925–1929 in the conflict between collective ensembles and written arrangements becomes clearer. While Armstrong was an improvisor of the first order, his achievements made collective ensembles more difficult to sustain. With the increased melodic and rhythmic risks being taken by a single soloist, the need for a set pattern behind the soloist became more compelling. This is particularly obvious in the climactic "routines" of the final choruses as Armstrong often stretches over the whole range of the trumpet. As Gunther Schuller and others have pointed out, the key to collective ensembles was that each instrument in the ensemble had an assigned range and function. With Armstrong stretching the range of his instrument, he increasingly bumped into other horns in the ensemble. Armstrong's extension of the individual solo made collective ensembles more difficult. The other options were the string of solos or a written arrangement. The string of solos worked fine on record but, as we have seen, relatively few locations were willing to book a band of only five pieces no matter how brilliantly they were played. This left the arranger and the big band to profit from Armstrong's innovations. Armstrong himself confirmed that direction starting in 1929 when he began almost fifteen years of recording and performing as the featured soloist within a big band setting.[41]

As is often the case in the mass media, the success of the Armstrong Hot Five recordings led other companies to look for a small super group or super soloist. RCA Victor turned to Jelly Roll Morton and his Red Hot Peppers who provided a very different response to the dilemma posed by Armstrong's innovations. In Gunther Schuller's words Morton was "the first of that precious jazz elite: composer . . . also a remarkably creative arranger."[42] Much of the beauty of the Red Hot Peppers sides comes from Morton's original compositions. His "King Porter Stomp" among others became jazz standards, but more impressive were the variety of textures that Morton achieved with his arrangements. As Gunther Schuller has pointed out at length, Morton provided an alternative to Don Redman's style of written arrangements for sections. Morton, instead, often worked with individual instruments, giving them a variety of roles in the pieces, improvised ensembles, written ensembles, solos, duets, and trios with other instruments.[43]

According to members of the Red Hot Peppers, these routines were often not written out but instead worked up by word of mouth between Morton and the musicians in rehearsal before recording dates. Morton's method relied to a great extent on the shared traditions of the musicians with whom he worked. Those who worked on the Chicago sides, with the exception of Louisville trumpeter George Mitchell, were from New Orleans and were aware of the distinct musical mix of that city.[44] This is one reason why the Morton method was difficult to standardize. Particularly in Chicago and New York, bands were less and less likely to consist of musicians from the same town with the same shared tradition. The great advantage of the Redman-Henderson arranged style and to a lesser extent the Armstrong string of solos approach, was that they worked even if all the musicians in the band did not share the same local traditions.

This may help to explain the problems that show up in Morton's New York recordings like the 1929 "Down My Way," on which he worked with musicians from various traditions. The combination of sounds needed the artistry of Morton to develop.[45] The Redman and Armstrong patterns by contrast could easily be reduced to formulas that other bands could adopt. The very uniqueness of Morton's artistry as a composer and arranger made it almost impossible for his contemporaries to reproduce it. It reappeared twenty years later in the modern arrangements for the Miles Davis

Nonette's "Birth of the Cool" sessions. As appreciation deepened for their musical mastery, the Chicago Red Hot Peppers sides have gained stature in jazz history, in contrast to the lukewarm response to their release.

Finally, of course, Morton's immediate impact was also limited by his abrasive personality. He did, however, make several important steps forward in the business world. His was one of the first black bands to get a contract with Victor Records, the leading company of the time, matching Jim Europe and predating Duke Ellington. Secondly, Morton's was the first black band to sign with the Music Corporation of America (MCA), the emerging leader in the band management field. Still, the bands he actually led for the dance jobs that MCA booked were not the all-star groups that recorded. It is unclear if this was a function of his abrasive personality, which made steady employment with him difficult, or if gaps in the bookings meant limited money, which made it impossible for him to recruit the same men for the dance jobs as he attracted for the recordings.[46]

Whatever the reason, Morton was viewed as a much bigger figure in the artistic development of jazz by the 1940s, when the Dixieland revivalists and jazz critics rediscovered and reinterpreted the importance of his recordings and musical achievements, than he was by his contemporaries in Chicago in the 1920s. Even the recordings themselves were not given as much attention by the Chicago players of the 1920s as they received later. It is possible that despite Morton's artistic achievement the recordings simply represented a style and taste too specialized and already old-fashioned to influence the Chicago black musicians who were so intent on making it as professionals by pleasing a mass audience.

Conclusion

The black jazz scene in Chicago in the 1920s was extremely active and complex. The actual working sounds of jazz often did not show up on records because the realities of the recording industry and the demands of live performances were very different. The dominant recording bands such as Jelly Roll Morton's Red Hot Peppers and Louis Armstrong's Hot Five did not exist as working bands, unlike the Fletcher Henderson and Duke Ellington groups in New York. Moreover, there were no real Chicago equivalents for the Roseland Ballroom or the Cotton Club until the opening of the Grand Terrace in December 1928. The dominant Chicago bands were not playing for the white upper or middle class but instead for the white working class in the ballrooms, the black community in the theaters, and the black and white underworld shadies in the cabarets. The Chicago bands were not able to influence the gatekeepers of culture and produce a national popular music like their New York contemporaries, but the Chicago musicians tapped a variety of experiences. This was reflected in the richness of their music, which has been appreciated over the years.

Dave Peyton in black theaters, Doc Cooke in Harmon's ballrooms, and King Oliver in the black cabarets created styles that matched specific conditions and did not easily fit a wider national audience. The age and personalities of these figures helped to keep them apart and delay the creation of a new synthesis comparable to the emerging style in New York Yet, the vibrant variety of Chicago sounds helped to shape the artistic perceptions of jazz, first through the white Chicagoans and the Austin High Gang and their contemporaries such as Benny Goodman and Gene Krupa, and later through the revivals and critical evaluations of the 1940s and after.

It is only after 1927 with the coming of talking pictures and the arrival of outside management at the Regal Theater and Savoy Ballroom that a new generation of Chicago musicians came forward to develop the synthesis of big band arranged jazz that New York had already produced. By 1929, with Armstrong moving on to success in New York, and Oliver and Morton facing failure there, the Chicago scene was turned over to Earl Hines, Tiny Parham, and Walter Barnes. Their music had a less distinct regional accent. Hines's Grand Terrace Band became the major Chicago band of the 1930s with a style strongly tied to national trends.[47] A few of the smaller groups remained, including bands led by Jimmie Noone and Johnny Dodds, but their influence was waning.

Even the establishment bands were losing their positions. A symbolic passing of the torch came on August 24, 1929, when Dave Peyton, the top theater band leader who had been part of the Chicago scene since 1903, was replaced as the music columnist of the *Chicago Defender* by Walter Barnes, a young leader of a Fletcher Henderson style band based in the Savoy Ballroom. Barnes continued Peyton's efforts to establish black musicians in the respectable professional part of the black class structure, but musically this was achieved through the New York synthesis.[48] At the same time, the black musician's union kept up the struggle to maintain a good standard of living for black musicians. The bandleaders continued to operate as individual entrepreneurs remaining their own bosses and competing as individuals.[49]

5

New York Scores
1923-1929

I N the fall of 1923, members of the gang of black musicians who had been regularly working recording sessions under Fletcher Henderson's leadership, heard of an audition at a white mid-town Manhattan cabaret that was changing from a Russian to a plantation theme. According to Don Redman, the group tried out and won the spot over Henderson's objections and then made him the leader "because he was a college graduate and presented a nice appearance."[1]

Redman's backhanded recommendation underestimates some of Fletcher Henderson's strengths, but it does come close to the mark. He was typical of St. Clair Drake's description of the black middle-class "respectable."[2] A light-skinned, well-mannered product of the small-town Georgia middle class, Henderson was handsome in a low-key sort of way. Appearance and manners were important to him, and deference, particularly to white authority figures, came perhaps too easily. His politeness got him in the door in many situations but often kept him from securing the most favorable terms in business dealings. Diffident seems the best overall description of him. Of course, he was the product of a time and place where it was dangerous for a young black male to be perceived as too aggressive, and this may have affected his approach.

Twelve years younger than Oliver and Morton, and two to three years older than Duke Ellington and Louis Armstrong, Henderson was on the front edge of the new generation of jazzmen. He could serve as the prototype of Hsio Wen Shih's model of the jazz innovator of the 1920s.

New York Scores, 1923–1929

> The typical innovator of the 1920s . . . was born about 1900, into a Negro family doing better than most, possibly in the Deep South but more likely on its fringe; in either case, his family usually migrated North in time for him to finish high school. If he had gone to college, and he often had, he had gone to Wilberforce or a fringe school like Howard or Fisk. He might have aimed at a profession and fallen back on jazz as a second choice. He was, in any case, by birth or by choice, a member of the rising Negro middle class.[3]

Except that his family remained in Georgia and he attended Atlanta University, this is a perfect picture of Fletcher Henderson.

Henderson, like many of the black migrants to New York, was a product of the Southeast, not the Deep South. He grew up in a black Southern middle-class family with a mother who taught music and a father who was a well-respected high school principal when this was one of the highest professional ranks a black Southerner could achieve. The young Fletcher received a degree in chemistry from Atlanta University and moved North for a career in chemistry. He found such careers closed to him and instead entered the music industry.[4]

Prior to its opening at the Club Alabam, the Fletcher Henderson Orchestra, like Louis Armstrong's Hot Five, had existed only in the recording studio. Beginning as musical director for the black-owned Black Swan record company in 1921, Henderson developed contacts with record companies that had helped establish his stable of black musicians. When the Henderson band became a live working unit, the change shaped its music and influence differently than similar transitions had affected the bands of Oliver, Armstrong, and Morton. These differences reflected gaps between black life and jazz music in Chicago and in New York.

The Club Alabam job led to a long decade of playing for white audiences at the Alabam and the Roseland Ballroom. These jobs earned the Henderson band prosperity, audience recognition, and respect from black and white musicians. The band's frequent recordings brought it to larger audiences, both black and white. All of this made the Fletcher Henderson Orchestra the dominant black musical group in New York in the 1923–1929 period. By the late 1920s, it was the most influential black jazz group in the United States. Together, Fletcher Henderson and his young musicians including Don Redman, Coleman Hawkins, and Louis Armstrong, developed the framework of big band arranged jazz that dominated American popular music through the Swing Era.

FROM JAZZ TO SWING

New York Trends

The success of the Henderson band reflected several trends: (1) the importance of records and radio, (2) increased opportunities for black musicians to play for white audiences, (3) more emphasis on playing for dancing, (4) the emergence of young black musicians for whom jazz was *the* black music, (5) increasing professionalism among jazz musicians, and (6) a tightening of the formal structure of the music business. All these general trends of the period were heightened in New York.

The New York jazz scene in the 1920s was affected by three basic realities. The Broadway theater and its surrounding cabarets provided black talent with a showcase to white audiences that was unparalleled in the country. The growth of Harlem into the largest single black community in the United States created an enormous pool of talent immersed in a very active African-American culture. Finally, the radio and record industries, headquartered in New York, helped New York's black cultural products to reach a national audience.

The success of Sissle and Blake's *Shuffle Along* in opening Broadway once again to black performers was discussed in chapter two. Throughout the 1920s at least one black show was usually appearing on the Great White Way. The music was played by large black pit bands directed by Ford Dabney, Will Vodery, Eubie Blake, and others. These composer-conductors of the old-line New York establishment had ties going back to the Clef Club. Broadway pit work required reading musicians with reliable work habits. Solo ability was rarely necessary. Only a few men, including Fletcher Henderson's lead trumpet Russell Smith, moved easily between Broadway and jazz. Broadway provided a sanctuary for older men who were losing ballroom and nightclub jobs to younger competitors. The pit bands were similar to Dave Peyton's group and the Chicago theater bands but had less direct influence in New York's black community since they were playing for white audiences outside the African-American neighborhoods. Pit players were important as models to black musicians, proving that written compositions and reading skills could provide professional opportunities. By the end of the decade, the younger men and the cabaret influence were coming into Broadway but Eubie Blake and Ford Dabney led the major black bands there until the Great Depression drove black shows and most other musicals off-stage after 1929.[5]

Broadway shows were important as an avenue opening up black music to white audiences. Intrigued by a black show, audiences might listen to black bands in mid-town cabarets like Henderson's at the Club Alabam and later Duke Ellington's at the Club Kentucky, or dance to the

Fletcher Henderson Orchestra at Roseland or other black bands playing in dance halls. Black New York bands had the widest access to white audiences of any groups in the country in this period.

White audiences flocked into selected locations in black neighborhoods, turning some nightspots into predominantly white or all-white establishments. This was the "When Harlem was in Vogue" era of the Harlem Renaissance. Jazz musicians in this period experienced problems and opportunities of access to white audiences similar to challenges faced by black poets, novelists, painters, and critics.[6]

The reasons for Harlem's popularity were complex. They were not as simple as James Lincoln Collier's quartet of "black exoticness, sex, liquor, and peppy black music."[7] One extremely important factor was that the arts, particularly music and entertainment, had been the one area in which black achievement had been tolerated and even expected. The stereotypes of African-Americans as natural musicians and entertainers dated back to slavery days and had been reinforced by the accomplishments of the first wave of black theater composers and later Jim Europe and his bands. Black talent was accepted by white audiences. "No exclusionary rules had been laid down regarding a place in the arts. Here was a small crack in the wall of racism, a fissure that was worth trying to widen."[8]

Another explanation was that blacks were a new and different element in the Northern urban scene. They were associated with the rural roots from which the majority of Americans had now moved. Many of the clubs of the 1920s had decor and names rooted in the rural South: the Plantation, Club Alabam, Club Kentucky, and Cotton Club. A combination of nostalgia for and relief at being away from those roots may explain why urban whites found black entertainers particularly appealing in the 1920s.

The lure of the forbidden may also have played a part. The new urban culture of the Roaring Twenties gloried in flaunting the rules and breaking the limits of traditional values whether in Freudian psychology and sex or in literary style and content. Contact with black culture represented another opportunity for rebellion. In the structured world of the ballroom and cabaret the contact could be limited and controlled. It is important to remember that many of the locations where black bands played in New York in the 1920s had virtually all-white clientele both through discrimination and high prices.[9]

This access to white audiences set conscious and sometimes unconscious limits on the experimentation of black musicians in New York in this period. The dense collective improvisation of the King Oliver Creole Jazz Band was so far removed from the experience of white audiences that it would have been difficult to assimilate. The arranged style of Henderson, Redman, and Ellington was much more accessible.

This arranged style also has a generational element. The Great Migration meant that many black Americans, born in rural areas, moved to the city for high schools or jobs. Better educational opportunities for their children was an important part of the Great Migration. Many families moved so that their children could finish high school in Northern cities. These youngsters as well as those who moved North to look for careers joined young natives like Benny Carter and Harry Carney. As a generation they all had a different perspective on black artistic opportunities. Jazz, heard as the music of their teenage years, continued as "their music" for decades.[10]

These men were Hsio Wen Shih's new wave of jazz innovators. They were often members of W. E. B. DuBois's "talented tenth," the best-educated youth of the black community. Having bumped into the bruising limitations of job discrimination, many turned for advancement, self-expression, and recognition to entertainment, the one profession in which whites did not find blacks too threatening. For these musicians, jazz was an opportunity for artistic exploration and economic and social advancement, a chance to make it into the mainstream of cultural and economic success. It was a way to advance themselves as well as "the race." "Not only was this tactic admirably suited to the ability and temperament of educated Afro-Americans, it seemed to be the sole battle plan affording both high visibility and low vulnerability."[11]

After the success of the Oliver and Henderson records of 1923, black jazz became a staple of the record industry. The concentration of studios and company headquarters in New York made it easier for bands there to get on record. At the same time, the new medium of radio began using live popular music, including jazz. The real pioneers in radio were the Kansas City Nighthawks, a white band led by Carlton Coon and Joe Sanders, who started broadcasting from the Muehlebach Hotel in Kansas City over WDAF in 1922. Their success created a demand for "sustaining programs," unsponsored, usually late-night live broadcasts from a club or hotel.[12] The new generation felt the influence of white radio bands. Reedman Rudy Powell remembers, "I used to listen to the radio bands from Chicago in the late 20's like Coon-Sanders. . . . I liked unity and finesse and the white bands had it."[13] Buck Clayton remembers being arrested for loitering when he stopped to listen to the music of the Nighthawks coming out of an open window.[14] The availability of white media models added to the merging of black and white musical elements in the music of this new generation of black New Yorkers.

The younger generation had a wider range of opportunities in New York because the rapid expansion of jobs available to black bands kept the older generation from exercising the power it had possessed in Chicago. Broadway pit orchestras and older society dance bands were entrenched in New York. Harlem theaters used theater organs, white bands, or touring black groups. A few small movie theaters had black pit bands, but there was no real New York equivalent to Dave Peyton and Erskine Tate's Chicago neighborhood theater bands. Fletcher Henderson and others found that there was plenty of room for younger men as well. The presence of large numbers of musicians from various parts of the country made the dominance by one regional tradition less likely. The concentration of radio and recording opportunities in New York meant that the new big band sound developing there could be mass produced and distributed around the country.

Fletcher Henderson and His Orchestra

All of this era's themes came together in the story of Fletcher Henderson and his orchestra. For all of the enormous impact of this group, perhaps no other major jazz figure remains as indistinct today as Fletcher Henderson. His hidden hand approach to running the band often makes him seem invisible.

Perhaps the key to understanding Henderson's real contribution to jazz is to focus on the "and His Orchestra" part of his record labels. First, it shows Henderson's concern with respectability. He usually avoided the flash and stereotypes of the Red Hot Peppers or the Hot Five or even the Creole Jazz Band. His first named sessions in 1921 were as Henderson's Dance Orchestra and after May 1, 1923, the simple, dignified "Fletcher Henderson and His Orchestra" was the most frequent label.[15]

Secondly, and more importantly, the secret to the group's impact is the whole unit rather than the leader. Like many black bands of the 1920s, the Henderson orchestra was essentially a cooperative effort that owed its success to the combined efforts of many people. Henderson was the front man and handled most of the business details. Perhaps his major skill was in hiring and keeping together a strong nucleus of players who represented the range of skills and interests in this new generation of jazzmen.

The Club Alabam location job required a substantial repertoire and solid personnel. These were the two key areas in which Henderson shaped his own orchestra. He hired and fired with a good sense of the kind of musician he wanted. He was a key influence in building the band's book of tunes. One of the Henderson band's effects on jazz was moving the repertoire from traditional tunes and multi-themed compositions to the mass-produced thirty-two-bar popular songs. As music director of Down South Music Company, Henderson had established good relations with Tin Pan Alley, from which he obtained new tunes for his band. The demands of white audiences and management at the Club Alabam and later at Roseland encouraged this use of these songs.[16]

Surprisingly few original compositions came out of the Henderson group until the late 1920s. Sidemen sometimes brought tunes from other groups. The most noticeable example of this was Louis Armstrong bringing "Dippermouth Blues" from King Oliver's Creole Jazz Band. Assimilating these tunes was difficult because of the significant differences among the traditions represented in the Henderson orchestra. It became the job of the chief arranger, Don Redman, to blend these styles together. The resulting transformation of "Dippermouth Blues" into "Sugarfoot Stomp" set the pattern for the future development of jazz into the Swing Era and emphasizes Redman's impact on the overall musical sound of the group.

At the time of his Club Alabam audition, Don Redman, a product of the border state of West Virginia, was twenty-three years old. He was a child prodigy from a musical family and was graduated from Storer College in Harpers Ferry, Virginia, with a music major in 1920. He had spent a year and a half in Pittsburgh with Billy Butler's dance band, which brought him to New York in 1923. He had been working with Henderson's recording band for months before the Club Alabam job. Redman's main instruments were clarinet and alto sax, but his key contribution to the Henderson band was as an arranger. Aware of the harmonic rules of European classical music, he also had roots in African-American brass band and church music. He combined those roots into a structure that could mesh the various regional traditions of Henderson's men for a white audience.[17]

His search for this synthesis and the band's growth was well documented by extensive recordings. Pre-Club Alabam sides showed the band going in a variety of directions, reflecting the varying backgrounds of its members and the different media models they heard. There were strings of solos, collective ensembles, and written arranged passages. At different points they sound like Ladd's Black Aces, Paul Whiteman, Jelly Roll Morton, or nothing heard before. With more sessions, the number of written passages, usually by Redman, increased. A key factor was the size of the band, which fluctuated from six to eleven pieces. The New Orleans polyphonic ensembles worked with three front line instruments that could stay in certain roles. With five or six voices, finding individual roles became much more difficult. By contrast, harmonized sections needed more than one voice in reeds or brass to work.[18]

Some early Henderson sides such as "Bull Blues" with just six or eight pieces used solo voices, often simply playing melody against harmonized section backgrounds, while "Linger Awhile" made with ten men was almost completely written section work with little solo space.[19] When Henderson's composition "Dicty Blues" was recorded with nine pieces in August 1923, Redman's arrangement used brass and reed sections against each other as well as written and improvised harmonies within sections for a marvelously varied orchestral texture, a perfect match for its "dicty" or high-toned title. With only seven pieces, a few months later, much of the section work disappeared and was replaced by strings of solos and collective ensembles.[20]

The Club Alabam job increased Redman's importance and opportunities, since the group grew to nine and then ten pieces. The demands of the dancers required lots of new tunes. Neither Henderson nor Redman was happy with the stock arrangements used by many white dance bands. In these arrangements, the rhythm section (piano, banjo, tuba, drums) ticked off the dance beat while the brass, (two cornets and one trombone) and reeds (clarinets and saxophones) tossed the melody and harmony between them. Occasionally, brief space was left for one instrument to shine through in the form of an Oliver style break rather than an Armstrong style solo. As with Jim Europe or W. C. Handy, the music was to be played as written.[21]

Redman began to connect the soloists and ensembles, drawing perhaps on the call-and-response tradition of the black church and African heritage. Recordings of the first nine months of 1924, the Club Alabam and early Roseland period, reveal this smoother sound. Examples include "Feelin' the Way I do," and "I Can't Get the One I Want." Written harmony sections became more common and the soloists were "singing" more with their instruments, perhaps reflecting the blues accompaniments they were doing both at the Alabam and in the studios.[22] Henderson's band was essentially a "dance orchestra" playing for white dancers. By combining more directly the written harmonies of European classical music with the improvised African-American tradition, and harnessing the whole thing to a dance beat, Redman answered the needs of musicians, dancers, listeners, and various levels of music managers.

The arrangements were musically interesting, took advantage of the knowledge and abilities of the band, and provided a propulsive dance beat that could be enjoyed by the dance audience. As Frank Tirro declared, "This style of arrangement is not dependent upon particular personnel. . . . Don Redman does not exploit the particular talents of individual instrumentalists, but simply leaves 'blank spaces' in his arrangements where available musicians may stand up and 'take a ride'."[23] This helps explain why the Henderson-Redman model became the source for the generic big band sound rather than a more personal style like Jelly Roll Morton's or Duke Ellington's. There were many players emerging around the country who could read well enough to play the Redman arrangements. An individual band could give all the solo space to whatever players were best qualified and still produce a saleable and distinctive sound.

Redman and Henderson's ideas were implemented and amplified by the other members of the band. The core of Henderson's recording group had been players about his own age, mostly from the New York-New Jersey area: Howard Scott and Elmer Chambers, cornets; Teddy Nixon or George Brashear, trombone; and Charlie Dixon, banjo. Dixon was key in setting the dance tempo for the band.[24] Scott modeled his work on two players who worked with Mamie Smith, first Johnny Dunn who was the king of the Eastern style from 1920 to 1923, and then the 21-year-old Joe Smith. Smith, who soon joined Henderson, was a product of Ohio whose strengths were his beauty of tone, melodic sense, and flexibility. He could read, play lead, and improvise. Like Redman, Joe Smith represented the new generation and new regional styles that were enlivening the New York scene.[25]

Redman's partner in the reed section was another young regional product. Coleman Hawkins was a 19-year-old Missourian who had worked in local bands before a Mamie Smith tour brought him to New York. He was also the product of a family with middle-class aspirations. Hawkins had a background in classical music including some formal music training at Washburn College in Kansas, but he had also been listening to early jazz and blues records. He fit in more easily with Mamie Smith than Henderson did with Ethel Waters. By 1923, Hawkins was a motivated professional with the ability to learn and grow. He proceeded to invent the use of the sax as a solo instrument in jazz.[26]

The Club Alabam job required Henderson to add a tuba player and a drummer. While these instruments were often inaudible during recordings and were left out of records at this time, they were essential to a live dance band. Rafael Escudero on tuba was one of the Caribbean musicians prized in New York for reading ability, technique, and legitimate tone. Drummer Kaiser Marshall was born in Georgia in 1902 but raised in Boston where he attended English High. Escudero and Marshall had been playing at the Club 'Bamville under the leadership of Shrimp Jones in the fall of 1922.[27] In 1924, Henderson added more regional voices to his mix when Charlie Green from Omaha replaced Nixon on trombone and Buster Bailey, a

Memphis-born veteran of the Chicago scene, was added as a third clarinet and saxophone.[28]

The key new arrival was Louis Armstrong, who joined in September 1924. Hiring Armstrong was the ultimate example of Henderson's ability to find the best new talent. It is unclear if Armstrong was his first choice and how much Armstrong's wife Lil pushed the two men together. Still, it was Fletcher Henderson who sent to Chicago to hire both Louis Armstrong and Lil Armstrong's Memphis buddy, Buster Bailey. At this point in the band business, it was unusual to go that far afield to get sidemen. Henderson's other regional players had already arrived in New York before he hired them. With Armstrong and Bailey, Henderson reached out and the players were willing to come, showing both the importance of Chicago as a jazz hub in 1924 and the growing popularity of New York opportunities.[29]

With Henderson, Armstrong moved from playing second cornet in the Creole Jazz Band ensembles towards becoming the soloist of the Hot Fives. He grew in confidence and experience as a featured player. According to Armstrong, at his first rehearsal Henderson threw him right into reading the third cornet part on "By the Waters of Minnetonka" a complex written showpiece arrangement.[30] Armstrong survived and proved to be a better reader than he thought he was. He improved with hard work and the challenge of Henderson's book of arrangements. At the same time, he stimulated fellow band members. Armstrong's enormous talents inspired Don Redman to make more solo room in his arrangements and pushed Armstrong's bandmates to new heights in their own work. Coleman Hawkins, who grew into the first true saxophone soloist in jazz remembered, "Man, when you took solos after guys like Louis . . . you just had to play something or go home."[31] At the same time, the Redman-Henderson arrangements gave Armstrong a clearer setting from which to stand than the collective ensembles and short breaks of the Oliver band.

The Henderson orchestra continued to record extensively from October 1924 to October 1925, the period in which Armstrong was with the band. These sides showed both his influence and the growth of the band in response to the demands of the large white dance audience at the Roseland Ballroom. The pattern of solos spotted in written arranged sections became much more pronounced. Clarinet trios, a favorite device of Redman, were more prominent. At this time, the sides made as Fletcher Henderson and His Orchestra used the full eleven pieces: three cornets, one trombone, three reeds, and four rhythm. In this setting Armstrong's solos frequently stand out, as on "I'll See You in My Dreams" and "Copenhagen." In many cases such as "Shanghai Shuffle," "How Come You Do Me Like You Do," and "Go Long Mule," he energizes not only his own work but also those of Green and Hawkins. Armstrong's own solos got stronger throughout the year, peaking with the "Sugarfoot Stomp" recording of 1925 on which he took over King Oliver's "Dippermouth Blues" chorus. Armstrong had an enormous impact on other musicians both in and out of the Henderson band, but he was not yet registering with the general audience. He was mentioned as "Lewis" in an article on the band but did not get special advertising billing.[32]

The whole Henderson band was enjoying enormous success at the Roseland with increased salaries.[33] This job increased the Henderson band's contact and exchange of ideas with white musicians. Like many other ballrooms, Roseland used two alternating bands to provide nearly continuous music for its patrons. During the 1920s, the other band was always white. Rex Stewart remembered the band that had the biggest impact on Henderson. "We were supposed to be the world's greatest dance orchestra. And up pops this Johnny-come-lately white band from out in the sticks, cutting us. . . . The facts were that we simply could not play with Jean Goldkette's Victor Recording Orchestra."[34] With the arrangements of Bill Challis, the unusual c-melody sax of Frank Trumbauer, and particularly the cornet of Bix Beiderbecke, the Goldkette band had a strong influence on Henderson and vice versa. The memories of men from both bands support this idea of a mutual admiration society. Henderson recorded several arrangements in tribute to Bix and recordings of both groups show reciprocal influences.[35]

The Goldkette band's impact was strong because the Henderson group rarely found a white band it regarded as equal competition. Still, Henderson's band was willing to borrow and learn not only from Goldkette's orchestra but also from other white groups that on the whole were below the level of the Henderson group. This tendency has been denounced by some later jazz critics who judged the music on their own strict standards of what is and is not jazz.[36] To Henderson's musicians, jazz was both art and livelihood. They were aware of their own roots in the black tradition and experience and did not feel a need to justify their music's purity. They saw their success as advancing the race. They were clearly as good or better at what they did than their white counterparts, Goldkette perhaps excepted. Their accomplishments were a basis for an "upsurge of Afro-American self-confidence . . . the emotional certainty that the very dynamism of the 'World's Greatest Negro Metropolis' was somehow a guarantee of ultimate racial victory."[37]

Henderson band members were professionals playing happy dance music to entertain a white audience and were willing to learn from others who were successful at that task. Like other black musicians of the period, the Henderson men respected musicianship displayed by anyone in any tradition. A possible problem was that the accepted criteria for judging musicianship were devised by white critics. Like other black artists of the 1920s, Henderson, Redman, and Armstrong were establishing black accomplishments according to rules set by whites. Armstrong's development of the solo forced whites to develop new criteria to judge the quality of improvisation, but Henderson's and Redman's achievements in composition and arrangement were judged by existing European-based norms. Their success, like that of black writers, was real and appreciated in the black community.[38]

Moreover, some of the alleged white influences on the Henderson band as seen by critics simply reflected Redman's previous breakthroughs. Many white bands borrowed extensively from Henderson and other black bands. Redman arranged many tunes for Paul Whiteman's orchestra and clearly influenced Bill Challis of the Goldkette band. This may be why the Henderson outfit could use Challis's arrangements.[39] This ability to cross racial lines musically was a major reason for the merger of jazz into the mainstream of American popular music in the Jazz Age of the 1920s.

While the black press praised Henderson's achievements as a pioneer crossover artist, the band played fairly rarely for black audiences. Throughout the 1920s, the Henderson orchestra remained based in white locations as it increased the number of one-nighters in the black community. The band's presence at Harlem affairs such as the opening of the Savoy ballroom became a symbol of an event's prestige.[40] A February 1926 Henderson appearance in Chicago got a rave review from Dave Peyton, who included the telltale line, "Those who should have packed the place missed a treat."[41] Apparently Henderson's New York sound and reputation did not translate into a large black turnout in Chicago.

The Roseland job provided economic success for the Henderson band. "A Henderson musician's weekly paycheck at Roseland came to about $80, except for Coleman Hawkins, who was paid $125, and Don Redman, who was paid additionally for arrangements—$25 per."[42] This was a source of pride in the black community. The *New York Age* in 1925 headlined "From $300 to $1,200 per week in less than 2 Years for Orchestra" and explained that this ranked Henderson with the top white bands.[43] In fact, Henderson's pay was well below the highest paid white bands like that of Paul Whiteman who paid Redman $100 each for twenty arrangements. It was well above other black bands and in the upper ranks of the band business as a whole.[44] Moreover, the Roseland base was supplemented by one-nighters and recordings. The splendor remembered by drummer Kaiser Marshall is impressive:

> We were in the money then, with a location job, plenty of recording dates, and other things. Sometimes after we finished playing at Roseland we'd go up to Harlem and play from 2 to 3 in the morning; it meant twenty-five dollars a man just for that hour of playing. We'd go to the Manhattan, Renaissance Casino, or over to Brooklyn to the Arcadia. We all lived high; we were a top band and we had top wardrobes. The boys used to wear English walking suits that cost a hundred-ten dollars, seven-dollar spats, and eighteen-dollar shoes. Things were good in those days.[45]

With this high life to offer, Henderson had his pick of players when he needed replacements or wanted to expand the band. Gradually the orchestra grew from nine to twelve, and some men like Armstrong and Redman moved on to other things. The core remained Henderson, Hawkins, and Marshall. Henderson added men from the territory bands and New York itself. His territory men were often reading sectionmen like trumpeter Russell Smith, a brass and theater band veteran, who took over the lead first chair. A technician and a teacher, Smith concentrated on tone, breath control, cohesion, phrasing, reading, and voice leading. Section leaders like "Pop" Smith gave black bands the cohesion, tone, and sound needed to impress white ballroom patrons. Trombonist Claude Jones, reedman Jerome Don Pasquall, who studied at the New England Conservatory of Music, and brass bassist June Cole, rarely soloed but were prized for their reading ability.[46]

Many of Henderson's new men like trumpeters Bobby Stark and Rex Stewart, trombonists Benny Morton and Jimmy Harrison, reedman Russell Procope, and the multi-talented Benny Carter were Henderson's own "second line." Many were members of a new generation, born around 1906. They had grown up or worked in New York listening to the development of big band jazz.[47] When they joined Henderson, they had already been influenced by Armstrong, Charlie Green, and Don Redman, respectively. Their hiring simply continued the already established direction and style of the band.

Armstrong's impact on Stewart was enormous: "I tried to walk like him, talk like him, eat like him, sleep like him. I even bought a pair of the bad policeman shoes like he used to wear."[48] He also developed a solo style in Armstrong's footsteps, which is evident when Armstrong and Stewart solo on "T.N.T." and "The Stampede," respectively.[49] By contrast, Carter strongly denies that he was influenced by Redman. "I always listened carefully to his writing, which I admired. But the occasion never arose for me to go directly to him for advice. Though he was a few years older, I have always thought of us as contemporaries."[50] Whatever the relationship, Carter filled some of Redman's roles both as reedman and arranger for Henderson when Redman left to take over McKinney's Cotton Pickers.

The flexibility of the Henderson-Redman style showed in two ways at this point. First, Redman could remain with the Henderson band on paper. His "book" of written scores continued to be an important part of Henderson's sound well after his departure. Secondly, the arrangements accommodated Stewart's Armstrong-style trumpet as well as the different approaches of Joe Smith or Bobby Stark. When necessary, space could instead be given to a different instrument. Coleman Hawkins on tenor became the star solo voice after Armstrong left.

Many of these men shared Henderson's middle-class values. As Benny Carter remembered, "We weren't violent or even given to obscenities. . . . Most of the musicians I knew were not rough characters . . . all gentlemen."[51] Russell Procope described a very middle-class adolescence. "As a teenager I had a very full schedule. Everything I did was supervised. I had to take music lessons and I played basketball on the church team. . . . My life was regulated and I was fortunate enough to have a good family life."[52] Procope, Carter, and others were trained in reading skills and musicianship by Lieutenant Eugene Mikell, the bandmaster of Jim Europe's 369th group. They were also inspired by the Henderson band, which had broken the "natural musician" stereotype that Jim Europe had not challenged. At Roseland, Henderson's men clearly read their parts from music stands.[53] Louis Metcalf recalls, "The sight of Fletcher Henderson's men playing behind music stands brought on a learning to read music kick in Harlem which hadn't cared before for it. There were two years of real concentration. Everybody greeted you with 'How's studying?' "[54] By 1926, the difference was clear to Doc Cheatham arriving from Chicago. "New York had its own style of music. It was more sophisticated. They had bandstands, music stands and books all full of stock arrangements."[55]

Other New York Dance Jobs

Young New Yorkers and territory men arriving in New York rarely moved directly into the Henderson band. Instead, they worked first with groups in dancing schools, taxi dance halls, and after-hours spots to get the experience and recognition necessary to land a spot with Henderson.

The most informal element in the New York black entertainment scene were the famous "rent parties" in private homes and apartments. The live music was usually a stride pianist like Fats Waller, Willie "the Lion" Smith, or James P. Johnson. Sometimes young musicians looking for a job would join in. This was a very loose music with lots of improvisation.[56]

Many black bands played taxi dance halls, the dime-a-dance haunts of the working class, even in mainly white neighborhoods. Early in the decade, some locations used five- to six-piece groups, but by 1928–1929, the nine- to ten-piece group using written arrangements had become the norm. June Clark, Bingie Madison, and Charlie Skeets were active leaders at this level during the 1920s. Clark's bands at the Tango Palace and Tango Gardens included many sidemen who went on to big name bands.[57] Madison and Skeets both developed bands in taxi dance halls only to lose them to better opportunities. At the Rose Danceland in the late 1920s, Skeets had a band of young Easterners like reedman Russell Procope and reedman-arranger Joe Garland. Jelly Roll Morton took over the band and the job to keep a band together between dates of his Victor recording contract. He added some New Orleans-rooted players including clarinetist Omer Simeon, cited by Procope as an influence. This band did, in fact, record a few dates for Victor. Thus, for a brief time, a taxi dance hall had a Victor recording band that mixed Jelly Roll Morton's style with young Easterners. In 1930, Skeets lost another band to Claude Hopkins who led it to fame.[58] Madison also led a Tango Palace band. His 1930 Broadway Danceland group became the core of the Mills Blue Rhythm Band for drummer Willie Lynch.[59]

In 1923, most of the black dances were still private, played by Happy Rhone and the other "society dance orchestras." The Savoy Ballroom really brought the public dance hall to Harlem. From its opening on March 12, 1926, the white owner, Jay Fagan, established it as the major black ballroom in the country. It was a very attractive job with strong public recognition, an appreciative and knowledgeable black dance audience, and good working conditions, but low salaries.[60] For its bands, the Savoy looked to younger New Yorkers and to territory bands working in the Henderson style. By 1926 there were plenty from which to choose.

The first two Savoy house bands were Fess Williams's Royal Flush Orchestra and the Savoy Bearcats. Williams's early career in the Southeast was covered in chapter three. He had organized this new band in Albany, New York, in 1924 with two friends from Louisville, Hank Duncan on piano and David "Jelly" James on trombone. He added men from Indianapolis, Washington, D.C., and Maryland. Merging regional lines, the band concentrated on a novelty band style that was a cross between Ted Lewis and the later Cab Calloway. Radio broadcasts over WGY in Schenectady caught the attention of Jay Fagan, who brought them to the Savoy. When Fagan sent Williams to Chicago to open the new Regal Theater, Fess left his Savoy band behind under his old Louisville rival Lockwood Lewis. Williams returned in 1929, and perhaps influenced by the Chicago theater bands, destroyed his popularity with jazz versions of classical overtures.[61]

Although billed as a Southeastern band, the core of the Bearcats included young New Yorkers like the brass team of Gil Paris, Demas Dean, and James Reavey. They stressed arranged dance music in the Henderson style. In fact, they used Henderson-Redman arrangements as well as originals by their pianist Joe Steele. Their few Victor records show a straight-ahead dance band that could keep the dancers happy. They are obviously using written arrangements playing off brass and reed sections. There is little variation among different takes, except for Joe Steele's stride piano solos.[62]

After the Bearcats left for a tour of South America, territory bands like Zach Whyte's from Cincinnati, Roy Johnson's from Richmond, Ike Dixon's from Baltimore, and Alonzo Ross's from Florida had brief runs at the Savoy, but none were successful. Even King Oliver leading the core of what became the Luis Russell band could not keep a steady job at the Savoy.[63] More successful were two other bands, the Scott Brothers' and Chick Webb's. The Scott band had grown in the 1920s, alternating between their Springfield, Ohio, base and New York. They followed the Henderson style to fit their New York audience. At the Savoy, they were successful because of their showmanship and danceable arrangements.[64]

Chick Webb led the last important Savoy band of the 1920s but had a hard time getting started. Arriving in New York from Baltimore in 1925, he found a cabaret job through the informal Baltimore-D.C. alumni association. By the time he started at the Savoy, he was leading a tight eight-piece dance band playing mostly improvised or "head" rather than written arrangements. Yet his band of East Coast men created an East Coast rather than a New Orleans style. Guitarist John Trueheart, like Webb, was from Baltimore. Pianist Don Kirkpatrick spent time there although he was born in North Carolina. The reedmen included Johnny Hodges and Howard Johnson from Boston and Elmer Williams from New Jersey. The one ringer, trombonist Bob Horton, was a Fess Whately-trained Alabamian. Later, Benny Carter and Hilton Jefferson, a youngster from

Danbury, Connecticut, briefly played in the reed section. As the personnel changes indicate, the Webb band was young, growing, and finding itself. It would leave the Savoy quickly for a variety of jobs before returning in triumph in 1933.[65]

Whether at the Savoy or in taxi dance halls, other black New York dance bands faced the same demands as Fletcher Henderson's at Roseland: a sound loud enough to fill the room; a flexible, familiar repertoire; and a steady beat for dancers. Not surprisingly, their answers produced similar music. The arranged big band style developed by Don Redman and Fletcher Henderson fit the audience's needs, and most groups used it. By the end of the decade, most groups had grown to ten pieces although a cheaper location might try to get by with a seven- or eight-piece group. Even with the smaller groups, the collective ensembles of the New Orleans style made little impact.

Bands all conducted business informally, usually through a single leader negotiating with a location owner. They filled long-term engagements, playing for dances every night for months at a time, which provided stability and built cohesive sections. This established a complex relationship between band, management, and audience. All of these elements contributed to the development of a distinct jazz style.

New York Cabaret Bands

Aside from the ballrooms and dance halls, the last major professional arena for black musicians in New York was the nightclub or cabaret scene. The structure of this world was similar to dance work. The lower levels were small black neighborhood clubs, and the top spots were the black-and-tans, large, exclusive locations featuring black entertainers for usually all white audiences.

The black nightclubs were scattered all over Harlem and changed names, locations, management, and entertainers frequently. The small black club owner rarely had the financial resources and clout to protect himself from the gangsters and police who represented the twin devils of the nightclub business during Prohibition. There were always plenty of nightclub jobs to keep musicians busy, although it was difficult to maintain a stable band in this setting. Instead, these small clubs were the main musical melting pot in Harlem. They often provided individual out-of-town musicians their first jobs and opportunities to test themselves and trade stylistic tricks with other migrants as well as local men. Jam sessions and cutting contests were a main feature of some after-hours spots and aided this process. The Rhythm Club actually set aside separate nights for individual instruments.[66]

The bands in these clubs ranged widely in size from trios up to ten pieces. Their styles are hard to judge because they rarely recorded. Many recordings by leaders like Thomas Morris, however, used men from these bands and may be representative of the sound. Early in the decade, there was more emphasis on collective ensembles and strings of solos, but as musicians began to see these unstable, low-paying jobs as steps to bigger bands like Henderson's, more emphasis was put on the arranged section style. Many Swing Era sidemen apprenticed in these groups. Although the groups may have played a little looser for black audiences, Elmer Snowden and June Clark among others moved easily from black cabarets into white dance halls. This was particularly true by the end of the decade when clubs like the Capitol Palace redecorated and expanded the size of their bands to get some of the overflow from the big three black-and-tans.[67]

Aside from Fletcher Henderson, the bands at three clubs, Connie's Inn, The Cotton Club, and Small's Paradise, were regarded as the most successful black bands in New York. They were also part of the arranged big band tradition but with some distinctions. The black-and-tan cabaret bands were in between dance and theater bands because they had to play for elaborate revues or floor shows as well as for dancing. They were bands with a flair for showmanship. Also, they were playing music to which people would listen as well as dance. This may be one explanation of the difference in styles between Duke Ellington's top cabaret band and Fletcher Henderson's top dance band. The cabaret bands were not as tied to dance tempos. They could experiment with mood pieces, which fit the artistic tempo and background of Duke Ellington.

Connie's Inn was a basement cabaret at the corner of 7th Avenue and 131st Street. It opened in 1921 as the Shuffle Inn to profit from the success of "Shuffle Along." At first, the entertainment was primarily blues singers, comedians, and pianists. In 1923, the cabaret was taken over by two delicatessen owners and gamblers, George and Connie Immerman, who featured elaborate floor shows, first-rate bands, and beautiful girls. Their first band was Wilbur Sweatman's vaudeville style group, which was quickly replaced by Leroy Smith's fourteen-piece Whitemanesque orchestra from Detroit. In 1926, this band left to go to a white midtown nightclub, the Club Richman, and then on to Atlantic City, New Jersey.[68] It was replaced by another large "symphonic jazz" orchestra led by violinist Allie Ross. By 1929, the club had imported Carroll Dickerson's Symphonic Syncopators including Louis Armstrong from Chicago. Armstrong's vocal on "Ain't Misbehavin' " helped the Connie's Inn *Hot Chocolates* revue to become a Broadway show and increase the club's reputation into the depression years.[69]

Pianist Charlie Johnson led the house band at Small's Paradise, 2294 1/2 Seventh Avenue, from its opening in 1925 until the mid-1930s, although he often shared the spot with other bands. His was a ten-piece group in the big band ensemble style, and from the memories of others and the evidence of a few recordings, it was an excellent one. "The Boy in the Boat" features fine muted plunger brass solos in what Duke Ellington would make known as the "jungle style," a shared trait of many New York cabaret bands. Gunther Schuller praised the collective improvisation of the last two choruses of "Hot-Tempered Blues." The band also revealed the changing nature of the Harlem scene. In 1925 Jenkins Orphanage alumnus Gus Aiken was the main trumpet man. By 1928, he had been replaced by Leonard "Ham" Davis from St. Louis and Sidney DeParis from Crawfordsville, Indiana.[70]

The Cotton Club, 644 Lenox Avenue, became the dominant Harlem nightclub. In many ways, it was a symbol of what was good and bad about the "vogue" for black culture in the Roaring Twenties. This was a gangster-owned club, openly flaunting Prohibition and well protected by muscle and graft. It had a segregated, white-only audience policy and a color-conscious, "high-yellow" hiring policy for chorus girls. It featured reviews, written and directed by whites, which played up the exotic jungle appeal of black culture. Still, it helped develop many fine black performers and gave them a major leg up to national recognition.

For most of the 1920s, the house band at the Cotton Club was led by Andy Preer, who had a young Southwestern territory band from St. Louis. After Preer's death, they toured the country as The Missourians. Under Cab Calloway's leadership, they returned to the Cotton Club in the 1930s as Duke Ellington's relief band. Their sound in their first Cotton Club period is hard to discern because there were few recordings and limited critical comments. They seem to have kept some of the Southwest riffs and growl trumpet work while moving to the big band style. Their situation at the Cotton Club had interesting parallels to that of Fate Marable and other St. Louis bands on the Strekfus riverboats. In both locations, black bands were playing for white audiences and very demanding owners. The results seem similar. Their sounds also resemble the other key black-and-tan bands, led by Charlie Johnson and Duke Ellington.[71] The development of the Ellington band, which replaced the Preer group at the Cotton Club in December 1927, will be discussed in chapter seven.

Conclusion

Between 1923 and 1929, the New York jazz scene took on a very clear form. While black jazz bands played a wide spectrum of music in ballrooms, theaters, cabarets, rent parties, recording studios, and elsewhere, some music and some jobs were more equal than others. The opportunities for what today would be called crossover play, reaching the white popular music audience, provided the most money, respect, and recognition for musicians and the black community as a whole. Access to that white audience was easiest with the arranged big band sound pioneered by Fletcher Henderson and Don Redman and elaborated by the other dance and black-and-tan cabaret bands. The rent parties and cabaret jam sessions continued to be the prime areas for the stride pianists. For other players, however, the parties and jam sessions were perpetual auditions for big band slots rather than the creation of an independent or competing musical tradition in the late 1920s.

This work situation shaped the styles and skills of the musicians. These bands mixed young, trained musicians from New York and the territories with older men including Clef Club and brass band veterans. They all shared certain skills, abilities, and attitudes. To hold their jobs, they needed to be able to read, master their instruments, and blend with other musicians. Punctuality and reliability were prime concerns both for the band leader and the location owner. Drunkenness and other bad habits that affected job performance were discouraged and could cost someone a job. Solo improvising ability was often not the major concern in hiring or firing. Most bands had only one or two main soloists, leaving five to nine sidemen to emphasize section work skills.

These skills and the professional attitudes that went with them became more prominent as players advanced. Jobs in New York formed an informal pyramid. They started out with neighborhood dances and pass-the-hat gigs and moved up through the taxi dance halls and cabarets toward the goal of a long stay at the Savoy, Roseland, Connie's Inn, or Cotton Club. This pyramid funneled many young musicians into careers in music. It taught them the abilities and values necessary to survive and weeded out those who did not fit. For New York players, the lower rungs provided the same seasoning as the territories. This process explains the prevalence in the 1920s of Hsio Wen Shih's model jazz innovator. The personality and abilities he describes are precisely those demanded by the New York business environment.

Moreover, the concentration of radio and recording opportunities in New York guaranteed that the new big band sound developing there could be mass produced and distributed around the country. New York bands like Henderson's and Ellington's had many more recording opportunities than bands elsewhere, including Chicago. As the decade went on, this significantly shifted the positions of these two jazz centers. In 1923, Chicago had several established styles and many recognized jazz players, while New York was still developing a distinctive style. By 1929, New York claimed the two leading jazz bands in the country and was rapidly drawing new musicians from everywhere. Henderson, Redman, Ellington and the other New York jazz innovators of the 1920s had found a synthesis of African-American and European-American musical elements in between Chicago's feuding establishment and collective ensemble styles.

After 1929, changes in the music business and national culture would make the New York style the dominant national sound of jazz. This reduced Chicago to another territory stop on national tours and laid the foundations of the Swing Era. In order to understand these developments fully, it is necessary to look first at the territories between 1923 and 1929. There, the same tensions seen in Chicago and New York were being worked out in a variety of ways.

6

Territory Scuffles 1923-1929

THE period 1923–1929 was the heyday of the territory band. The *Chicago Defender* entertainment pages for these years mentioned more than 250 bands active in the territories. Musicians' memories indicate that there were hundreds more.[1] By their very nature, these bands have been poorly documented, and any study of them is just sketching the outlines of the iceberg. Still, such a study is very important because it shows how the new urban culture that was so visible in Chicago and New York was also developing in Cleveland, Atlanta, Kansas City, Omaha, and Los Angeles and reaching out from these cities to change American small towns. The territory jazz bands were a very important part of the cultural revolution of the Roaring Twenties that transformed America from a local, rural, homemade culture to a mass-produced, national, urban, media culture. The territory bands brought these two cultures together much more than the jazzmen of the major urban centers.[2]

Part of this revolution could be seen in the changing nature of entertainment in the territories. In the prosperity of the Roaring Twenties, the new mass media of radio, motion pictures, and the phonograph combined with the automobile to transform America. Local personal contacts and institutions were replaced by national models. Even live national institutions suffered. At the beginning of the decade, minstrel and tent shows still roamed the nation. By 1929, many had folded and most that remained were in the Southeast where a few were active into the 1940s. The vaudeville circuits felt increasing competition from films although the black TOBA circuit prospered, perhaps because of the lack of black faces on film. TOBA was strong in the South, the middle-sized cities of the Midwest, and the black neighborhoods in major cities like Chicago and New York.

The real growth industry for musicians and the core of life for the territory bands was playing for dancing. The Lynds's study of Muncie, Indiana, showed the importance of dancing in this period. "Cards and dancing are the standard entertainment of Middletown. . . . In general, dancing holds the position of pre-eminence with the younger group before marriage."[3] Local ballrooms and dance halls grew up in cities around the country to fill this need, while smaller towns organized dances in schools, gymnasiums, and even tobacco barns.

The desire for dancing was fed by recordings and radio broadcasts coming from the major cities. Until late in the 1920s, most of the bands creating this media music remained in the major cities with long location jobs. This created a void which was filled by the local "territory bands." A major dilemma facing them was how to combine local demands and skills with the mass media tastes generated by radio and records. Their various answers to this dilemma created a spectrum of six regional territory styles in the Roaring Twenties. The following discussion will show how local realities created distinctions among regions. The final summary will focus on the shared experiences that united the territory musicians of this period.

East Coast

Life in the East Coast territory was dominated by the presence of New York City. This area was the earliest to experience the impact of the New York bands and their style. Although this area turned out many very talented musicians during the 1920s, it was very difficult for a territory band as such to survive here. Before national tours began, New York bands took round-the-world tours, hitting jobs in Philadelphia, Baltimore, and Washington, D.C., or New England. The Duke Ellington band played summer jobs in Boston and the New England area as early as 1926, which may help to explain why Bostonians, Johnny Hodges and Harry Carney, both became key Ellingtonians. Charlie Johnson and Leroy Smith played frequently in Atlantic City and Philadelphia.[4]

The readily available recordings and radio broadcasts of New York bands kept their names and styles in front of local musicians, so the local players developed in the Henderson-Redman New York style. This situation also denied record opportunities to East Coast territory bands. However, by the late 1920s, New York City had drawn in so many good young, players from Washington, D.C., Baltimore, New Jersey, Boston, and Philadelphia that the style there might be more accurately labeled East Coast. Boston was the home of great sax players. Johnny Hodges, Harry Carney, and Charlie Holmes moved to New York between 1924 and 1926, while Howard Johnson arrived in 1928. Hodges in fact began commuting to New York for weekend jobs even before he left home. Duke Ellington and others helped land New York jobs for later migrants from the Washington, D.C., area like Chick Webb, John Trueheart, and Claude Hopkins. Young players who left New Jersey in the 1920s for New York included Count Basie, Herb Gregory, and Sonny Greer, who detoured by way of D.C. to become a charter Ellingtonian. Rex Stewart, Charlie Gaines, Doc Cheatham, and Wilbur and Sidney DeParis came to the Big Apple by way of Philadelphia.[5]

The departure of so many good young players made it very difficult to maintain local bands, but despite the odds some leaders survived for long periods of time. George Tynes in Boston, Doc Hyder in Philadelphia, Doc Perry in Washington, D.C., Bobbie Brown in Newark, Eugene Primus and George Warmack in Buffalo, and others kept bands going in this territory in the 1920s. Claude Hopkins's band led a split existence in the period, alternating stints as a territory band in D.C. and New Jersey with vaudeville tours and trips to Europe.[6] The absence of recordings or clear descriptions makes it difficult to get a clear picture of the sound of these East Coast bands, particularly early in the decade. The ease with which these men fit into the New York big bands, however, suggests that the music in this territory was compatible with the New York style.

Southeast

The majority of the black population still lived in the Southeast, and it is not surprising that this area had the most territory bands in the 1920s. More than seventy-five are mentioned in the *Chicago Defender* and many more bands existed that were never documented, particularly in small towns and rural areas. Due to their isolation, a much smaller percentage of bands here recorded than in other territories. This makes it tough to discern the regional styles from recordings. This is particularly unfortunate since the range of styles in the Southeast was the widest in the nation. Not only was the territory large but also the cultural gaps between city and country and among states such as Mississippi and North Carolina as well as middle and working class blacks created great musical variety. Jazz was not the dominant black music in much of the Southeast at this time. As Paul Oliver has pointed out, very distinct country blues styles had developed to provide private enjoyment and some public entertainment to rural blacks.[7]

The tent shows, minstrel shows, and circuses with their brass bands and blues singers continued to tour this territory and were the only professional entertainment in some small towns and rural areas. This was changing as early as the fall of 1926. Veteran showman Coy Herndon complained in January 1927 that at least nine minstrel tent shows had "gone bust" in the last four months. He blamed it on the poor prices in the cotton market and labor troubles in the coal mines.[8] While the rural South was not sharing in the prosperity of the Roaring Twenties, these failures reflected the impact of the radio, motion picture, and automobile and the waning of traditional entertainments. In medium-sized towns, the black TOBA vaudeville circuit continued to provide a steady diet of stage shows accompanied by pit bands, some very good and some very awful. These bands often played for dancing and were important on the territory scene. Two of the best recorded, Eddie Heywood, Sr.'s band from the 81 Theater in Atlanta and Charlie Williamson's group from Memphis's Palace Theater. They show solos and an improvised ensemble style in touch with both the ragtime and blues traditions that continued in this area in the 1920s. The Williamson band was only a six-piece group, while Heywood had seven. All of the players except the drummers took solos somewhere in the recordings. These included several minstrel type banjo solos and slap-tongued baritone sax work. Except for a few harmonies in the Williamson records, the ensembles are collectively improvised polyphony. Pianist Heywood and his band as a whole were quite comfortable with the blues as shown on "Trombone Moanin' Blues." This is not surprising since in addition to playing in Atlanta, the Heywood band often toured with the blues act of Butterbeans and Susie. A veteran of W. C. Handy's band, Williamson on trumpet along with James Alston on piano showed strong ragtime influences particularly on "Scandinavian Stomp" and "Memphis Scronch."[9]

The loose, small band style represented by these TOBA pit groups was typical of the many small dance bands scattered around the Southeast in places like Fayetteville, North Carolina; Paris, Tennessee; Columbia, South Carolina; Vicksburg, Mississippi, and many small towns and rural areas.[10] In the rural areas, in fact, the line between jazz bands and folk music was still very blurred in the 1920s. Groups in the style of the Memphis Jug Band or Dixieland Jug Blowers provided much of the dance music. Virtually none of these groups recorded, so it is difficult to actually document their sound.[11]

Three small groups that did record were the Triangle Harmony Boys, Frank Bunch's Fuzzie Wuzzies, and the Blackbirds of Paradise, all from Alabama. All three groups included music students. Bunch's group claimed two of Fess Whately's students from Birmingham, while the Blackbirds and Harmony Boys included some Tuskegee Institute students. The Blackbirds were rare among these groups in that they frequently played a white country club. Philmore "Shorty" Hall, the trumpet soloist for the Blackbirds, later became a music teacher in North Carolina where he taught a very young Dizzy Gillespie. Still, taken as a whole, all their recordings showed strong African-American folk elements. All three groups had a heavy blues feel as they mixed strings of solos and improvised ensembles. There were few written passages and almost no section work, even when an alto and clarinet or two cornets and trombone were playing. Tunes played were primarily originals, mostly based on the blues.[12]

These records fit the memories of musicians from this area where many dance bands played for black audiences. In the segregated South, black artists' access to white audiences was more limited. Black folk traditions were evident in the music, which resembles the early New Orleans sound. It is unclear if this is the result of direct influence, similar development, or the impact of the records of King Oliver's Creole Jazz Band, the ODJB, or others. Despite the string of solos, the 1927 Southeastern recordings show that the model for cornetists in this area was still King Oliver rather than Louis Armstrong. Armstrong's expansion of tone and direction were not yet accepted here.

Given that connections of the small Southeastern bands to the New Orleans tradition, it is interesting to see that the two New Orleans bands that traveled in the territory were expanding the New Orleans tradition by adding sax sections. These bands were led by Oscar Celestin and Sam Morgan. Both men had long careers in New Orleans that dated back before World War I, and were well-versed in the New Orleans style. By the mid-1920s, however, both were leading larger dance bands that often played outside of the Crescent City, often in Mobile, Alabama. Both recorded and showed a New Orleans collective ensemble sound with nine or ten pieces. All the musicians in both bands came from shared New Orleans traditions, so the collective ensemble roles were clearer. Also in several places, either the brass or the reeds improvise as a section; for example, two trumpets and trombone, or alto and tenor, or alto and clarinet with roles influenced by the traditional cornet, trombone, and clarinet line-up. Sam Morgan's recorded repertoire included three spirituals, which raises the question of whether these were played for dances or if his band played other types of jobs as well.[13] It is not known if there were other traditional regional styles in this area that were not recorded.

FROM JAZZ TO SWING

While all of these strains represented continuing local traditions, the last trend in the Southeast was the emergence even here of bands influenced by the style developing in New York and popularized by radio and records. At least seven Southeastern bands expanded from eight to ten pieces between 1927 and 1929. Most of these bands contained a core of college students from one of the black institutions in the region. In fact, several were official college groups. The use of musical groups to raise funds for black colleges was well established, going back to the Fisk Jubilee singers of the late nineteenth century. By the 1920s, jazz bands were filling this role. In many of these institutions, the emphasis on musical reading skills and sophistication made Fletcher Henderson's orchestra their model.[14]

Two of these bands recorded, and the results were clearly in the New York arranged big band style. Alonzo Ross's De Luxe Syncopators started as a five-piece band in Jacksonville in 1925 led by a ragtime pianist, but made its reputation at Della Robia Gardens in Miami as a ten-piece band playing for white dancers. Its 1927 Victor recordings show a band obviously influenced by but unable to capture fully the style of Don Redman. The similarities to the Henderson band came both from recorded influence and a similar social and economic situation. Ross's band was made up of young ambitious black musicians from many regions playing for white dancers. The arrangements by Bob Cloud, a reedman from Terre Haute, Indiana, were very heavy on written section work, and the solos did not swing despite the presence of several future jazz stars. The group included at various times reedman Ed Hall from New Orleans, trumpeters Cootie Williams from Mobile, Alabama, and Melvin Herbert, and bassist Dick Fulbright from Texas. Neither Hall nor Williams are on the records. The band took a crack at New York in 1928 but failed to click and broke up, leaving the players to make it on their own there.[15]

J. Neal Montgomery led a group of Atlanta University students that built a reputation playing for white dances around the Atlanta area. Their two 1929 sides "Atlanta Lowdown" and "Auburn Avenue Stomp" show them to be firmly in the Redman-Henderson mold, and they seem to have been very conscious of this. The group included George Robinson, Pete Clark, and Wayman Carver, none of whom apparently were on the records. They all became Swing Era sidemen in New York. Carver, who recorded the first jazz flute solos with Chick Webb, was already experimenting with that instrument while playing with Montgomery. This band did show a little more awareness of the blues than the Ross group, though that may just be an accident of the recorded repertoire. The Montgomery band stayed in the Southeast, although some of the players eventually found their way to New York.[16]

Similarly, Roy Johnson's Happy Pals of Richmond, Virginia, kept their base in that city through the late 1920s and into the early 1930s even though they were well received in several New York appearances including at the Savoy Ballroom. Their two 1929 records also show strong written ensemble and section work.[17]

Two fascinating bands that did not record were the C. S. Belton and Smiling Billy Stewart groups. Both were based in Florida and led by tent show brass band veterans. These successful bands were known for their showmanship. Frequent letters from their leaders kept them well covered in the *Chicago Defender*. Belton replaced Ross at Della Robia Gardens when Ross took his group to New York. Belton also split time between society jobs and broadcasts in West Palm Beach and tours of small towns throughout Florida, Georgia, and the Carolinas. Stewart's group was the official band of Bethune Cookman College and competed with Belton in the same territory. The style of both seems to have been a blend of brass band and Redman-style big band playing that stressed section work and showmanship.[18]

The Southeastern band that would gain the greatest national success also began as a college group. In 1926 Jimmie Lunceford and several classmates at Fisk University in Tennessee began playing in the area. After taking a teaching job in Memphis, Lunceford formed a band combining some of his college friends and high school students. It became popular in the area. Its earliest recordings, in 1929, show a strong blues and church influence, although the tunes such as "In Dat Morning" with "preaching" by bassist Moses Allen may not present the band's full style at this time. In its Swing Era career the band stressed section work and was known for its strict musical and moral standards.[19]

Clearly, the Southeast styles in the 1920s ranged from small blues-influenced groups close to the folk roots through theater and dance bands to the young college groups with their versions of the Henderson sound. Each style emerged out of audience demands and musician creativity with only the later groups reflecting any strong impact from media influences outside the region.

Midwest

The Midwest spectrum of styles was much narrower. Most Midwestern bands were playing for dancing. While there were some smaller groups, ten-piece bands playing homophonic arrangements in sections predominated. Midwest big bands were competing strongly with New York by the late 1920s. Springfield, Ohio, central Indiana, and Detroit were exporting bands to Chicago, New York, and Los Angeles, and several Midwestern bands were building national reputations. By 1927, all of these bands were operating in the big band style set by Don Redman and the Fletcher Henderson Orchestra. In that year, Redman came to Detroit to take over leadership of McKinney's Cotton Pickers, the most successful Midwestern band.

The reasons for the success of Midwest bands are difficult to pinpoint. Dancing was a very important recreation in the Midwest as the Lynds showed in *Middletown*. The growing black communities of the Great Migration provided a base, but there was also ample access to white audiences. Big cities like Detroit and Cleveland with their large black populations could support several ballrooms and bands at the same time. Both had at least four active black dance bands at one time. Also, the cities were close enough that bands from Toledo, Detroit, Cleveland, and Columbus, for example, could play in one another's home turf and add to the competition and blending of sounds. They could also complete with bands from smaller towns both for one-nighters in those towns and for gigs in the bigger cities. The concentration of black colleges in the Wilberforce-Central State area of Ohio was unusual for the North. Finally, national touring shows brought bands from New York and the East Coast into the territory. Summer resorts in Indiana and Michigan provided another source of jobs. Michigan particularly had several important areas that were primarily black middle-class resorts.[20]

The performance situations and the skills and interests of the players combined to create a parallel to the New York synthesis. The Springfield, Ohio, bands led the way. Both the Scott Brothers and McKinney expanded early in the decade. The Scotts started rotating summers in New York with winters in the Midwest in 1925. Their experience at Harlem's Capitol Palace demonstrated that to be more successful they needed to grow beyond their six-piece novelty band format. Touring back into the Midwest, they added members including trombonist Dickie Wells. By the time they recorded in New York in 1927, they were a ten-piece band working in the big band section style of Redman and Henderson. This style won them acceptance at the Savoy Ballroom, though they also continued occasional tours back to the Midwest. Further recordings in 1929, particularly "Springfield Stomp," show strong arranged sections and good solos by Wells and trumpeter Bill Coleman. By 1929, the Scott band, now Cecil Scott's Bright Boys, had finally shifted its base to Harlem, where it remained into the early 1930s, enjoying moderate success and launching long careers for Coleman, Wells, Scott, Frankie Newton, and others. Its achievement served as a model for many other Midwest bands.[21]

The most influential Midwestern band was the Scotts's old Springfield competitor, McKinney's Cotton Pickers, which by 1927 had settled in Detroit after touring the Ohio area with stops in Dayton and Toledo. They were taken over by Jean Goldkette, a white band manager, who imported Don Redman as music director. The band became a regional and national force from its Greystone Ballroom base. Before Redman arrived, the band expanded to nine and then ten pieces and used written arrangements by pianist Todd Rhodes and trumpeter John Nesbitt. Redman was responsible for a much smaller percentage of McKinney's arrangements than Henderson's since Nesbitt and others also contributed, but all of the music is in the section work style that Redman had pioneered.

These arrangements, section work, and entertaining vocals of George "Fathead" Thomas and Redman were the strengths of the McKinney band. The solo talents of the players were featured less than with Henderson or most other bands of the period. Still, John Nesbitt showed good "cool" cornet work influenced more by Joe Smith and Bix Beiderbecke than Louis Armstrong, while Redman contributed good alto solos.

The recorded picture of the Cotton Pickers is somewhat confused because after November 1929, recordings were often made in New York by Redman with the McKinney arrangements played by New York allstars Fats Waller, Coleman Hawkins, and others. Also, some of the actual Detroit group's most interesting recordings, "Paducah," "Birmingham Breakdown," and "Stardust" were made under the Chocolate Dandies pseudonymn. The recordings and memories of the period, however, indicate that the Cotton Pickers were a tight ensemble playing straight-ahead dance music that pleased its white dance audience and also impressed scores of young Midwestern musicians.[22]

Vic Dickenson, Teddy Wilson, and Speed Webb were just a few of the young men who were impressed by the smooth ensemble sound of the Cotton Pickers. They were part of a second line of young Midwestern black dance bands in the mold of McKinney and the Scott brothers, influenced by Redman's Cotton Pickers and white recordings. All grew to ten-piece groups stressing arrangements, tight section work, and a smooth ensemble sound playing for both white and black dance audiences.

Speed Webb organized such a band in Indiana in the early 1920s and took it to the West Coast. He returned to the Midwest late in the decade and organized another one.[23] Vic Dickinson remembered, "Seven guys arranged in that band . . . and every week we had seven new arrangements.

111

We played everything in the way of dance music in those days."[24] Teddy Wilson, who worked with Webb, listed the Bix Beiderbecke recording of "Singing the Blues" as an early influence, while bandmate Vic Dickenson acknowledged a debt to Miff Mole.[25] Wilson also remembered that "The (Bill) Warfield group was very unusual. These fellows, from memory, specialized in playing the Red Nichols repertoire."[26]

Other Midwestern bands included those of Willie Jones and Alex Jackson. The Jones band played in Ohio, Michigan, and Wisconsin. Its recording of "Michigan Stomp" shows how white some of the black Midwestern bands could sound. They were a very tight ensemble with strong section work playing a complex arrangement with limited solos.[27] Jackson's Plantation Orchestra often worked white dances in Cincinnati in the mid-1920s. Their "Jackass Blues" reflected an arranged big band sound with a little more of a blues edge to it. Both groups profited from another advantage of Midwestern bands, the hometown recording studio of Gennett Records in Richmond, Indiana.[28]

Perhaps the best of this second wave of bands was Zach Whyte's Chocolate Beau Brummels, based in Cincinnati in 1928 and 1929. It featured the first work by young Sy Oliver, a major arranger of the Swing Era. The son of college professors, Oliver clearly followed and enlarged on Fletcher Henderson's style. He took "Mandy, Make Up Your Mind," a 1923 Fletcher Henderson tune, and gave it an up-to-date 1929 arrangement that improved on Redman's original. "West End Blues," the Louis Armstrong showpiece, was also given a strong big band treatment. Whyte's group could hold its own with any band in Chicago or New York. They defeated several groups with greater national reputations in local "battles of the bands."[29]

The sound of jazz in the Midwest in the 1920s was that of the ten-piece band playing arranged big band jazz with good section work for dancers. The quality of the Midwestern territory bands of the 1920s can be traced in the long list of Swing Era stars who served their apprenticeships in these bands. Teddy Wilson, Sy Oliver, Roy Eldridge, Vic Dickenson, Quentin Jackson, and many other key swing band sidemen came out of this territory. Many of the young men like Claude Jones, Zach Whyte, Speed Webb, and Teddy Wilson had some college education, and most shared Sy Oliver's view about professional musicians. "I don't consider it the vagabond life everyone claims it to be. Most of them are mature members of the community who have to pay insurance premiums and worry about getting that house in the country just as a doctor or lawyer would."[30]

Northwest

The Northwest territory in the twenties had plenty of land, few people, and few bands. Omaha, Minneapolis, and Milwaukee supported several black bands. They competed with several others without permanent locations for local dance jobs. Only thirty to forty bands were active here in the 1923–1929 period. The territory had a slow pace and informal atmosphere.

> Jumps were short—from 20 to 75 miles. A number of the places we played furnished a big midnight supper for the band. In many cases, dancers would follow the band for almost a week. I often wonder when some of those youngsters slept. By playing repeated engagements, the bands made many friends and life in general was pretty pleasant.[31]

The small black population of this area meant that these bands spent much of their time working for white audiences with no awareness of African-American culture. The fact that a very young Lawrence Welk was a key competitor for the black bands in this territory captures the musical tastes here. The major cities were too small for long-term location jobs to support the bands. So these groups spent much of their time doing one-nighters in small towns and farm areas, usually booked informally by the band and a local promoter. One exception was the Stecker brothers' Wisconsin Music Circuit, a group of jobs organized by the Stecker brothers. "Wisconsin and Upper Michigan were divided into seven territories. Each band played a territory for two weeks and then moved on to the next."[32]

The bands of Eli Rice and Grant Moore of Minneapolis and Lloyd Hunter and Red Perkins of Omaha were the top groups, followed by Ted Adams's band and the Virginia Ravens. The Art Simms-Bernie Young group of Milwaukee was an extension of the Chicago scene. Live models were replaced by records. Eddie Barefield worked in one Minnesota group that made a feature of playing the Fletcher Henderson arrangements copied from records.[33] His own group, which became the core of Eli Rice's most successful band, was strongly influenced by the Frank Trumbauer-Bix Beiderbecke sides. Eli Rice, a Kansas-born minstrel show veteran, began his career as a territory band leader in 1925 when he was almost fifty years old and worked successfully into the Swing Era. Besides the Stecker brothers' circuit, he worked Iowa county fairs and other small-town jobs from bases in Milwaukee and Minneapolis. His early groups were small, apparently with a ragtime feel. By the late 1920s, he had a group of young

113

musicians centered around Eddie Barefield who were influenced by New York big band recordings.[34]

Grant Moore came to Milwaukee from Arkansas in 1921 and started his band with five pieces in 1925. In October 1927, he took ten pieces into the Coliseum Ballroom in Minneapolis. They worked other Twin Cities locations including the Wigwam, Marigold Gardens, and Palace Ballroom. In the spring of 1928, they escaped the cold by working in Hot Springs, Arkansas, and then returned to Minneapolis.[35]

Red Perkins's early career was described in chapter three. Lloyd Hunter emerged as competition by 1924. Both bands began with six pieces and grew to eight. In the 1920s both were small groups, though they tried to use doubling to give a fuller sound. Perkins stressed entertainment, with vocals being a main draw. Hunter was apparently stronger musically although he also tried to use vocalists like Victoria Spivey when he got the chance. The closeness of this territory is evident in the fact that many musicians worked in two or more of these groups, as their paths often overlapped.[36] None of these groups recorded before 1931 so it is difficult to tell how they actually sounded in the 1920s. The musical level of the Northwest in the 1920s is definitely backwater, quite below that of the rest of the country.

West Coast

The West Coast continued to import musicians throughout this period. The earlier settlers were joined by young Midwesterners like Les Hite, Lionel Hampton, and Speed Webb. This created a generation gap. In 1923 older leaders like the Spikes brothers, Curtis Mosby, and Sonny Clay remained influential, but by 1929 a new group of younger men were being heard. Los Angeles continued to be the center of the action with the largest black community and a very active music scene. The Los Angeles area had perhaps the highest percentage of New Orleans musicians outside of the Crescent City, and their influence was still strong in this period.

Sonny Clay had continued success merging the New Orleans sound of soloists such as Nenny Coycault with non-New Orleans men. His 1926 record of "Slow Motion Blues" has a strong New Orleans collective ensemble sound equal to most Chicago groups. As late as January 12, 1928, Coycault is spitting out neat solos and the whole group grafts a great collectively improvised out chorus on to a written arrangement of the pop tune "In My Dreams."[37] Two days later, the group left for an Australian tour that ruined Clay's career. He was deported for misconduct over a party involving six of his musicians and six white women. Clay was blamed by the black press for setting back the race, and he moved briefly to Mexico to sit out the scandal. Eventually, he pulled his California career back together but the momentum and drive had gone.[38]

Job requirements in the West Coast as elsewhere were pushing bands in different directions. In the middle of the decade, the Spikes brothers and Mosby both moved into long-term theater jobs. They began playing mood music for the movie studios, and after 1927, made a few appearances in the new sound films. Mosby probably appeared in and played for *Hallelujah*, the first all-black talking picture. These jobs demanded larger groups, and the older bands began moving toward an arranged big band style. Mosby's October 1927 version of "In My Dreams" had written section work and solos without the collective ensemble of the Clay version. Mosby's "Tiger Stomp" from the same session still shows collective improvisation and all the usual "Tiger Rag" solo tricks.[39]

The new generation of West Coast men were young imports from elsewhere like Lawrence Brown, Lionel Hampton, Les Hite, Marshall Royal, Leon Herriford, George Orendorf, and Charlie Lawrence; they began playing on the West Coast between 1925 and 1927. Many had classical training and most had middle-class ambitions. Andrew Blakeny remembers, "It was a 100% white audience. L.A. was a fairly segregated city and what little mixing was in the coloured section. . . . Then, we did . . . a taxi dance hall . . . catering mostly for Phillipinos (*sic*) in the Mexican section."[40] Eventually, many of the young musicians worked for white promoter Frank Sebastian at his Los Angeles area version of the Cotton Club. The shows and dancing at his club required the arranged big band style, and these young musicians provided it. Sebastian signed many of them to personal contracts playing with the club no matter who was the nominal leader of the band. Recordings in 1929 under the leadership of tenor player Paul Howard used arrangements by Charlie Lawrence such as "Charlie's Idea" that pointed the club group in the Henderson-Redman direction. The recordings also showed George Orendorf's interesting trumpet, Lionel Hampton's scat vocal, and Lawrence Brown already developing the trombone style he would bring to Duke Ellington. "The Ramble," arranged by Lawrence Brown, and "Overnight Blues" suggest the Bill Challis style of the Bix Beiderbecke-Frank Trumbauer recordings.[41]

The West Coast continued to show a fascinating diversity, but despite its relative isolation, this region too was changing with increased importance given to the big band format.

Southwest

In this period, the entire Southwest was alive with bands creating some of the most exciting jazz of the 1920s. Walter Page's Blue Devils, Bennie Moten's Orchestra, and the bands of Alphonso Trent, Troy Floyd, and Jesse Stone ranked with the best in the nation, while Jap Allen, Terence "T." Holder, and Paul Banks were not far behind.

The success of the Southwestern bands of the 1920s rested on a dual foundation of social and musical factors. The Southwest combined the urban growth of the Midwest with the sizeable black population of the Southeast because the Great Migration movement of blacks from the farm to the city took place primarily within the Southwest itself. The booming Texas and Oklahoma cities drew largely from their own rural hinterlands rather than from other areas. Rural migrants not content with these locations often ended up in Kansas City or St. Louis rather than farther afield. The result was a stability of population that brought shared rural traditions to the shock of urbanization.

All of the key Southwestern bands of the 1920s were dance bands. The dancing craze struck the Southwest hard. Ballrooms sprang up not only in the large cites but also in small towns and rural areas, providing many opportunities for black musicians. Kansas City, St. Louis, San Antonio, Amarillo, Dallas, and Oklahoma City all supported local bands with long-term location jobs supplemented by one-nighters in the surrounding rural areas. These locations provided jobs for the established territory bands and starts for young local musicians.[42]

All of these bands had specific positions in the tight pyramid of the Southwest in the 1920s. As trumpeter Ed Lewis remembered,

> You had your own territory to play in and you didn't play anywhere else unless you got permission from the leading band in the territory. For example, Walter Page's Blue Devils in the Oklahoma City-Wichita, Kansas area . . . T. Holder, Troy Floyd and Alphonso Trent in Texas. Jesse Stone from Kansas City stayed mostly in the Sioux Falls-Lincoln, Nebraska touring areas . . . George E. Lee also . . . since many of those cities had no bands at all.[43]

Below these were local bands trying to make names for themselves. The Blue Moon Chasers of Dallas, the Royal Aces of Austin, the St. Louis Merrymakers of Wichita Falls, and McCloud's Night Owls of Sherman, Texas, produced a bumper crop of young jazzmen who reached the national scene in the Swing Era. These rising players included Carl "Tatti" Smith

(Aces), Buster Smith, Lamar Wright, Lloyd Glenn (Aces), Walter Page, Jimmy Rushing, and Keg Johnson (Chasers). The territory produced so many tenor sax stars that the term "Texas tenor" became a label of high praise for Ben Webster, Herschel Evans (Merrymakers), Buddy Tate (Merrymakers-Night Owls), and Budd Johnson (Chasers), among others.[44]

They came from a variety of backgrounds but they shared a common goal of using music to gain a better life. For Lester and Lee Young, "music was better than blacksmithing."[45] Lem Johnson chose it over the carpentry career his family had picked for him, while Ed Lewis and LaForest Dent saw music as the best way for a young married high school graduate to support a family.[46] Buster Smith, the eldest of five sons of a share cropper, summed up the ideal of the musician for blacks in the Southwest: "Musicians were respected in those days, just like a doctor or lawyer. We were happy; everybody was just like brothers and the music was the only thing we cared about."[47]

This homegrown crop of musicians shared strong musical traditions. They could jam for hours because they brought the same folk roots of spirituals and blues to their playing. This produced a distinctive, rhythmic, riff-based, blues-drenched music. Still, there was no shortage of reading musicians in the area due to the work of kid bands and music teachers like Mrs. P. Washington Pittman of Dallas and William L. Dawson of Kansas City.[48] The large number of bands in the area also increased the pressure to learn to read to secure a job. Players often moved from band to band getting familiar with the styles of many bandmates.

In the 1920s, several musical styles existed in the Southwest. Many groups grew from six to ten pieces and in the process moved from collectively improvised ensembles to written sections. This often created instrumental ensembles strongly immersed in the vocal traditions of the blues. This became the hallmark of the Bennie Moten and later Count Basie bands of the 1930s. In the 1920s, this riff style was most audible in the work of lesser-known bands such as Jesse Stone and his Blues Serenaders. Stone's two 1927 sides, "Starvation Blues" and "Boot to Boot," show strong blues-influenced solos in strong written arrangements by Stone himself. They are recognized as classics of 1920s big band jazz and are particularly representative of the Southwest since they feature men such as Al Hinton and Druie Bess who never left the region.[49]

Jesse Stone also arranged the 1929 sides of George and Julia Lee's Kansas City-based band. This group had been a small combo playing improvised ensembles and strings of solos in 1927. Stone brought them an arranged style that still carried a strong blues feel on "Ruff Scufflin'" and "St. James Infirmary." The guitar-based rhythm section was unusual for the period and forecast the Swing Era with a feel closer to 4/4. This Kansas City band also reflected the migration within the territory since it featured a Texan, Budd Johnson, on sax.[50]

Walter Page's Blue Devils, an Oklahoma-based group, provided key figures to the Swing Era Count Basie orchestra. In this period, the Blue Devils were the dominant band in the Southwest outside of Kansas City and Dallas. The two excellent sides recorded by this band in November of 1929 represent highlights of the Southwestern tradition. The solos by Buster Smith and Oran "Hot Lips" Page, both twenty-one and beginning extensive careers, are inventive and expressive. The real strength, not surprisingly for a band led by a bass player, is in the rhythm section. On "Blue Devil Blues" Walter Page plays tuba, but on "Squabblin" he plays string bass and a solo on baritone sax. Combined with the guitar and drum work, this group offers a swing feel even when it is still in two-beat time.[51]

This blues-rooted style was blended with other elements by the region's best-known bandleader, Bennie Moten. Moten's group through the 1920s led the way in Kansas City with the best location jobs and many more recordings than any other territory band. The Moten recordings of the 1920s present a band that followed formulas and routines with ensembles and solos often fitting into the same structure to create a "safe," peppy sound. The Moten band became the Southwestern version of the "businessman's bounce" sweet bands of the Swing Era. The 2/4 beat of the tuba anchored the sound and often dragged it away from the swinging pulse that was becoming the hallmark of the region. This was particularly true after the Moten band toured the East in 1928. Rather than bring the Southwest to New York, Moten transferred elements of Henderson-Redman arrangements to the Southwest. Moten and his imitators began to rely more on clarinet trios and other borrowings from Redman and Eastern arrangers. This did not seem to hurt Moten's popularity too much, in part because he was increasingly playing white and black middle-class jobs where this turn away from the blues base was not objectionable.[52]

Moten's was not the only Southwestern black band working middle-class jobs. These bands had wide access to the white middle- and upper-class audiences, which was surprising in legally segregated states. Although it has been argued that racial attitudes were a little looser in the Southwest than in the Southeast, that is difficult to document. Still, location jobs at white hotels or ballrooms were a major part of the prestige and success of many Southwestern bands, something they had in common with the New York bands.

Alphonso Trent started this trend in 1924 at the Adolphus Hotel in Dallas, the leading white hotel in the region. He turned a two-week commitment in the second ballroom there into a year-and-a-half job. The band also successfully played other white hotels, ballrooms, proms, and society affairs. From all reports and later recordings, the Trent group relied strongly on written arrangements played with a style and sophistication that rivaled and perhaps surpassed even Henderson and Ellington. They broadcasted frequently and their influence may have been enormous, but it is very difficult to document. Like the Moten band, Trent's group also toured out of its territory, but this seemed to strengthen the Trent outfit. As early as the spring of 1927, they began extensive touring and the personnel changed. Even by the time of their first recordings in 1928, they could be considered a national rather than territory band. Trumpeters Peanuts Holland from the Jenkins Orphanage band and Mouse Randolph from St. Louis, and violinist Stuff Smith from Ohio had joined the group. Smith enhanced the solo work and showmanship, adding to the strength of the arrangements.[53]

The Troy Floyd group of San Antonio also worked extensively for white audiences but developed a different sound. It featured the solo work of a young New Orleans trumpeter, Don Albert (Albert Dominique), and a unique soprano saxman, Siki Collins. The few Floyd band recordings and several blues accompaniments featuring Collins and Albert rely heavily on the blues and collective improvisations but soften the impact with the use of mutes by Albert and a sweet tone by Collins that could reach the white ballroom audience.[54]

Terence "T." Holder led two fine groups in the Texas-Oklahoma area between 1925 and 1929, but since they did not record under his leadership it is unclear exactly where they fit into the Southwest spectrum. Holder had worked with Trent and began his Dark Clouds of Joy in Texas in 1925. By 1927, it was an eleven-piece group. In January 1929, Andy Kirk took over the band from Holder, and in the Swing Era it was a major national band. By March 1929, Holder was leading a new band of some of the best young Texas talent, including Keg and Budd Johnson and Booker Pittman. He had the added help of Jesse Stone as his arranger.[55]

While the jazz reputations of Kansas City and Texas grew, St. Louis was beginning to decline as a jazz center. This was partly because it had already exported significant talent. By 1923, many of the New Orleans men like Louis Armstrong, who had come through St. Louis with the riverboats, had moved on to Chicago or elsewhere.[56] Moreover, many of the younger local musicians left the city quickly including trumpeters R. Q. Dickerson, Louis Metcalf, and Leonard "Ham" Davis; and the good section reedmen Jerome Don Pasquall, Boyd Atkins, Gene Sedric, and Walter "Foots" Thomas. Andy Preer's Cotton Club Orchestra, one of the first territory big bands to be successful in New York, was a St. Louis export.[57]

While the riverboats and clubs of St. Louis continued to host jazz-men, they no longer were as close to the cutting edge of the music. This period was the heyday of the St. Louis trumpet school of Charlie Creath, Dewey Jackson, and Ed Allen. They played in the pre-Louis Armstrong style that reflected their own roots and the influence of King Oliver. In small club bands in the city they worked in a collective ensemble setting. On the riverboats, they led seven- to ten-pieces playing dance music to fit the tastes of the Streckfus brothers and their audience.[58] Like New Orleans earlier, St. Louis in this period went through a generational conflict with many of the younger players leaving for better jobs and living conditions while the older men remained. Here, St. Louis's position on the edge of the Southwest territory and the legally segregated states may have had an impact. Unlike Kansas City, Missouri, which faced Kansas and the lightly populated West, St. Louis was linked by rail and road to Chicago and the path to New York.

The Southwest presented the widest variety of styles and experiences of all of the territories of this period. Its richness is a mirror of the overall reality of the territory experience. Here was the real "jazz revolution," where the values of small communities and folk traditions blended and conflicted with the realities of new entertainment media, which reflected the diversity of the urban environment.

Conclusion

This survey of the black territory bands of the 1920s shows a wide range of styles and experiences in the six different territories. Some of these reflect the influence of individuals such as Don Redman or Walter Page; others are a result of geography and demographics.

Still, the most important characteristics of territory bands were shared on a national basis. First, their enormous success was due in part to limited live competition. Bands remained essentially in their own areas with only occasional challenges, which were more frequent in the Southwest than elsewhere. The national black bands and white groups that helped shape musical tastes through radio and records rarely ventured out of New York or Chicago. The territory bands were left to provide, in person, music that reflected the media trends.

The impact of the media models and the acoustic demands of the bigger ballrooms explain the expansion of bands from five to eight to ten players from 1923 to 1929. This expansion pulled jazz bands from loose, collective ensemble performances to tighter routines relying more on written arrangements with improvised solos. Arrangements and Louis Armstrong's virtuosity fueled the demand for technical proficiency both in music reading and instrumental mastery. All these changes sharpened the generation gap between younger musicians with more technical training and middle-class values and older musicians with different goals, habits, and abilities. This conflict could be felt in various ways around the country.

Black band leaders were mainly individual entrepreneurs handling their bands' business and financial affairs on an informal, personal basis. Some leaders like C. S. Belton provided both musical and business leadership. In other bands like Red Perkins's Dixie Ramblers, musical and business duties were split between a partnership. Still other groups were cooperatives who operated on consensus and assigned responsibilities to most band members.[59] Musical and business decisions were typically worked out within the bands rather than imposed from outside, regardless of the leadership arrangements. The occasional agent, manager, or ballroom chain was the exception rather than the rule for the business.

The life of the black territory bands of this period reflected the small town societies that spawned most of the players. Decisions were still made on a personal, face-to-face basis with local factors taken into account. Small-town lifestyles are mirrored by the regional differences of the territory bands of this period.

This situation changed dramatically after 1929 as the jazz world and its styles were standardized by the electronic media and national business trends. The events of the depression era after 1929 led to the swing revolution of 1935.

7

The Rise of the National Bands 1929-1935

O N July 2, 1929, the Duke Ellington Orchestra opened on Broadway as a featured act in Florenz Ziegfeld's *Show Girl*. At the same time, the Fletcher Henderson Orchestra was coming apart over the failure of its leader to protect his own men in Vincent Youmans's show *Great Day*. Manager Irving Mills had correctly steered the Ellington band out of Youmans's show. Henderson took the job but soon found himself and his band fired and replaced by white musicians in a show that flopped on Broadway after extended tryouts in Philadelphia and Atlantic City.

Henderson's failure to speak out strongly against the firing either directly to the show's producers or through the union or press, cost him respect in the black press and the black community. Many of his men left the band, forcing him to reorganize. The loss of the pit band job compelled Henderson to scramble for dance and theater dates, which were below his usual standards.[1]

At the same time, Henderson lost his access to the record industry. The Henderson band had recorded two sides in April and May of 1929 but did not return to the studios until October of 1930. This time gap represented the first time in six years that the band was out of the studio for more than five months. While the onset of the Great Depression was a factor here, business skill and popularity also played a part. In those same seventeen months, the Duke Ellington Orchestra recorded more than fifty-five sides. The summer of 1929 marked the passing of black big band jazz leadership from the Henderson to the Ellington orchestra.[2]

These incidents were important because the climb to the top by Duke Ellington and his white manager Irving Mills signaled a significant shift in the structure of the band business, which brought jazz much more clearly into the world of popular entertainment. This new structure changed the environment in which black jazz musicians worked. Their options were increasingly limited by white gatekeepers in the entertainment world. The summer of 1929 began the journey toward the summer of 1935 and the official arrival of the Swing Era.

Working conditions for black jazz musicians and the music that they played changed profoundly in this six-year period. Many of these changes were linked to the new elements arriving on the jazz scene with the Ellington-Mills combination. The local variations of the territories were replaced by a uniform national structure and sound distributed by the mass media of records, radio, and motion pictures. Bands began to tour on a national level supported by complex publicity machines and highly organized schedules of bookings. New York-based bands appeared increasingly on the home turf of the territory bands, forcing them to adapt or vanish.

Duke Ellington and Irving Mills

The two men who created this revolution were, on the surface, unlikely revolutionaries. Irving Mills was a Jewish music publisher looking for a band to play his songs. Edward Kennedy "Duke" Ellington was the product of a black Washington, D.C., family with middle-class aspirations. According to his somewhat self-produced legend, he turned down a Pratt Institute scholarship to pursue the music business and girls, not necessarily in that order. The core reality was that like Henderson and so many of Hsio Wen Shih's other jazz innovators, Ellington sensed less hostility and more opportunity in music than in other fields.

As discussed in chapter three, Ellington began his career as a bandleader in Washington, D.C. He came to New York early in the 1920s with fellow Washingtonians Otto Hardwick on sax, and Art Whetsol on trumpet, and New Jersey-born Sonny Greer on drums. They worked briefly in theaters and cabarets under the leadership of Wilbur Sweatman and then Elmer Snowden. While they were at the Hollywood, later renamed the Kentucky Club, a white midtown cabaret similar to Henderson's Club Alabam, Duke Ellington took over the group.[3]

FROM JAZZ TO SWING

Comparisons between the careers of the Ellington and Henderson bands in the 1920s are both inevitable and enlightening. While Henderson began his career in New York in 1920 with Pace-Handy, Ellington got started in 1923. The first two years at the Kentucky Club were the Ellington band's apprenticeship period, similar to Henderson's 1920–1923 experiences in the record business. While the Snowden-Ellington band was apparently into its cabaret before Henderson actually arrived at the Alabam, the Henderson band was larger, ten pieces to Ellington's seven, and had more name recognition because of its recordings. Henderson moved from the Alabam after six months to the Roseland Ballroom, while the Kentucky remained Ellington's base almost until his move to the Cotton Club in December 1927.[4]

The Ellington band released only ten sides before November 1926, while Henderson made more than 140 records between January 1924 and November 1926. This imbalance makes comparison difficult, but a few things do stand out. Although Abel Green's early review of the band cites Ellington as pianist-arranger, it is clear from description and records that the Washingtonians at first stressed solos and collective ensembles much more than written arrangements. The small size of the band, its youth, and the demands of the club, which stressed entertainment and a loose environment, explain this contrast to the tighter Henderson Alabam-Roseland sound. Ellington's band was accompanying singers and a floor show more than it was playing for dancing. Much of this work was table hopping by Ellington and drummer-singer Sonny Greer. Several records were made with the usual group expanded, which produced a lack of cohesion. Still, as Mark Tucker and Gunther Schuller pointed out, even these early Ellington pieces have flashes of promise.[5]

By the spring of 1926, the Ellington band was a solid cabaret band competing with Elmer Snowden, Bill Brown, and June Clark, but well below Fletcher Henderson and the Harlem stars of Connie's Inn and the Cotton Club. Like other New York bands, Ellington worked the East Coast territory. Summer tours of New England for Charles Shribman in 1926 and 1927 provided growth for the band. This was a circuit of ballrooms like the Stecker Brothers' Wisconsin Music Circuit. This extensive course in playing for white dancers rather than shows increased the cohesion of the band.

On a summer tour, trumpeter Bubber Miley turned the phrase "Oh, Lewandos," after a local cleaners, into the band's first theme, "East St. Louis Toodle-oo." Miley had been born in South Carolina but moved to New York as a child. His muted trumpet work became the core of the band's early "jungle" style and was echoed on trombone by fellow

New Yorkers Charlie Irvis and later Joe Nanton. Miley's improvisations stimulated Ellington's composing. Bostonian Harry Carney joined the reed section for the 1927 summer tour and remained for more than forty years. He was joined by Johnny Hodges in May 1928. These additions to the core of Washingtonians turned the group into an East Coast band.[6] The 1927 arrivals of New Orleans bassist Wellman Braud, St. Louis trumpeter Louis Metcalf, Chicago reedman Rudy Jackson and his replacement New Orleans native Barney Bigard, who arrived from King Oliver's Chicago Dixie Syncopators, made the band national in background.[7]

The most important impact of the New England tours may have been that Ellington's success with Shribman made him more open to the management suggestions of Irving Mills. The question of exactly when Mills and Ellington began working together may never be completely resolved. Mark Tucker's evidence for a date in the 1926–1927 season after the first Shribman tour is stronger than James L. Collier's argument for a 1925 date.[8] Mills placed Ellington in the upper reaches of the New York scene with his move to the Cotton Club in December 1927.

Irving Mills set the pattern for band management from 1927 through the Swing Era. Before Mills, band leaders and members had managed themselves informally. Mills changed that. He set up an Ellington corporation with 45 percent each owned by Mills and Ellington and 10 percent held by a lawyer. From this organizational base, Mills turned band management into a full-time business with career planning and public relations as a major focus. Most importantly, Mills worked on a national scale extending the range of Ellington and his later clients such as Cab Calloway's Orchestra and the Blue Rhythm band. Mills discovered the economic advantages of exploiting media-based reputations with tours into the territories.[9]

Mills provided a model for success under the new conditions created by improved transportation and the increased importance of the electronic media in the band business. The three factors in Mills's model were national exposure through recordings and radio broadcasts, streams of publicity to build interest, and national tours to reap the profits of a band's reputation.

Perhaps his key contribution was inventing new ways to get publicity for his clients. Before Mills, public relations in the band business had been a haphazard affair. Leaders and promoters provided posters and newspaper advertisements for dances and engagements. Leaders and sidemen wrote to the entertainment pages of black newspapers, particularly the *Chicago Defender*, to plug themselves and their bands and to look for jobs and other musicians. These chatty letters gave the *Chicago Defender* of the

125

mid-1920s the flavor of a small-town newspaper in which everyone knew everyone else.

The systematic thoroughness of Irving Mills completely transformed this side of the band business. It seemed at times as if his sole concern was to grind out press releases and pictures plugging his bands. He flooded both the black and white papers with his releases, swamping the other letters in the process. The *Chicago Defender* and other papers acquired a homogeneous appearance as the same releases showed up in many places.[10]

This public relations flood supported a structured career pattern that Mills developed for the Ellington orchestra and later copied for Cab Calloway and others. From the Club Kentucky base, frequent recordings and a local radio wire laid a foundation for Duke Ellington's move to the Cotton Club and the CBS national network. More recordings followed and Mills then moved into high gear, arranging high-priced theater tours across the country, accompanied by a high-pressure advertising campaign. He even extended Ellington's career into motion pictures, first a short, *Black and Tan Fantasy*, and then a feature with the radio team of Amos "n" Andy, *Check and Double Check*. Each of these steps was highly publicized, pushing Duke Ellington into national prominence. By 1930, Ellington's was the best-selling dance band on the number one record company, Victor, and was recognized as the best black band in the country and one of the top two or three bands of any race. In 1933, Mills and Ellington achieved international success with a European tour.[11]

The Ellington orchestra relied more heavily on original compositions from within the band than did other groups, reflecting Ellington's interest in composing. The first wave of classics such as "Black and Tan Fantasy," "Creole Love Call," and "The Mooche," came from the interaction of Miley and Ellington. By 1930, the interaction between Ellington and his soloists Barney Bigard, Johnny Hodges, Harry Carney, Cootie Williams, and Joe Nanton were creating very personal music that also reached a large popular audience. Some, such as the prescient "It Don't Mean A Thing If It Ain't Got That Swing" were consistent with the popular developments of the period. Other pieces like "Mood Indigo" reflected Ellington's artistic interest in tonal color. Several of these early attempts to move his version of jazz into the realm of art music were fought by Mills as diluting his popular appeal, but Ellington succeeded in including them in his repertoire. "Creole Rhapsody" (1931) was an extended composition of more than five minutes released on two sides of a 78 rpm record so that it had to be turned over in the middle. "Sophisticated Lady" (1932), a moody piece stressing tone colors, emerged as a popular song with words added and represented a savvy gamble by Ellington to express his feelings in his music. Piece by piece, new compositions were incorporated into the Swing Era: "Harlem Speaks" (1933), "Solitude" (1934), and the four-part extended "Reminiscing in Tempo" (1935).[12]

Changing Business Conditions

While these compositions began Duke Ellington's lasting contribution to American music, the immediate impact of his band's success on jazz in 1929 was quite different. For many in the band business, Mills rather than Ellington was the key. Mills's system exposed the new complexity of the band business and the increased role of the gatekeepers including recording executives, theater managers, ballroom owners, and radio executives in the career of a band. A full-time professional manager was needed to deal with those various elements. No longer did one man have the time to lead a band and handle its business affairs. Even splitting jobs in the old cooperative format became ineffective. Business tasks—publicity, booking, scheduling—were now more specialized and required business practice and training rather than musicianship.

Increasingly, managers were white businessmen like Mills, Joe Glaser, and Harold Oxley rather than black musicians. Once established, the Mills system could easily be applied to several bands as Mills did for Ellington, Cab Calloway, and the Blue Rhythm Band. This pattern was followed on a even larger scale by Jules Stein's Music Corporation of America (MCA). The profit to be made with bands and their movement into theater tours brought booking agencies like Rockwell-O'Keefe and William Morris into the field. Although they mainly booked white bands, their activity deeply affected black bands. These managers and agencies had the contacts and resources to influence local ballroom owners and dance promoters. Increasingly, decisions for theaters and radio stations were being made at the network or chain level, often in New York, where the managers' skills and contacts were dominant. Even recording opportunities were more available to bands with management representation than to those without.[13]

Thus Mills and Ellington symbolized economic and social changes that were remaking jazz in this period. Black musicians were competing in an increasingly national marketplace where white gatekeepers and bureaucrats controlled their access to both black and white audiences. These national developments in the music business were sharpened by the Great Depression. Hard times hit rural and small town areas well before the stock market crash of October 1929. Farmers had not shared in the prosperity of the 1920s. Lean years on the farms limited the market for tent shows and black vaudeville. After the crash, the July 1930 failure of Chicago's black-owned Binga Bank indicated that money was drying up in the urban black communities too.[14]

The switch to sound films beginning with the 1927 release *The Jazz Singer* hurt both vaudeville and theater bands. By 1929, most movie theaters were controlled by several large chains, MGM-Loew's, Paramount-Publix, Warner Brothers-First National, and Radio-Keith-Orpheum. These groups were increasingly conscious of costs because of the depression and because they needed to invest in the new sound technology. Like other corporations, they responded to the depression with layoffs. In 1928, hundreds of smaller theaters including the Metropolitan, Pickford, and Owl on Chicago's South Side fired their orchestras. Just a few years before Dave Peyton had recommended these groups as the most secure sources of jobs.[15]

From 1929 on, many movie and vaudeville theaters began to replace their house bands with touring dance bands that could play a week or two and then move on. Many ballrooms and nightclubs around the country also began to shift from continuous extended engagements by local bands to appearances by national touring bands ranging in duration from one night to two weeks. Both changes increased the power of band managers and the reach of national bands while hurting local territory groups. The stories of Chicago's Regal Theater and Savoy Ballroom reveal the consequences of this shift. From its opening in February 1928, the Regal was the pride of the black South Side, supplementing films with stage shows and its house orchestra led by Fess Williams or Dave Peyton. In late 1929, the management began to add nationally known black stars such as Mamie Smith, Nina Mae McKinney, and Ethel Waters to the bill on a weekly basis. The most successful bills were those featuring bands or musicians such as Louis Armstrong, Jimmie Noone, Fats Waller, and Earl Hines. By early 1931, jazz bands with national reputations such as McKinney's Cotton Pickers and the orchestras of Duke Ellington, Earl Hines, Fess Williams, and Lucky Millinder dominated the Regal bills, and Dave Peyton's house band was fired.[16] This trend was national. Even Harlem theaters dropped house bands for weekly stints by touring jazz bands.[17]

Similar events were occurring in the ballrooms, and again Chicago is a good example. Its Savoy Ballroom next door to the Regal had opened in November 1927 featuring local bands. It was, in fact, at the Savoy that Louis Armstrong had his regular job as a member of Carroll Dickerson's big band, playing music that was moving in the Fletcher Henderson direction at the exact same time his own small recording group, the Hot Five, was stressing solo work. The Savoy provided opportunity to a new generation of Chicago musicians who followed the Henderson-Redman style more closely than any previous Chicago groups. However, this proved to be a liability after 1929 when touring bands such as McKinney's Cotton Pickers, which had helped develop that style, increasingly took the prime dates and limited the action for local bands.[18] A key factor was that the Savoy audience after 1929 preferred the national style over the local traditions, reversing the reaction Fletcher Henderson had received on previous visits. Across the United States ballrooms were looking for the arranged big band sound. "There was nothing but band traffic up and down the road in those days. Most music was live and everyone got a chance to hear live bands. . . . They didn't consider a band under twelve pieces. If you went into a town with a ten-piece outfit you might just as well forget about a crowd."[19]

Several factors were involved in this shift. Some improvements in automobiles and the highway system made long distance travel by car or bus more practical and cheaper, increasing the mobility and availability of touring bands while worsening living conditions particularly for black musicians. While at least one black band had a bus as early as 1928, the years 1929–1930 saw a rush to the bus. As the jumps between towns became longer, the musicians found themselves living totally on the road, eating and sleeping in their buses or cars for weeks at a time. This was particularly true for black bands, who could never be sure when prejudice would deny them a place to eat or sleep in the North and who knew that Jim Crow would always severely limit their access to public accommodations in the South.[20] The amount of time bands spent on the road coupled with the pressures they were under increased the dangers of travel. After the late 1920s, automobile accidents were accepted as an occupational hazard. The decline of the Fletcher Henderson orchestra, for example, may be traced to a 1928 accident in Kentucky in which Henderson was injured. The Earl Hines and Alphonso Trent orchestras and McKinney's Cotton Pickers, among others, all lost men or material to accidents or theft on the road.[21]

Conditions in the locations where the bands played were often as bad as those where they stayed, particularly in rural areas. In the Southeast, dances often took place in tobacco barns and other improvised locations. Many permanent clubs and juke joints were fire traps. The most famous example of this for black musicians was the 1940 Natchez, Mississippi, nightclub fire which killed ten members of the Chicago-based Walter Barnes Orchestra.[22]

Barnes, writing in the *Chicago Defender*, had seen the trend to national tours by March of 1931.

> Times have changed—and how. Bands, I mean big bands are now taking to the road rather than hold one stand indefinitely. There's more money on the road and in barnstorming, even in one-night jumps. . . . Radio has so popularized good music that the smaller towns want and are willing to pay to hear good bands in person. Big name bands who are barnstorming or will soon be are . . . Duke Ellington, on a theatrical tour, Noble Sissle, Eubie Blake, Dave Peyton, Andy Kirk, George Lee, Bennie Moten and any number who could get steady stands if they wanted them. But the road calls both with more appreciative audiences and bigger do-re-mi.[23]

Barnes's analysis includes two key factors in this period—money and radio. Many bands went on the road looking for better pay, often because the depression was drying up funds in their own neighborhoods. Bands from rural areas including the C. S. Belton and "Smiling Billy" Stewart groups from Florida extended their tours from the Southeast to other parts of the country looking for deeper pockets. Other bands like those of Fess Williams and Dave Peyton went on the road after losing location jobs to talking pictures or local poverty. In this sense, some touring bands resembled the Okies of the Dust Bowl, hitting the road for the elusive pot of gold. The key difference is that many of the touring bands were pleasantly surprised when they actually found gold on the road, making more than they had in their location jobs.[24]

This was particularly true of bands that matched the model set up by Irving Mills and Duke Ellington. Here, the role of records and radio became crucial. The recording industry suffered greatly in the depression. Many of the small jazz or blues-oriented labels such as Vocalion, Brunswick, Paramount, Gennett, and Okeh either disappeared or were taken over by the two remaining giants, RCA Victor and Columbia.[25] This limited black access to recording time in some ways. True, top names such as Duke Ellington and Louis Armstrong still recorded frequently between 1929 and 1931. Also, many territory bands were able to make one or two sides in the 1929–1933 period. Still, black bands had less access to studio time and fewer chances to get records released in the early depression years than they did in the 1920s. Enough black bands were recorded to show changes in the national styles. Bands prized recording reputations even if they were tied only to one or two sides. A "recording orchestra" label for publicity was a source of pride and higher asking prices.

Radio

Radio was one of the few segments of the economy to escape severe damage from the depression. National networks began in the late 1920s, and their new sponsored programs such as "Amos N' Andy" and "Rudy Vallee's Fleishman Yeast Hour" created profits and national impact. Both networks and local stations had plenty of open time, much of it filled by late night and late afternoon sustaining (non-sponsored) broadcasts from hotels, nightclubs, and ballrooms. These "sustainers" gave black bands good radio exposure in the early 1930s, both in New York and in the territories.[26] Also, they provided access to audiences that could be tapped on tours, supporting Barnes's idea that "radio has so popularized good music that the smaller towns want and are willing to pay to hear good bands in person."[27]

The opportunity for even more radio exposure for black bands was halted by conflicts among the various bureaucracies involved in the band business. During the 1930–1931 season the major radio networks, NBC and CBS, attempted to move into the band-booking business. This led to a full-scale war between the networks and the big booking agencies. Although the agents eventually won with a big assist from the musicians' union, the bands, particularly black bands, were the big losers. Bands such as Duke Ellington's and Cab Calloway's were caught in the middle, and suffered the most from lawsuits, cancelled engagements, union fines, and lost air time.

This last was particularly disappointing because the conflicts erupted just as Ellington, Calloway, and Armstrong were peaking in popularity and under consideration for sponsored network shows. Such a breakthrough for black artists into the mainstream of the entertainment industry would have been comparable to the arrival of Bill Cosby and Diahann Carroll on prime time television in the 1960s. The radio opportunities offered economic gains and wider acceptance for blacks within society. Black "firsts" in radio were eagerly promoted in the black press and seen as advancing the race in significant ways.

The booking war, however, stopped the plans for programs for Ellington, Calloway, and Armstrong. Although the Mills Brothers and the Don Redman Orchestra did eventually headline the Chipso Soap program, there was no sequel to this breakthrough. It is unclear if the unfulfilled promise was the result of racist reaction, such as that which greeted Nat King Cole's television program of the early 1950s, or just business uncertainty created by the booking war. Black bands did not get the full advantages of radio network time that the bands' popularity merited. Still,

131

some network exposure was sufficient to create a demand for the live services of Ellington's and Calloway's bands around the country.[28]

Conditions in the depths of the depression helped a select group of black bands gain more recognition and financial success than did any other group in the history of jazz. Leading this effort were Duke Ellington's band and McKinney's Cotton Pickers. In January 1931, Eli Oberstein of RCA Victor announced that these two bands had been the best-selling dance bands on that label in 1930. Ellington's theatrical tours in the 1930–1935 period often broke attendance records set by the Paul Whiteman Orchestra, the 1920s king of jazz. The cost of an Ellington appearance in this period went up from $3,500 to $5,000 a week.[29]

Along with theatrical tours, black bands in this period made serious inroads into the previously white preserve of private parties and proms. Between 1929 and 1932, McKinney's Cotton Pickers played lucrative prom dates at Yale, Cornell, Princeton, Amherst, Northwestern, Stanford, and the universities of Ohio, Illinois, Indiana, Pennsylvania, Michigan, Wisconsin, and West Virginia. These gains were not limited to any particular section of the country. In the early 1930s, Andy Kirk's Clouds of Joy played dances at the universities of Arkansas, Missouri, and Kentucky as well as Texas A&M, Oklahoma A&M, Harvard, Yale, and Cornell.[30]

Racism and Segregation in the Depression

Breakthroughs often put considerable pressure on the musicians as they bumped against the color line. Some colleges, including the University of Kentucky and Texas A&M, denied admission to black students at this time. Others had only token black enrollments. On many of these prom dates, black musicians had to stay in private homes or drive great distances because there were no rooms for them on campus or nearby. On theater tours in segregated states, black bands often played to all-white crowds or where blacks were limited to the balcony. Some black bands of this period played in hotels where the musicians could not rent rooms because of their race.[31]

There was little overt agitation by entertainers against these restrictions. The reasons for this reticence were varied. The musicians frequently felt that their positions were precarious and that protests would have negative effects. They viewed their appearances before white audiences as a way to raise the prestige of blacks and to siphon off some white money into black pockets.[32] Still, the treatment clearly grated on many musicians. Their memories of small indignities remained many years later, and bands that could took pains to cushion themselves against these blows. Some bands simply would not tour in the South. Ellington refused until the band could afford to make the tour in its own private railroad car. Since they could not be fed in the railroad dining car even with a private rail car, band members cooked meals in the baggage car in an attempt to be totally independent of the country through which they were traveling.[33]

Ellington and Ethel Waters, among others, eventually used their drawing power to "encourage" some hotels and theaters, particularly in the North, to change their policies, either by asking for a room or threatening not to fulfill an engagement if a room request was denied. The impact of such actions seems to have been very limited, even after the celebrated integration of the hotel bandstand by the Benny Goodman, Teddy Wilson, Gene Krupa trio at the Congress Hotel in Chicago in 1936. Throughout the Swing Era of 1935–1945, black members of white bands (Billie Holiday with Artie Shaw and Roy Eldridge with Gene Krupa) were often denied rooms or food with the band in white locations.[34]

Even the enormous success of black jazz bands in the early depression years may have its roots in racial stereotypes. There were no hot white dance bands in the early 1930s until the Casa Loma, Dorsey Brothers, and, above all, the Benny Goodman orchestras came along. Goodman's appearance at the Palomar Ballroom in Los Angeles in 1935 is taken as the official beginning of the Swing Era. All the important white dance bands of the early 1930s, led by Paul Whiteman, Guy Lombardo, and Ben Bernie, played sweet, soft, slow dance music. The hot white jazz musicians of the 1920s such as Bix Beiderbecke, Red Nichols, Gene Krupa, the Dorseys, Goodman, and Frank Teschemacher had either died or been reduced to being sidemen in big, sweet bands.

This left the black bands without competition as the purveyors of hot dance music because the white band styles were no different. Frequently, white and black musical groups shared an evening, each dispensing a distinct musical style, as when the Guy Lombardo and Jimmie Lunceford orchestras played a Cornell dance.[35] After 1935 these arrangements were rare, and many black bands saw their prom dates being picked off by the white swing bands.

If the success of the black bands proved that there was a demand for this hot style, why did it take the white musicians so long to cash in on it? Black bands such as Ellington's, Henderson's, and McKinney's (Redman) began developing the swing style as early as 1931, and by 1933 it was established and learnable. Some white recordings of 1933 show an awareness of the style but the great white wave of swing does not arrive until the summer of 1935. One reason for this delay was the caution of the

the gatekeepers in the new band business structure. Swing might prove successful, but Sweet was already profitable, so why change?

Beyond this, the subtle influence of racism intrudes. Black bands were perpetually labeled as "hot" bands reflecting the happy-go-lucky, Sambo, and natural rhythm stereotypes that have been inflicted on blacks and particularly black entertainers for generations. Even the band names of the period, McKinney's Cotton Pickers, Andy Kirk's Dark Clouds of Joy, Zach Whyte's Chocolate Beau Brummels, and the Chocolate Dandies, reflected this image. Black musicians were aware of this. The Black Rock Collegians of Atlanta were criticized roundly in the *Chicago Defender* for their "Uncle Tomish" name until they proved it came from a fancy country club rather than a stereotype.[36] By 1935, most black bands had settled on the simple "Name and his Orchestra" pattern followed by most white bands. In the early depression years, these stereotypes may have conditioned responses to popular music, making the happy sound of swing an acceptable reaction from black but not white musicians in the midst of the national economic calamity.

The Impact of National Bands

All of the changes in the music industry in the 1929–1935 period built an audience for a national style of jazz and made it easier for national bands to reach territory audiences with personal appearances. These developments directly challenged the regional variety of the territory bands. The attempt to sell a national style through the mass media directly cut across the local styles that were the stock in trade of the territory bands. Live competition by national bands presented both an economic threat and artistic stimulation that had not existed prior to 1929. When Duke Ellington could earn $3,800 in one week in Omaha, the audience left over for Red Perkins, Lloyd Hunter, and Ted Adams became limited.[37]

The effects of these changes and the responses of the local bands varied from territory to territory and often from band to band. Many territory bands of the 1920s broke up, but new ones were formed. Some bands moved to New York or toured nationally, while others moved into a specific territory. The number of territory bands did not necessarily decrease, and with the growth of the Swing Era and the expansion of the size of bands, there may have actually been more black jazz musicians playing in the territories in 1935 than there were ten years before. However, the position of the black musicians in the jazz community had changed dramatically. Territory bands lost reputations and independence as they endured direct challenges from national bands. The clear result was increased standardization of the sound as well as the working conditions of black jazz musicians. This encouraged the development of the big band sound, which set the core of the Swing Era.

Band Business Pyramid

From 1929 on, the band business adopted an informal structure resembling professional baseball with major leagues and various grades of minor leagues from AAA down to A. The major leagues were the national bands, Ellington, Cab Calloway, Louis Armstrong, McKinney's Cotton Pickers, and later Jimmie Lunceford and Count Basie, who toured extensively and also received frequent radio time and recording opportunities. Class AAA bands were top territory outfits who occasionally toured elsewhere such as Bennie Moten in the Southwest, Les Hite on the West Coast, and Zach Whyte in the Midwest. Next came the class A bands, those recognized as supreme in a particular city or region, Rud Perkins in Omaha, Grant Moore in Minneapolis, Boots Douglas and Don Albert in San Antonio.

The lowest level in the chain were the local bands trying to make names for themselves. These groups were often amateur or semi-pro groups of young musicians seeking experience and money.[38] These young musicians looked up the pyramid hoping to move beyond the local territory band level. Preston Love remembers seeing things this way from Omaha.

> Well, with inferior buses and small nightly grosses, and the other hardships, life for the scuffling territory band was sometimes very difficult, so all the musicians in these bands had the incentive to make it to the name bands which meant so much better conditions. This made us admire and idolize the men in the name bands even more, and made every young musician strive harder to prepare himself for the eventual big break—graduation to a name band. . . .
>
> We all shared one obsession—to make it to a Basie, a Lunceford or a Duke or one of the name bands. Actually I think it was the desire for recognition more than an obsession to escape the "Sticks" which gave us our incentive.[39]

Love makes several excellent points, and two further concepts should be added. The goal of joining a name band made the styles of the younger swing players more homogeneous because they emulated their idols and prepared to play in big band arranged swing settings. They wanted to avoid the plight of Lester Young, who was sent home by Fletcher Henderson because his style was too strikingly different from that of his predecessor, Coleman Hawkins.

There were some exceptions to this pattern. A few excellent musicians chose for personal reasons to remain in the territories. This was often true of leaders or teachers like Fess Whately, but even sidemen like Buster Smith turned down name band offers to stay off the road and on their own turf. Also, a few unique individuals like Lester Young followed their own muses. Young eventually made it to the national scene but others remained lost in the territories.[40]

Players seemed to understand their positions in this system, but they did not always accept them. Frequently musicians and whole bands tried to move up the pyramid through a "Battle of Music" or by extending their touring territory. The top roll of the dice was a move to New York. Such gambles paid off for Cab Calloway, Chick Webb, and Jimmie Lunceford, but failed for the Alonzo Ross De Luxe Syncopators and the Fess Williams Royal Flush Orchestra. The two keys in making it in New York were good management and the ability to fit the arranged big band style of the music in vogue there.

The Emergence of the Swing Style

The business changes of the 1929–1935 period were matched by changes in musical style. Black bandleaders, musicians, and arrangers helped transform the established big band arranged jazz style of the 1920s into what became known by 1935 as swing. Swing was above all an arranged jazz style, and black arrangers were extremely influential in its development. They included both the stalwarts of the the 1920s style, Don Redman and Duke Ellington, and a horde of younger musicians from New York and the territories, Sy Oliver, Edgar Sampson, Eddie Barefield, and Eddie Durham.[41]

On a practical level, several changes in instrumentation gave the arrangers new sonorities with which to play. First, around 1928, the guitar and string bass began replacing the banjo and tuba in the rhythm section. This was tied to the advances in electric recording that made it easier to record these instruments. Since breath patterns no longer had to be taken into account, a steady 4/4 rhythm could replace the bouncy 2/4 of the 1920s. This change in the rhythm section provided a more horizontal feel to the music, which is the most noticeable difference between the swing style and its predecessors.[42]

The size of the band continued to grow until by 1935 it was up to fourteen pieces. Aside from the four-piece rhythm section of piano, guitar, bass, and drums, this included five brass, typically three trumpets and two trombones, and five reeds, usually one clarinet, two alto, and two tenor saxes. The second tenor gave a fuller, deeper tone to the reed section. The Ellington, Lunceford, and Moten-Basie bands used the baritone saxes of Harry Carney, Earl Carruthers, and Jack Washington, respectively, to anchor the reeds.[43] An important factor here is that section men now often outnumbered soloists in many big bands. The surroundings that encased the solos became as influential as the solos themselves. Moreover, black section men with good reading skills and work habits found more work than the improvising soloists could find. Dave Peyton's famous "Old, ace musicians" were finding less and less room in the new world of the swing band.

Instead, the swing band was the home of the new generation of middle-class, well-educated sidemen and arrangers, described by Hsio Wen Shih as the key innovators of this period. Many of the national sidemen of the early 1930s had some college education. A few examples include Willie Smith, Earl Carruthers, and Ed Wilcox, all of the Jimmie Lunceford Orchestra and Fisk University, and Wardell Jones and Edgar Hayes of the Blue Rhythm Band and Wilberforce University. Eddie Thompkins in Lunceford's group went to the University of Iowa, and Crawford Wetherington of Blue Rhythm attended the University of Illinois. Arrangers and leaders such as Sy Oliver, Fletcher Henderson, and Claude Hopkins were all the sons of educators. All of these men brought very professional attitudes to their music as well as good reading and often writing abilities.[44]

Still, the most important change in the emergence of swing was not the size or make-up of the sections but the way in which they were used. By March 1931, the Fletcher Henderson Orchestra had recovered from the *Great Day* fiasco and was in the midst of a recording binge of over thirty sides between February and August. One of these, "Hot and Anxious" arranged by Henderson's younger brother Horace, stands out as a forecast for the future. As Gunther Schuller has pointed out, it was a blueprint for the swing sound consisting of a three-part structure that many arrangers and bands would follow for the next ten years and more: "The formula consisted of three primary elements: (1) a steady four-to-the-bar 'chomp-chomp' beat, unvaried and relentless in all four rhythm instruments; (2) simple riffs whose melodic contours could fit any of the three major steps (I,IV,V); and (3) the gradually receding 'fade-out' ending, preferably with bent blue notes in the guitar."[45]

"Hot and Anxious" was an anomaly in March 1931, as the other recordings of this period show. The swing style elements did not begin to appear regularly in even the Henderson band's repertoire until 1932–1933. New York bands were moving towards the swing synthesis in 1931 but had not yet reached it. This is evident in sides such as Cab Calloway's "Minnie the Moocher" (March 1931), Don Redman's "Chant of the Weed" (September 1931), or the Mills Blue Rhythm Band's "Wild Waves," arranged by Harry White (May 1932). In each of these tunes the new elements have not yet fused, the vertical 2/4 feel of the 1920s remains, and the interplay of the sections and soloists is still incomplete.[46]

Gradually, arrangers and musicians figured out how to put the pieces together. Fletcher Henderson led the way. After Benny Carter, his chief arranger, left, Henderson himself began doing more of the band's arrangements, increasingly relying on and improving the formula expressed by his younger brother Horace in the "Hot and Anxious" arrangement. While his band never reclaimed its number one position, Fletcher Henderson arrangements set a standard for black bands developing the swing synthesis. They were supple and universal. They could be adapted to the needs of any personality and array of soloists. These qualities helped them to shape the whole Swing Era as a major part of the book of arrangements of the white Benny Goodman Orchestra in 1935.[47]

Coming to swing from another direction were the December 13, 1932, recordings made for Victor by Bennie Moten's Kansas City Orchestra in Camden, New Jersey, at the end of a long and hard road trip. The band and the country were in bad straits that month. The band had incurred debt in a date at the Pearl Theater in Philadelphia, was losing its bus, and had not eaten a good meal before the marathon recording session. After the session, a local promoter got them a feast of rabbit stew and greens served on a pool table. Anchored by the solid 4/4 bass of Walter Page, and featuring other Blue Devil alumni including Count Basie and Jimmy Rushing and the riff-filled arrangements of Eddie Durham, the nine classic sides exude a vitality and confidence that is hard to reconcile with the disastrous conditions of the country and the band at the time. The records also contain the core of the elements seen in "Hot and Anxious," the 4/4 rhythm which is stronger and faster here than with Henderson, the riffs, and the fade-out endings often using riff figures.[48]

Conclusion

Moten or Henderson, the territories or New York, the new style and new business conditions intersected, and the results transformed jazz. Everywhere an informal, locally based art form became the product of a national industry.

Rise of National Bands, 1929–1935

Moten's men in Kansas City and Fletcher Henderson in New York were refining the basic big band format that Don Redman and Henderson had developed to reflect new technological changes. The resulting style would become a national one as the result of the new business conditions pioneered by Duke Ellington and Irving Mills. This standardization limited regional creativity. It replaced local personal business operations with a national scene that increased the role of white gatekeepers: radio and record executives, band managers, and location owners. It increased the rewards of national success but made the odds against achieving it much greater.

8

The Impact of the National Bands

THE impact of the business changes described in the previous chapter was felt nationally. The reactions in New York and the territories were different. New York City became a revolving door. As established bands such as Duke Ellington's and Fletcher Henderson's began national tours, other bands and musicians flocked into New York looking for their big opportunity. Some made it and some did not. The stories of Louis Armstrong, Cab Calloway, Fess Williams, Luis Russell, Claude Hopkins, Chick Webb, and Jimmie Lunceford illustrate some of the factors involved.

New York: Home of National Bands

Louis Armstrong arrived back in New York in June 1929 with Carroll Dickerson's big band. He was briefly involved with Fletcher Henderson's band in the *Great Day* fiasco but emerged on his feet, moving with Dickerson's band into Connie's Inn in Harlem. In the fall, he also began appearing on Broadway in *Hot Chocolates* playing and singing Fats Waller's "Ain't Misbehavin'" accompanied by Leroy Smith's pit band. This was the engagement that made Armstrong a popular music star with a strong following among white audiences. His live performances and recordings featured his distinctive and engaging vocals as well as his virtuoso trumpet playing. He worked exclusively in the big band format as a featured artist, and the bands began to take his name. He appeared and recorded with the Luis Russell orchestra and the Mills Blue Rhythm Band before moving to Frank Sebastian's Cotton Club in Los Angeles and fronting the Les Hite band, with whom he recorded extensively. Returning to Chicago in 1931, he was backed up by what had basically been Bernie Young's band with Zilner Randolph doing the arranging and musical directing while John Collins managed Armstrong and the band. Armstrong toured the United States with this band for a year and then went to Europe. There he also fronted bands organized for him. By the fall of 1935, back in the States, he was fronting the Luis Russell band. This arrangement would last for most of the Swing Era.

At his point, Armstrong was the best-known black jazz musician in the world. Throughout this period, he left the musical direction of his bands to others. Perhaps for this reason, they have weak reputations which are not always deserved. Armstrong's own virtuosity grew at this time as did his influence on all soloists. By expanding the range of the soloist, Armstrong indirectly gave the arrangers of this period, including his own Zilner Randolph, new goals. His influence on the development of swing should not be underestimated, but Armstrong's very dominance tended to turn his own bands into stage sets simply supporting him.

His personal and business affairs were complex, as his managers and wives, Lil Hardin and Alpha Smith, fought over him. He followed the Ellington-Mills pattern of developing an international reputation with the aid of a series of white managers including Tommy Rockwell and John Collins. Armstrong's business life stabilized with the 1935 arrival of Joe Glaser as his manager. His personal life took longer to clarify. Armstrong had been transformed by his 1929–1930 New York appearances from a successful jazz performer to an international entertainment super star, and he had successfully adapted to both the musical and business conditions of the period.[1]

Similarly, Cab Calloway began as an unknown dancer and became "the King of Hi-De-Ho" between 1928 and 1935 as a result of New York appearances. Calloway had signed on as front man and vocalist with Marion Hardy's Alabamians in Chicago. As he remembered, "I brought the Alabamians from Chicago to New York in late 1928 and we went to work in the Savoy Ballroom. We were a big flop because we were playing Chicago-style jazz and they didn't like it too much in New York. . . . The kids couldn't dance too good to our music and they really didn't like it. . . . but they went for my vocals."[2]

After a Savoy Ballroom music battle against Lockwood Lewis and the Missourians, a manager switched Calloway to the more successful Missourians to get the best leader-band combination. By July of 1930, the band was known as Cab Calloway and his Orchestra, and Calloway's vocals and visual effects on the bandstand were increasing the band's popularity. It quickly became Irving Mills's number two band, filling in at the Cotton Club when Duke Ellington toured and benefiting from the Mills publicity machine. Soon, the Calloway band was also reaping large profits from national tours based on frequent recordings, radio broadcasts, and movie appearances.

Calloway was even more of an entertainer than Armstrong, and his band served as a backdrop for his act. Calloway possessed the charisma of a Michael Jackson or Prince in the early 1930s. His light skin color and dance moves had tremendous visual appeal with just a little hint of the forbidden. His songs touched on subjects such as drugs ("Minnie the Moocher," "The Reefer Man"), but his humor made them acceptable, perhaps with the aid of racial stereotyping. The band was a solid group that developed a reliable ensemble style. Its arrangers, including Harry "Father" White, a D.C. competitor of Duke Ellington's, and Eddie Barefield, a graduate of the Eli Rice and Bennie Moten bands, adjusted quickly to the new developments of the swing style. By 1935, the Calloway band was eminently successful. Like Duke Ellington, it lost an opportunity for national radio exposure in a battle between managers and networks, but it was extremely popular and well paid. It rested near the top of the band business pyramid as one of the major national bands as a result of Mills's management, Calloway's showmanship, and the band's adjustment to swing style, all stemming from New York engagements in 1929.[3]

In contrast to these success stories, New York was less kind to another musician who returned there in 1929. Fess Williams had been a star at Harlem's Savoy Ballroom in the mid-1920s before moving to Chicago's Regal Theater in January of 1928. In March of 1929, he left the Regal, perhaps because it was beginning to trim its payroll for sound movies, and returned to the Savoy. He got a Victor recording contract and made over thirty sides between April of 1929 and July of 1930, including an interesting version of Armstrong's hit, "Ain't Misbehavin'." Still, he never recaptured the glory years of the 1920s. He lost $60,000 on a 1930 tour he booked himself and had bad luck with several different agents. He made no records after July 1930 although he continued as a band leader in the New York area. Williams had clearly dropped to the second or third level in the music world. He was not able to fit into the new business environment or keep up with changing musical tastes. His recordings show a continuation of the peppy 1920s novelty style with echoes of Wilber Sweatman, Wilton Crawley, and Ted Lewis, which no longer fit the developments in black jazz.[4]

Impact of the National Bands

The Luis Russell band is well respected by many jazz critics and historians but did not fully survive this period. The reason for both the respect and the downfall may be that it broke too many of the rules of the period. It was in many ways the last New Orleans-influenced band to try for national success before the revival of that style in the 1940s. The core of the band was Luis Russell on piano, Henry "Red" Allen on trumpet, Albert Nicholas on clarinet, George "Pops" Foster on bass, and Paul Barbarin on drums. All were New Orleans musicians who had come to New York in 1927 under King Oliver's leadership.

This group recorded extensively between 1929 and 1933 under the names of Luis Russell, King Oliver, Red Allen, Louis Armstrong, Jelly Roll Morton, and Wilton Crawley. Under Russell's name and leadership the group built a strong reputation by 1931 with the strong swing propulsion of its rhythm section and the excellent solos of Allen, Nicholas, and trombonist J.C. Higginbotham. Manager Tommy Rockwell was worried that the band was too small and too different with no star personality As he tried to exploit the band along accepted lines with theater tours in 1932–1933, the rules held. The small group that was so powerful in a nightclub or record studio seemed lost in a cavernous theater or ballroom. The very looseness that appeals to critics and historians today was a weakness with the theater and ballroom audiences of 1932–1933. The concert and club audiences that supported the New Orleans revival were not in place yet, and the audience demands of the early 1930s did not fit the strengths of the Russell band. Russell saw the flaws too and with Rockwell's urging expanded the band to thirteen pieces by 1934 and changed to a section-oriented arranging style more in tune with the developing Swing Era. While these changes saved the band financially, its musical uniqueness was lost. In October 1935, the Russell band came under Louis Armstrong's name as his regular working band although Russell continued as musical director. The band prospered as a national touring band throughout the Swing Era, but the individual musicians were not able to shine as they had in the brief glory days of the early 1930s.[5]

By contrast, the Claude Hopkins Orchestra was quite successful from the early 1930s through the Swing Era by fitting its time well. Hopkins, the college-educated son of members of the Howard University community, spent much of the 1920s playing, musically and socially, in Atlantic City and Europe. In 1930, after a period with a black touring show, Hopkins took over a New York taxi dance hall band led by Charlie Skeets and began to move it up the band pyramid. The key break was an extended engagement at the Roseland Ballroom as a replacement for Fletcher Henderson's band. This also involved extensive radio exposure, which along with some recordings built a strong audience for the band. With white management, Hopkins prospered in the 1931–1935 period from tours and location jobs.

The band became one of the first to completely absorb the swing style, and Hopkins kept his arrangements rigidly in that format. The sections were given strict roles and solo space was limited. The band did not sport great soloists except for Edmond Hall on clarinet. Hopkins's band has been criticized for lack of personality and limited arrangements, but these were the result of conscious decisions by Hopkins rather than an absence of ability. Unlike Luis Russell, Hopkins had a realistic under-standing of the middle-brow tastes of the ballroom and theater audiences and he satisfied them. By 1933–1934, he was successful with both black and white audiences employing a very serviceable and entertaining swing style without any personality of its own. However, partly because of this lack of distinction, Hopkins, along with other second-line national black bands like the Mills Blue Rhythm Band, suffered more acutely than others when white swing competition arrived in 1935.[6]

The Blue Rhythm Band was the ultimate manager's band. It was the third group in Irving Mills's management stable and even carried his name. It had been a New York taxi dance hall band led by Bingie Madison before undergoing some quick leadership changes and Mills's adoption. Mills used the Blue Rhythm Band to fill in at the Cotton Club for Duke Ellington and Cab Calloway when they were on tour, and it developed a second-line reputation. From 1930 on, the musical director was pianist Edgar Hayes, who provided serviceable arrangements. The group also fit Hsio Wen Shin's model. Publicity stressed that nine band members were college-educated. This too was clearly a swing band, although as their 1932 record "Wild Waves" showed, it took some time to master the style. Harry White provided that arrangement before going on to Cab Calloway's band where he did his best work. This group worked under wraps even more than Hopkins's band since it was not supposed to compete with stablemates Ellington and Calloway.[7]

Chick Webb had arrived in New York in the mid-1920s from Bal-timore and worked in a variety of settings. By March 1931, when the Webb band recorded its first releases, it was a solid big band with a late 1920s sound. In October 1931, Webb moved in as the house band at Harlem's Savoy Ballroom. It soon became a real favorite of the black dancers there, and on its home turf successfully battled many national bands. When the band returned to records in 1933, it was clearly a swing unit. Spurred by the Savoy dancers, the rhythm section including Webb and bassist John Kirby, and arrangers including Edgar Sampson, developed a very danceable version of the swing synthesis. Webb standards such as "Stompin' at the Savoy," and "Don't Be That Way" were featured in the books of Benny Goodman and other swing bands.

The unique chemistry between the frail Webb's band and the dancers at the Savoy did not travel well. While the band toured before 1935, it was not in the first line of national bands. This changed during the Swing Era with the discovery at a Harlem amateur hour of a very young Ella Fitzgerald. With her vocals increasingly dominating, the Webb band became a national success, setting attendance records in a 1938 tour, which was followed by Webb's death, the decline of the band, and Ella's establishment of a solo career. The Webb band's story in the early 1930s is another example of how a black band could find success with the swing sound and good management, both more accessible in New York than elsewhere.[8]

The last important big band to arrive in New York during this period was Jimmie Lunceford's. As mentioned in chapter six, this group started in Memphis in the 1920s with Lunceford, a high school music teacher, and several of his students and college friends from Fisk University. From the beginning they aspired to the big time and sought radio and record exposure. Two sides recorded in 1930 show a strong blues influence and ties to the Southeastern sounds within an arranged big band format. After local jobs, they moved their base to the Cleveland-Buffalo area in 1931. There, with an eye on New York, the Lunceford band developed its style in a national direction, adding musicians from several regions. The most important was trumpeter-vocalist-arranger Sy Oliver, from Zanesville, Ohio. This young, middle-class Midwesterner confirmed the focus of the band on arrangements and vocals, updating the approach of McKinney's Cotton Pickers to the tastes of the 1930s.

In 1934, the band went to New York City, recorded for RCA Victor, and signed with Irving Mills, who put them into the Cotton Club while Cab Calloway toured. That summer, apparently wanting more personal attention, they signed with Harold Oxley, who sent them on a theater tour that netted the band an infusion of mostly Southwestern territory men. With the new men, Oxley's management, and a Decca record contract, the Lunceford band finally achieved national prominence and remained one of the major black bands throughout the Swing Era with a unique style and a constant schedule of road tours. The tours were necessary because Lunceford rarely had the luxury of the long location jobs that Ellington and Calloway enjoyed. The steady grind of touring as well as Lunceford's concentration on entertainment values explain the band's unique sound. The arrangements of Oliver and others including pianist Ed

Wilcox, trombonist Eddie Durham, and reedman Willie Smith were the band's strength. On records particularly, solo space was limited. The band specialized in unorthodox treatments of popular songs.[9]

In the midst of this new wave of competitors, Fletcher Henderson rebuilt his band and re-emerged as an important figure. He failed to regain the dominance he had before 1929, in part because he was never quite comfortable with the new management style and longed to remain independent and low-key, but he did rebound from the depths of the *Great Day* disaster. In the 1930–1931 season, his band had its one year as a Harlem group based at Connie's Inn. In January 1931, the band made headlines by flying to a dance in Cincinnati. More tours, however, were unsuccessful. Between 1931 and 1934, Henderson kept missing one more big break at the same time he was developing some of the key swing arrangements. A record session and some dates organized by John Hammond produced interesting music but little income. By 1934, Fletcher Henderson disbanded his group and concentrated on selling his arrangements. Many of them became key parts of Benny Goodman's 1935 "book" when that band began the official Swing Era.[10]

The national bands that succeeded in New York in this period all shared a desire for national recognition and the ability to adapt to the musical and business demands of this period. The groups that failed and those that remained in the territories lacked one or more of those characteristics.

East Coast

Chick Webb, Claude Hopkins, and Jimmie Lunceford are reminders that, as indicated in chapter six, the Northeast was the most affected by New York dominance of all the territories. Its best players easily moved to New York and its regional style was, in fact, the New York style. Theater bands here were the first to be influenced by New York competition, with the theater tours amplifying the impact of talking pictures. Despite all this, a few bands survived in this area. George Tynes and Eddie Deas both led Boston-based bands that lasted for most of the 1929–1935 period. "Docs" seemed to thrive in Philadelphia, with Cheatham, Hyder, and Wheeler leading bands there, usually at the Pearl Theater, which was also home to Charlie Gaines. As in the early modern era, it was also the entry point to the North for some Southeastern musicians including Jimmy Gorham's band. Still, the region has no real distinct personality by this period.[11]

Chicago

It is not surprising that three of the key leaders discussed in the New York section came from Chicago. The changes occurring in the band business and in the music were felt perhaps most deeply in Chicago. The drying up of movie and vaudeville theater jobs hurt badly in Chicago where many musicians had relied on the Regal and other locations. Also, the sharpening of tensions over Prohibition in Chicago after the 1929 St. Valentine's Day Massacre undermined the nightclub jobs of black musicians there. The entire black economy of Chicago was devastated by the depression, represented by the 1930 collapse of Jesse Binga's black-owned bank. All events had a negative impact on opportunities for Chicago musicians who responded in various ways.

After 1927, King Oliver, Jelly Roll Morton, Jimmie Wade as well as Fess Williams, Carroll Dickerson, Louis Armstrong, and Cab Calloway all tried New York. Only Armstrong and Calloway really succeeded. Walter Barnes's Royal Creolians, and groups led by Dave Peyton and Sammy Stewart attempted to become Midwestern territory bands without success. By 1933, the entire old-line Chicago establishment had been destroyed. Dave Peyton, Erskine Tate, Doc Cooke, Charlie Elgar, and Jimmy Wade had all left the band business, and the careers of Jelly Roll Morton, King Oliver, and Sammy Stewart were in decline.[12] Apparently, the failure of Chicago bands to participate fully in the New York synthesis and business changes limited their potential for success in the new conditions.

Even the younger band leaders had to expand their turf. In 1929, Walter Barnes, a twenty-four-year-old native of Vicksburg, Mississippi, led a twelve-piece band regularly at the white Arcadia Ballroom. From late 1929 to July 1930 the Barnes band worked at Al Capone's brother's club in Cicero. From the summer of 1930 on, however, Barnes began extensive tours, first into the Midwest and next into the Southeast. By 1932, his Southeastern tours were so extensive that he made Jacksonville, Florida, his winter base. Well into the Swing Era, Barnes toured areas usually skipped by the national bands. He found economic success and musical survival by identifying those few geographic areas in which the conditions of the 1920s remained and leading a territory band that could survive on individual bookings and musical copies of national band hits. Unfortunately, as described in chapter seven, this route for Barnes eventually led to the deadly Memphis cabaret fire.[13]

Job opportunities for black musicians in Chicago were complicated by infighting between the white and black locals of the musicians union. The white Local 10 was led by the very aggressive James C. Petrillo. He later served as president of the national American Federation of Musicians sparking costly fights with other parts of the music industry. In August 1931, Petrillo blocked Irving Mills from bringing the Ellington, Calloway, and Blue Rhythm bands into dates at the Congress Hotel by fining them for violating union rules and threatening action against the hotel. The action may have been simply an early example of Petrillo's belligerent defense of his union's turf. It was viewed, however, by many black musicians and the black community, perhaps correctly, as an example of active racism in the North. The contracts had been approved by Chicago's black Local 208.[14]

As job opportunities in Chicago for black musicians declined, some groups continued and new bands were born. Some small bands enjoyed success in Chicago nightclub settings. New Orleans veterans like Johnny Dodds and Lee Collins kept playing in clubs and Chinese restaurants. When Jimmie Noone's group toured ballrooms it had to expand to eleven pieces and lost the core of its sound. Young Chicagoans like Ray Nance and new players from the territories developed their styles in small band settings. Bands led by Cassino Simpson and Tiny Parham mixed small group, blues, and big band styles in unique ways that won fans in Chicago but had limited recording or touring opportunities. Bernie Young led a 1930 band with Zilner Randolph and Eddie Barefield as arrangers that became the core of one of Louis Armstrong's big bands.[15]

The most important Chicago band was that of Earl "Fatha" Hines, the Louis Armstrong of the piano. He led a band that was often undisciplined but sparked by a mixture of New Orleans veterans like Omer Simeon and young Chicagoans like Cecil Irwin. Hines developed a pre-swing style that was competitive with the national bands. He remained in Chicago because of economic and perhaps personal pressure connected with his location at the Grand Terrace and its possible underworld ties.[16] Their absence from the road and recording studios kept Earl Hines and his Orchestra below the top national ranks, but it was clearly a major band. To reach national prominence Hines's group gradually lost its local color, becoming a more standardized big band as the Swing Era approached.

Midwest

In the rest of the Midwest, the area's commitment to arranged big band jazz and its abundance of middle-class sideman served it very well. The Detroit-based McKinney's Cotton Pickers was one of the few national bands to operate without New York as its base. It was one of the leading black bands in the country until 1931, when its musical director, Don Redman, left to form his own New York-based band and took the national reputation with him. With Redman as leader of course, the McKinney band was directly in the center of the arranged big band style Redman had developed with Fletcher Henderson. It was in fact the first real arranger's band, featuring not only Redman's scores but those of John Nesbitt and others. After Redman left, drummer Cuba Austin and pianist Todd Rhodes kept McKinney's Cotton Pickers touring the Midwest and South with less success.[17]

Other Midwestern bands like Speed Webb's and Zach Whyte's competed with national bands by providing a similar style with young bright musicians. The key problem with this approach was that musicians such as Roy Eldridge and Teddy Wilson with Webb and Sy Oliver with Whyte could succeed with national bands. They often moved up the pyramid, leaving their bandmates behind or forcing groups to disband entirely. While many musicians went on from the Midwest to New York for the Swing Era, no new major bands developed from within that territory.[18] Cecil Scott's national band almost returned to territory status with extensive local tours.

Southeast

The changes of the Swing Era had perhaps the most profound impact in the Southeast. Here, the failure of the farm economy to participate in the prosperity of the Roaring Twenties and the Jim Crow laws had already limited opportunities for black musicians. The onset of the Great Depression shrank the market for bands in this area even more. Moreover, the demand for big band jazz could not be met by most of the groups in this area. Bands led by Smiling Billy Stewart and C. S. Belton, both based in Florida, gradually expanded their tours to the Midwest and even the Northwest, attempting to become national touring bands. They failed because they lacked the musical and business muscle of their New York-based competition. The groups of J. Neal Montgomery, Charlie Williamson, Eddie Heywood, and many others broke up as theater and dance jobs became scarce. Blues musicians filled the void in some areas, and national touring bands also worked this region, often reluctantly.[19]

Three young groups developed from regional institutions. Taylor's Dixie Serenaders were mostly students at Johnson C. Smith University in Charlotte, North Carolina. They recorded two sides in 1931, reflecting the New York-based arranged big band style. Jimmy Gunn took over the group in 1934, and they recorded again in 1936. Band members Leslie Johnakins, Skeets Tolbert, and Harry Prather had later careers in New York.

The Carolina Cotton Pickers were alumni of the Jenkins Orphanage and had started as one of several official groups for that institution. Their records launched the career of Duke Ellington's trumpeter, Cat Anderson, but are limited in overall value.[20]

Erskine Hawkins's 'Bama State Collegians, the only national band to come directly out of the Southeast, also began as one of three official groups for Alabama State College. Even though the group emerged late in the Swing Era and reflected its style, the 'Bama State Collegians showed more ease with the blues than did many of its contemporaries. The group featured Hawkins's high-note trumpet work and Avery Parrish's blues-rooted piano. Some Alabama State musicians were former students of Fess Whately's who continued his teaching and band leading in Birmingham throughout this period, moving to a big band swing style.[21]

Northwest

In the isolated Northwest, it was easier for band leaders to ignore the big time and to remain in place, but this just increased the pressure within the bands. In 1930–1931, Eli Rice had built a tough band of brash, bright, ambitious young musicians including Eddie Thompkins and Joe Thomas on trumpet, Keg Johnson on trombone, and Eddie Barefield as arranger-reeds. Barefield provided strong arrangements, and the band had strong section work and brass solos influenced by Louis Armstrong. As the band's drummer, Eli's son Sylvester Rice remembered, "This was really a precision band. We figured that we were ready for the big time in the East and were willing to sacrifice to do it, but Eli vetoed the idea and as a result, the group disbanded."[22] Eli Rice put more groups together, but Thompkins, Thomas, Johnson, and Barefield all left to find jobs with national bands.[23]

Not only national bands but Southeastern bands like Smiling Billy Stewart's and Southwestern bands like George E. Lee's raided the Northwest. Isolation, however, allowed the older generation of bandleaders—Red Perkins, Grant Moore, Eli Rice, and Lloyd Hunter—to survive. They were joined in 1936 by Nat Towles who brought a band up to Omaha from Texas. The senior leaders eventually modeled themselves more closely on national styles and were more aware of their place as minor league feeders for national bands. Their sound grew closer to the media models, and they came to expect the loss of some of their best men and songs to the national market. This was reflected in 1931 recordings by three groups. Lloyd Hunter's version of Henri Woode's "Sensational Mood,"a tune that arranger Woode took to Chicago's Earl Hines band, was a tight swinging arrangement that fit the needs of dancers and the national model. The Grant Moore band recast "Original Dixieland One-Step" and "Mama Don't Allow" towards swing with strong section riffs that drove the dancers up the walls of the Minneapolis ballrooms, but fit anywhere. Red Perkins's small group kept more of a 1920s regional sound, but "Old Man Blues" with its vocal trio came right out of the Ellington repertoire.[24]

West Coast

On the West Coast as in Chicago, changes in musical tastes and business practices hurt the older territory bands. The Spikes Brothers, Sonny Clay, and Curtis Mosby bands all folded in this period.[25] The core of Frank Sebastian's Cotton Club group survived, led by Leon Elkins and later Les Hite. They backed up Louis Armstrong when he performed in Los Angeles and made some of his more impressive early big band recordings, but he left them behind when he went back East. The Armstrong West Coast recordings kept a few unique touches such a Ceele Burke's Hawaiian style guitar reflecting his actual experience in the islands, and Lionel Hampton's experiments on vibes, but the main direction was the national arranged big band structure. Sebastian replaced Hite with a white band and members began to drift away. Trombone star Lawrence Brown joined Duke Ellington and Lionel Hampton experimented with his own West Coast band before he took a small step for social revolution by joining Benny Goodman in 1936 as the second black musician with a white national band. Other musicians remained on the West Coast where their isolation kept them even more obscure. The Les Hite Orchestra recorded only four sides in the 1930s under its own name, and they were not released. Gradually the West Coast bands were recognized more for the stars they had lost to national bands than for players they retained.[26]

Southwest

The Southwest, as usual, was somewhat different. The Pendergast Prosperity of Kansas City's political machine and wide-open town and the territory's blues bias provided a shelter for local groups. The Kansas City scene lived, in part, on the death of the Texas-Oklahoma bands: Kansas City bands toured more into the territory, creating more competition for local bands; they lured away young talent with direct offers and the excitement of Kansas City life. The Blue Devils and bands led by Jap Allen, Troy Floyd, T. Holder, Jesse Stone, and Alphonso Trent, as well as many lesser groups, all collapsed in this period.[27] Many of the bright young sidemen of the 1920s were already leaving for Chicago and New

York. The Johnson brothers of Dallas are a case in point. Trombonist Keg Johnson jumped from Texas to Kansas City, to Eli Rice and Grant Moore, and then to Chicago to the touring Louis Armstrong who took Johnson to New York where he settled into Cab Calloway's band for the whole Swing Era. Tenor player Budd Johnson took the Texas, Kansas City, Chicago route to the Earl Hines band where he remained for much of the swing period. Several members of the Nat Towles band moved from Texas to Omaha, Nebraska.[28]

Still, new bands and strong music continued to originate in this area. Paul Banks, Clarence Love, Tommy Douglas, and the Thamon Hayes band, taken over later by Harlan Leonard, all survived in Kansas City with a Southwestern sound moving towards swing.[29] However, hard times and business changes affected the players here. Clarence Love remained regional in part because he turned down an MCA management offer, had union problems, and never landed a record contract.[30] Tommy Douglas swore he lost his shot at the big time when his group turned down a shot at KVOO in Tulsa where Bob Wills's white band remained and became a national figure in Western swing.[31] For whatever reason, Douglas missed the connection with a gatekeeper who might have opened the door to national success. Love and Douglas, as well as the more successful Southwestern bands including Bennie Moten's, Alphonso Trent's, Andy Kirk's, and Don Albert's, extended their touring territory so much that they became, in effect, national bands based in Kansas City or Texas rather than New York. They even followed the same use of radio and records to advance their fame.[32]

The Alphonso Trent band presents a puzzle. It disbanded in 1934 and had recorded only four sides. Yet the tunes are excellent music and show very clearly the move from the "peppy" jazz of the 1920s to the smoother swing sound of the 1930s in "Clementine" and "I Found a New Baby." The musicianship is uniformly high. The arrangements are tight and the solos exciting. The Trent band seems ahead of their contemporaries. Their "Clementine" sounds closer to the later Jimmie Lunceford style than the Lunceford 1930 cuts, while "Baby" is even closer to later Basie than the Moten 1932 sides. Relying on recordings as documentation sometimes raises more questions than it answers. Despite their few records, the Trent band toured and broadcast extensively. They are well remembered by musicians. Do these records simply reflect the national changes that were taking place, or was the Trent band in fact one of the key creators of this new style? Unfortunately, that question will probably never be answered.[33]

The 1932 sides of Bennie Moten's orchestra have been mentioned earlier. Moten had rebuilt his band in this period by buying players from bands in smaller markets who were being hurt by the hard times. The core of his 1932 band, Oran "Hot Lips" Page, Jimmy Rushing, Count Basie, and Walter Page, were in Page's Oklahoma City-based Blue Devils in 1929. Moten lured away Rushing and Basie with better salaries. Page tried to maintain the Blue Devils but his replacements did not fit, and he was faced with union, booking, and financial problems. Consequently, he gave up band leading to join Moten. The new Moten band moved much closer to the swing synthesis, as its 1932 recordings show, but it still had limited financial success, in part because it was not based in New York where Moten could maintain direct contact with the national gatekeepers. He was not able to translate the 1932 records into great success as Calloway or Lunceford did. Any attempt for the Moten band as a unit to move from Kansas City ended with his death in 1935. The core members of the band made it big in the Swing Era under Count Basie's leadership, while "Hot Lips" Page, Ben Webster, Eddie Barefield, and Eddie Durham had national careers with other bands.[34]

Andy Kirk succeeded as a Kansas City-based national band. Kirk like Jimmie Lunceford was a product of the Denver public school music program headed by Paul Whiteman's father. Kirk took over Terence Holder's band in Texas in the late 1920s and moved it to Kansas City. A few 1929–1930 sides show a good Southwestern band of the period. The band did not record again until 1936 by which time it was clearly in the swing mold. Without recordings, Kirk's musical development is more difficult to chart than Moten's but his professional progress is unmistakable. Apparently Kirk concentrated on the business side, allowing pianist-arranger Mary Lou Williams to develop the musical shape of the band. Kirk managed the group for much of this period, 1929–1939, gradually supplementing Kansas City locations with tours. By expanding tours slowly he avoided some of the hard times that the Moten band faced on its 1932 trip. He made breakthroughs into many white locations and took advantage of contacts with white managers, eventually landing a record contract in the early Swing Era, which established the band as a national power. Meanwhile, Mary Lou Williams had moved up from wife of band member to relief pianist, then to pianist and chief arranger. She gave the Kirk band a unique big band sound with her arrangements. Kirk was one of the last successful examples of the bandleader as an individual entrepreneur.[35]

In Texas, even more than in Kansas City, unique conditions allowed white musicians like Bob Wills and Milton Brown to create a distinctive merger of jazz and country traditions known as Western swing. Conditions also allowed black bands to maintain some regional sounds while keeping an ear on the national synthesis. The stories of Don Albert and Boots Douglas illustrate this.

Don Albert's band toured nationally from its Texas base but never reached national name band status as Kirk's did. Albert was originally from New Orleans and his band combined New Orleans and Texas players. He had been part of the Troy Floyd Orchestra. After that group broke up in 1932, Albert established the leading band in San Antonio. A lack of recordings makes it difficult to determine what the band sounded like in this early period, although memories indicate it had more of a collective ensemble sound. Several of its members, including reedmen Louis Cottrell and Herb Hall and trumpeter Alvin Alcorn, later played in the New Orleans revival or Dixieland bands. Apparently, ballroom audiences and bookers demanded closer ties to the prevailing styles. By the time the band recorded in 1936, it had moved to a swing style with a bit of a regional accent established by pianist-arranger Lloyd Glenn. Albert (like Kirk) gradually increased his touring area to gain money until he had touched much of the United States and even visited Canada and Mexico.[36]

His frequent absences from San Antonio left room for drummer Clifford "Boots" Douglas to develop his group, Boots and his Buddies. Their extensive recordings, which date from 1935–1938, are definitely in the swing style but alternate wildly. Some sides continue the Southwestern territory tradition. Others imitate virtually every national style in existence. These records reveal how the territory bands after 1929 needed to deal with the dominance of national bands in the music industry and the ears of their own regional audiences.[37]

In St. Louis times were even rougher than they were elsewhere in the Southwest. Many of the older men either left town or left the business. Even the younger members of the St. Louis trumpet tradition, Shorty Baker, Mouse Randolph, and Joe Thomas, departed quickly. Oliver Cobb led a group that became the Crackerjacks and lasted until 1938, but Cobb, an Armstrong-influenced player, drowned in 1931. Later recordings by the Crackerjacks and the Jeter-Pillars band show groups that had neither strong regional accents nor the potential to fit smoothly into the national style. Perhaps St. Louis's closeness to the Midwest and the routes to Chicago and New York made it more difficult to maintain a unique sound, but the local ties of the musicians who stayed made it tough to adjust to the national model.[38]

While the Southwest easily remained the most successful territory, it could no longer ignore the national sounds, and the changes that tied jazz into the national entertainment business.

Conclusion

The problems of the territory bands everywhere reflected the success of the national bands. The key factor was the increased role of the mainly white gatekeepers: band managers, recording executives, theater managers, ballroom owners, and radio executives. Band managers fulfilled the need for a full-time professional to deal with the band business bureaucracies. The Irving Mills system adjusted to the increasing complexity of managing a band. His important contacts with other gatekeepers opened doors for his clients, the black musicians who were creating the musical product. Access promoted success; denial of access usually assured failure. The rise of managers between 1929 and 1935 brought wholesale changes that fundamentally altered the nature of the band business. It was transformed from a hodgepodge of informal local arrangements to a highly structured national entity. In this process, the ability of individual bandleaders and musicians to determine their own fates was limited, but the chances for both success and failure increased greatly.

The factors involved in these changes were simple although their interactions often became quite complex. They included: (1) the increasing popularity of dance music; (2) the movement of theatrical booking agencies into the field of band booking; (3) the decline of vaudeville, leaving a void in the entertainment world; (4) the existence of mass media—radio and records to reach a national audience; and (5) improvements in roads, and automobiles which made travel cheaper and easier.

Together these factors produced a unified national band business pyramid that affected black jazz bands. On the top were a few very successful national bands earning excellent salaries and fine reputations. These bands built their names through recordings and radio broadcasts, with careful nurturing by managers. This name recognition was then exploited for financial gain during national tours of ballrooms, nightclubs, and theaters. On the next level, less successful national bands followed the same pattern on a smaller scale. Still lower, the territory bands continued, but they were definitely marked as minor league, copying the styles of the national bands and losing their most talented musicians to the lure of the big time.

While this new structure hurt many black bands, it also offered chances for unparalleled economic success and prestige to others. This was particularly true because the white bands emphasized the sweet style in this period. The black bands' development of the hot swing style represented a major musical accomplishment and left black musicians without any competition as the dispensers of hot dance music. Bands like Ellington's, Calloway's, and others prospered, and many black musicians graduated to a higher standard of living and greater recognition. White bands eventually mastered the hot jazz style to dominate the core of American popular music from Benny Goodman's 1935 arrival into World War II.

Although the dominance of the white bands brought black musicians up against the harsh reality a racial discrimination, there was little open discontent. Black musicians seemed satisfied to use their success and wealth to score recognition points for "the race" without overtly protesting the limits placed upon them. This acquiescence reflected their hopelessness about the willingness of white Americans anywhere to change their patterns of prejudice.

The demands of the national music industry established the professional, educated, middle-class musician as the dominant figure in the national bands and therefore on the jazz scene. Self-discipline, punctuality, good appearance, and reliability were as important as musical ability. Musical standards also shifted toward greater emphasis on reading and ensemble playing for most players. Solo abilities were required only for certain key performers. The swing style was complex, using written arrangements that demanded full technical control by the musician of his instrument. For all these reasons, the position of the black musician playing jazz-dance music changed considerably between 1929 and 1935.

This was the last stage in the gradual transformation of jazz from a primarily local music rooted in black folk traditions to the tightly managed product of a national industry controlled by white businessmen and aimed at a predominantly white mass market. This development paralleled the changing nature of American society and the changing roles of African-Americans in that society. The Great Migration brought blacks into the urban environment at precisely the time that the cities became the dominant reality in American life. The ability of the black jazz musicians to catch the spirit of that period created music that became the core of American popular culture in the Swing Era. Many of these musicians achieved economic and artistic success, but their accomplishments were muted by the constant awareness of the limits placed on African-American progress not only by legal segregation in the South but also by informal discrimination in the North and West.

Commercial success with white audiences made it more difficult for black musicians to define the musical boundaries of jazz in African-American terms. New solutions to those problems emerged with modern jazz during and after World War II. Varying business conditions and artistic expressions created a different jazz reality that supplemented and in some ways supplanted the swing synthesis created by the great jazz innovators of the 1923–1935 period.

Notes

Chapter 1

1   For the general transformation of American society in this period, see: Howard P. Chudacoff and Judith E. Smith, *The Evolution of American Urban Society,* 3d ed., (Englewood Cliffs: Prentice-Hall, 1988) pp. 76–150, 207–259; Mary Beth Norton et al., *A People and a Nation,* 3d ed., (Boston: Houghton Mifflin, 1990) pp. 523–577, 695–725; Paul S. Boyer et al., *The Enduring Vision,* (Lexington, MA: D.C. Heath, 1990) pp. 640–707, 828–865. For a general picture of how these changes affected African-Americans, see John Hope Franklin, *From Slavery to Freedom,* 6th ed., (New York: Alfred A. Knopf, 1988) pp. 251–264, 277–290, 324–338, 376–377; David R. Goldfield and Blaine A. Brownell, *Urban America: From Downtown to No Town,* 2d ed., (Boston: Houghton Mifflin, 1990) pp. 221–233.

2. Goldfield and Brownell, *Urban America,* pp. 222–223.

3. Herman Autrey with George W. Kay, "Herman Autrey Recalls the Early Days," *Jazz Journal* 22, 10 (Oct. 1969) p. 10; Reunald Jones with Valerie Wilmer, "Reunald Jones—Follow My Leader," *Jazz Journal* 16, 11 (Nov. 1963) p. 5; Ed Lewis with Frank Driggs, "Kansas City Brass, the Story of Ed Lewis," part 1, *Jazz Review* 2, 4 (May 1959) p. 16; Nathan W. Pearson Jr., "Political and Musical Forces That Influenced the Development of Kansas City Jazz," *Black Music Research Journal* 9, 2 (Fall 1989) pp. 180–188, *Chicago Defender,* July 2, 1910, p. 3.

4. *Chicago Defender,* March 13, 1915, p. 3; Aug. 18, 1917, pp. 1–2; David Halberstam, "A Day with Satchmo," *Jazz Journal* 10, 8 (Aug. 1957) p. 3; Harold Holmes with John Norris, "Harold Holmes, His Story," *Coda* 4, 4 (Nov. 1961) p. 23.

5. *Chicago Defender,* Aug. 18, 1917, pp. 1–2.

6. Melvin "Sy" Oliver with Frank Driggs, "Sy Oliver," *Sounds and Fury* 1, 1 (July–Aug. 1965) p. 49; George Hoefer, notes on Gene Sedric, Eugene Sedric file, Institute of Jazz Studies (IJS) files, Rutgers University; George Washington with Grayson Mills, "George Washington," *Jazz Journal* 13, 11 (Nov. 1960) p. 17–18.

7. James L. Collier, *Louis Armstrong: An American Genius*, (New York: Oxford University Press, 1983) p. 35–43; John Chilton, *A Jazz Nursery: The Story of the Jenkins' Orphanage Jazz Bands*, (Chicago: Chicago Public Library, 1980); *Chicago Defender*, Feb. 1, 1911, p. 1; July 27, 1912, p. 10; July 12, 1913, p. 5; July 19, 1913, p. 1; June 14, 1913, p. 1; May 22, 1920, p. 7.

8. *Chicago Defender*, July 10, 1910, p. 3; August 13, 1910, p. 1; Jan. 7, 1911, p. 1; Oct, 25, 1911, p. 6; April 20, 1915, p. 7; March 18, 1916, p. 1; April 1, 1916, p. 1.

9. Paul Oliver, *The Story of the Blues*, (Philadelphia: Chilton Book Co., 1969) p. 49–57.

10. For detailed stories of the two top black bands in this circuit see Clifford E. Watkins, "P.G. Lowery and His Musical Enterprises: The Formative Years" in George R. Keck and Sherrill V. Martin, *Feel the Spirit: Studies in Nineteenth-Century Afro-American Music*, (New York: Greenwood Press, 1988) pp. 61–81, and W.C. Handy, *Father of the Blues*, (New York: Macmillan, 1941) pp. 32–51. See also, Garvin Bushell with Mark Tucker, *Jazz From The Beginning*, (Ann Arbor: University of Michigan Press, 1988) pp. 2–3, 11–13; Garvin Bushell with Nat Hentoff, "Garvin Bushell and New York Jazz in the 1920s," part 2, *Jazz Review* 2, 2 (Feb. 1959) pp. 9–10; Franklin S. Driggs, "Red Perkins and His Dixie Ramblers," *Jazz Journal* 17, 11 (Nov. 1964) pp. 14–16; Joe Darensbourg with Peter Vacher, *Jazz Odyssey: The Autobiography of Joe Darensbourg*, (Baton Rouge: Louisiana State University Press, 1988) pp. 11, 23–25, 33–38, 46–49; Joe Darensbourg with Wallace Umphrey, "New Orleans in Seattle," *Jazz Record* (Dec. 1944) pp. 10–11; Amos White with Bertrand Demeusy, "The Amos White Musical Career," *Record Research* 69 (July 1965) p. 3; Paul Oliver, *The Story of the Blues*, pp. 58–65; Nathan W. Pearson Jr., *Goin' to Kansas City*, (Champaign: University of Illinois Press, 1987) pp. 5–12.

11. Garvin Bushell and Nat Hentoff, "Garvin Bushell," part 1, *Jazz Review* 2, 1 (Jan. 1959) p. 8.

12. Two cuts by the 369th are on *Steppin' On The Gas* (New World Records NW 269); and three are on *Sissle and Blake's Shuffle Along* (New World Records NW 260). These can be compared with *The Souza and Pryor Bands* (New World Records NW 282). For New Orleans, see William J. Schafer, *Brass Bands and New Orleans Jazz*, (Baton Rouge: Louisiana State University Press, 1977). His discography on pp. 102–105 covers the revival recordings. See also the Sam Morgan cuts on *Steppin' On The Gas* or in *Sound of New Orleans*, (Columbia Records JC3L 30). For rural bands, see Frederic Ramsey, Jr., *Music From The South, v. 1: Country Brass Bands* (Folkways Records FA 2650).

13. Count Basie as told to Albert Murray, *Good Morning Blues, The Autobiography of Count Basie*, (New York: Random House, 1985) pp. 31–33; Michael W. Harris, *The Rise of Gospel Blues: The Music of Thomas Andrew Dorsey in the Urban Church*, (New York: Oxford University Press, 1992) pp. 40–42.

14. Albert F. McLean, *American Vaudeville as Ritual*, (Lexington: University of Kentucky Press, 1965) pp. 38–65.

15. Athelia Knight, "In Retrospect, Sherman H. Dudley: He Paved the Way for T.O.B.A.," *The Black Perspective in Music*, 15, 2 (Spring, 1987) pp. 153–181; *Chicago Defender*, Jan. 28, 1911, p. 3; Aug. 17, 1912, p. 3; Oct 26, 1912, p. 5; Nov. 29, 1913, p. 6; July 19, 1914, p. 6; Nov. 7, 1914, p. 6; Feb. 6, 1915, p. 6; Sept. 15, 1917, p. 6; June 5, 1920, p. 7; Jan. 29, 1921, p. 4; Feb. 12, 1921, p. 5; Paul Oliver, *The Story of the Blues*, pp. 69–71; Tom Riis, *Just Before Jazz; Black Musical Theater in New York, 1890–1915* (Washington: Smithsonian Institution Press, 1989) pp. 24–28, 141–149, 167–171.

16. Dave Peyton, "The Musical Bunch," *Chicago Defender*, April 3, 1926, p. 6; Joe Darensbourg with Peter Vacher, *Jazz Odyssey*, pp. 14–15; Garvin Bushell with Mark Tucker, *Jazz From The Beginning*, pp. 35–36; Michael W. Harris, *The Rise of Gospel Blues*, pp. 40–42; Nathan W. Pearson, Jr. *Goin' To Kansas City*. pp. 12–16.

17. W. E. B. DuBois, *The Philadelphia Negro*, (New York: Shocken, 1967) pp. 234–321; St. Clair Drake and Horace R. Cayton, *Black Metropolis: A Study of Negro Life in a Northern City*, rev. ed., (New York: Harcourt Brace, 1970) pp. 22–24, 47, 55–56, 71; Chudacoff and Smith, *Evolution of American Urban Society*, p. 91; Leroy Ostransky, *Jazz City: The Impact of our Cities on the Development of Jazz*, (Englewood Cliffs: Prentice-Hall, 1978) pp. 18–19, 27–28, 33–39, 44, 59, 74–75, 79, 136.

18. Author's interviews with Eubie Blake, Brooklyn, N.Y., Nov. 15, 1971, and with Willie "the Lion" Smith, New Brunswick, N.J., Nov. 8, 1971; Frank Tirro, *Jazz: A History* (New York: Norton, 1977) pp. 88–113. The story of piano ragtime is a separate area covered in Rudi Blesh and Harriet Janis, *They All Played Ragtime*, (New York: Oak Publications, 1971), William J. Schafer and Johannes Riedel, *The Art of Ragtime*, (Baton Rouge: Louisiana State University Press, 1973).

19. William J. Schafer, *Brass Bands and New Orleans Jazz*, pp. 7, 49, 106–124. Schafer's treatment is an excellent addition and revision to New Orleans jazz historiography, which goes back to Fredric Ramsey, Jr., and Charles E. Smith, eds. *Jazzmen*, (New York: Harcourt, Brace, 1939). Samuel B. Charters, *Jazz: New Orleans, 1885–1957*, rev. ed. (New York: Oak Publications, 1963) is a key resource for information on individuals, bands, and locations. Leroy Ostransky, *Jazz City*, pp. 2–59, connects the city with the music. Nat Shapiro and Nat Hentoff, *Hear Me Talkin' To Ya*, (New York: Rinehart and Co., 1955) pp. 3–62 contains some musicians' memories of the time and place.

20. William J. Schafer, *Brass Bands and New Orleans Jazz*, p. 49.

21. Joseph Robichaux with Tony Standish, "Joseph Robichaux—Those Early Days," *Jazz Journal* 12, 4 (April 1959) p. 11.

22. Sam Charters, *Jazz: New Orleans*, pp. 17–57; Leroy Ostransky, *Jazz City*, pp. 50–63, Alan Lomax, *Mr. Jelly Lord*, (New York: Grove Press, 1950) pp. 46–

50, 56–69, 76–85; Jack V. Buerkle and Danny Baker, *Bourbon Street Black*, (New York: Oxford University Press, 1973) pp. 2–24.

23. Allan H. Spear, *Black Chicago: The Making of a Negro Ghetto, 1890–1920*, (Chicago: University of Chicago Press, 1967) p. 12; Drake and Cayton, *Black Metropolis*, pp. 9–18, 51; Goldfield and Brownell, *Urban America*, pp. 222–223.

24. Unlike many earlier black newspapers, Robert Abbott's *Chicago Defender* was not essentially a political or a religious voice. Instead, it was modeled on the new mass newspapers of Hearst and Pulitzer with an emphasis on sports, entertainment, and other parts of daily life, so that it provides a strong picture of the development of the black entertainment world in Chicago after 1909. In fact, the paper's entertainment pages became a national black entertainment trade paper, giving information on and notices of job opportunities for the black entertainment world around the United States. As such it is a major source for this book.

25. Drake and Cayton, *Black Metropolis*, pp. 516–525, 710–715, particularly the charts on p. 525 and 711, sketch out this structure. By the 1930s, 5 percent of black Chicago was upper class, 30 percent middle class, and 65 percent lower class. The shadies made up about 10 percent of the upper class, more than 20 percent of the middle class, and a much larger portion of the lower class. The extended discussion on pp. 516–715 develops the interaction of these groups and the importance of decorum and "front." Michael W. Harris, *The Rise of Gospel Blues*, pp. 52–62, 93–110, describes the impact of this conflict of both the musical and religious communities and analyzes its impact in detail.

26. Drake and Cayton, *Black Metropolis*, p. 710.

27. Thomas J. Hennessey, Chicago's Black Establishment," *Journal of Jazz Studies* 2, 1 (Dec. 1974) pp. 15–45; John Lax, "Chicago's Black Jazz Musicians in the Twenties: Portrait of an Era," *Journal of Jazz Studies* 1, 2 (June, 1974) pp. 116–118; Chadwick C. Hansen, "Social Influences on Jazz Style: Chicago, 1920–30," *American Quarterly* 12, 4 (Winter, 1960) pp. 493–497.

28. *Chicago Defender*, July 2, 1910, p. 3; Oct. 1, 1910, p. 4; Nov. 5, 1910, p. 6; Nov. 19, 1910, p. 2; Nov. 26, 1910, pp. 2, 3; Dec. 3, 1910, p. 2; Dec. 31, 1910, p. 1; Jan. 7, 1911, pp. 1, 2, 5, 6; Sept. 9, 1911, p. 2; Jan. 6, 1912, p. 1; Oct. 11, 1913, p. 6.

29. *Chicago Defender*, Aug. 6, 1910, p. 3; Jan. 7, 1911, p. 5; Feb. 4, 1911, p. 4; Allen Spear, *Black Chicago*, pp. 30–33; Alan Lomax, *Mr. Jelly Lord* pp. 63–65, 72-73.

30. *Chicago Defender*, Aug. 13, 1910, p. 1; George E. Dulf, interviewed by Louise Henry, "A History of Local 208 American Federation of Musicians," Illinois W.P.A. Writers' Files, Chicago Public Library; F.H. Robb, ed., *The Intercollegian*, (Chicago, 1927) p. 180; Clark Halker, "A History of Local 208 and the Struggle for Racial Equality in the American Federation of Musicians," *Black Music Research Journal* 8, 2 (Fall, 1988) pp. 207–211.

31. *Chicago Defender*, July 22, 1911, p. 3, July 2, 1910, p. 8; Aug. 6, 1910, p. 3;

Nov. 5, 1910, p. 6; Dec. 10, 1910, p. 2; Jan. 4, 1911, p. 4; March 4, 1911, p. 4; March 11, 1911, p. 3; May 4, 1911, p. 3; May 11, 1911, p. 3; June 3, 1911, p. 3; June 10, 1911, p. 3; June 17, 1911, p. 3; July 8, 1911, p. 5; April 13, 1912, p. 3; Nov. 2, 1912, p. 5; Nov. 23, 1912, p. 6; A good early biography of Dave Peyton is given Jan. 29, 1916, p. 6; Dempsey J. Travis, *An Autobiography of Black Jazz* (Chicago: Urban Research Institute, 1983) pp. 11–15, 25–30; John Chilton, *Who's Who of Jazz*, (Philadelphia: Chilton Book Co., 1972) pp. 116, 287–288, 370, 371; Allan Spear, *Black Chicago*, p. 76; Paul Oliver, *The Story of the Blues*, pp. 73–74.

32. *Chicago Defender*, Nov. 7, 1914, p. 6; Nov. 28, 1914, p. 6; Dec. 5, 1914, p. 6; Jan. 23, 1915, p. 6.

33. *Chicago Defender*, Aug. 6, 1910, p. 3; Oct. 1, 1910, p. 4; Nov. 19, 1910, p. 2; Feb. 25, 1911, p. 6; March 4, 1911, p. 3; Aug. 12, 1911, p. 4; July 7, 1912, p. 2; John Steiner, "Chicago," in Nat Hentoff and Albert J. McCarthy, eds. *Jazz* (New York: Rinehart, 1959) pp. 140–142; Lucille Hegamin and Leonard Kunstadt, "The Lucille Hegamin Story," *Record Research* 39 (Nov. 1961) pp. 1–4; Paul Oliver, *The Story of the Blues*, pp 76–84.

34. *Chicago Defender*, Aug. 6, 1910, p. 3; Oct. 1, 1910, p. 2, Nov. 19, 1910, p. 2; Nov. 26, 1910, pp. 2, 3; Jan. 7, 1911, p. 2; Sept. 9, 1911, p. 2; Oct. 11, 1911, p. 6; Oct. 28, 1911, p. 6; Oct. 25, 1911, p. 6.

35. Allon Schoener, ed., *Harlem On My Mind* (New York: Random House, 1968) p. 11; Jervis Anderson, *Harlem: The Great Black Way* (London: Orbis, 1982) pp. 3–48; Morroe Berger, Edward Berger, and James Patrick, *Benny Carter: A Life In American Music,* (Metuchen, N. J.: Scarecrow Press, 1982) pp. 18, 32–33; Gilbert Osofsky, *Harlem: The Making of a Ghetto* (New York: Harper and Row, 1968) pp. 3–123; Leroy Ostransky, *Jazz City* p. 192.

36. Chudacoff and Smith, *Evolution of American Urban Society*, p. 110. For a discussion of southern regional blues styles and migration patterns see Paul Oliver, *Story of the Blues*, pp. 18, 46, 125–134

37. Eileen Southern, *The Music of Black Americans* (New York: Norton, 1971) pp. 294–304; Anderson *Harlem*, pp. 30–41; Tom Riis, *Just Before Jazz*, pp. 33–141. Riis provides copies of sheet music of many of these songs on pp. 234–302.

38. Samuel Charters and Leonard Kunstadt, *Jazz: A History of the New York Scene* (New York: Doubleday, 1962) p. 26.

39. R. Reid Badger, "James Reese Europe and the Prehistory of Jazz," *American Music* (Spring, 1989) pp. 48–67; Charters and Kunstadt, *Jazz: New York*, pp. 23–41, 51; Albert J. McCarthy, *Big Band Jazz*, (New York: G. P. Putnam's Sons, 1974) pp. 10–11; Tom Riis, *Just Before Jazz*, pp. 59, 131, 135, 137.

40. James Reese Europe, "A Negro Explains Jazz," *Literary Digest*, April 26, 1919, p. 28.

41. Ron Welburn, "James Reese Europe and the Infancy of Jazz Criticism," *Black Music Research Journal*, 7 (1987) pp. 35–44.

42. Author's interview with Eubie Blake, Brooklyn, N.Y., Nov. 15, 1971.

43. Frank Tirro, *Jazz: A History*, pp. 111–113; Tom Davin, "Conversation with James P. Johnson," in Martin Williams, *Jazz Panorama* (New York: Collier, 1964) pp. 45–54.

Chapter 2

1. Florette Henri, *Black Migration: Movement North, 1900–1920* (New York, Doubleday, 1975) pp. 49–80; Goldfield and Brownell, *Urban America*, pp. 222–223.
2. Paul Oliver, *The Meaning of the Blues* (New York: Collier, 1960) pp. 24, 27, 36–37, 51–59, 63, 75, 79, 82–89, 185, 205–207, 234, 337–338; Gilbert Osofsky, *Harlem: The Making of a Ghetto*, p. 30; Allan Spear, *Black Chicago*, p. 13.
3. Florette Henri, Black Migration, pp. 18–22; Chicago Commission on Race Relations, *The Negro In Chicago: A Study of Race Relations and a Race Riot* (Chicago: University of Chicago Press, 1922) pp. 80–84; Robert A. Divine et al., *America Past and Present*, 3d ed., (New York: Harper Collins, 1991) pp. 488, 589; John Hope Franklin, *From Slavery to Freedom*, pp. 235–238.
4. Florette Henri, *Black Migration*, pp. 11–18, 32–58; Chicago Commission, *The Negro In Chicago*, pp. 84–103; Charles Edward Smith, booklet to *History of Classic Jazz* (Riverside RB-005) p. 7; John Hope Franklin, *From Slavery to Freedom*, pp. 235–238, 279–282, 305–306; Gary Nash et al., *The American People: Creating a Nation and a Society*, (New York: Harper and Row, 1990) pp. 778–779.
5. Florette Henri, *Black Migration*, pp. 58–60, 62–66, 67; Chicago Commission, *The Negro In Chicago*, pp. 86–92.
6. For TOBA see note 15, chapter 1. Lawrence Gushee, "How the Creole Band Came to Be," *Black Music Research Journal*, 8, 1 (1988) pp. 97–100; Tom Riis, *Just Before Jazz*, pp. 24–28, 167–171; Robert Sklar, *Movie-Made America*, (New York: Random House, 1975) pp. 12–18, 30–32, 40–47.
7. Kathy Peiss, *Cheap Amusements: Working Women and Leisure in Turn-of-the-Century New York*, (Philadelphia: Temple University Press, 1986) pp. 88–114 describe the development of social dancing in the urban working class. Lewis A. Erenberg, *Steppin' Out: New York Nightlife and the Transformation of American Culture, 1890–1930*, (Westport, Conn: Greenwood Press, 1981) pp. 146–175 cover the rise of middle class cabaret culture. Kathy J. Ogren, *The Jazz Revolution: Twenties America and the Meaning of Jazz*, (New York, Oxford University Press, 1989) pp. 78–80.
8. Maria W. Lambin and Leroy S. Bowman, "Evidences of Social Relations as seen in Types of New York City Dance Halls," *Journal of Social Forces* 3 (1924–1925) p. 289.
9. Ibid.
10. Ibid., p. 290.
11. Ibid.

12. Ibid.
13. Kathy J. Ogren, *The Jazz Revolution*, pp. 37, 57, 79.
14. Charters and Kunstadt, *Jazz: New York*, pp. 33–41; Marshall Stearns and Jean Stearns, *Jazz Dance*, (New York: Macmillan, 1968) pp. 96–98; Frank Tirro, *Jazz: A History*, pp. 60–61; *Chicago Defender*, Feb. 23, 1918, p. 4; Vernon and Irene Castle, *Modern Dancing*, (New York: World Syndicate Co,. 1914); Lewis Erenberg, *Stepping Out*, pp. 146-175.
15. Charters and Kunstadt, *Jazz: New York*, pp. 33–41; Albert J. McCarthy, *Big Band Jazz*, (New York: G.P. Putnam's Son's, 1974) pp. 10–11; R. Reid Badger, "James Reese Europe," pp. 49–55; Kathy Ogren, *The Jazz Revolution*, p. 79; *Chicago Defender*, Feb. 23, 1918, p. 4.
16. *Chicago Defender*, Feb. 23, 1918, p. 4.
17. Frank Driggs and Thornton Hagert, "Jerome Don Pasqual," part 1, *Jazz Journal* 17, 5 (May, 1964) p. 24.
18. Walter C. Allen, "Freddie Keppard, Jazz Giant," Freddie Keppard file, Institute of Jazz Studies, Rutgers; James L. Collier, *The Making of Jazz*, (Boston: Houghton Mifflin, 1978) p. 72.
19. Frank Tirro, *Jazz: A History*, pp. 171–174; Brian Priestly, *Jazz On Record: A History* (New York: Billboard Books, 1991) pp. 1–10; John Steiner, booklet to *The Sound of Chicago* (Columbia, C3L32) p. 15.
20. Walker C. Allen, *Hendersonia: The Music of Fletcher Henderson and his Musicians*, (Highland Park, N.J.: Walter C. Allen, 1973) pp. 7–8; Charters and Kunstadt, *Jazz: New York*, pp. 83, 86, 102; Robert M. W. Dixon and John Goodrich, *Recording the Blues*, (London: Studio Vista, 1970) pp. 6–19; *Chicago Defender*, May 10, 1919, pp. 9, 14, 15; Brian Rust, *Jazz Records, 1897–1942*, (New Rochelle: Arlington House, 1978) pp. 378–380, 512–513, 1515–1518; Brian Priestly, *Jazz On Record*, pp. 10–23; Roland Gelatt, *The Fabulous Phonograph*, (Philadelphia: Lippencott, 1955).
21. Frank Tirro, *Jazz: A History*, pp. 175–179; Gunther Schuller, *Early Jazz* (New York: Oxford University Press, 1968) pp. 180–187.; Charters and Kunstadt, *Jazz: New York*, pp. 121–126
22. Lawrence Gushee, "How the Creole Band Came To Be," pp. 97–100; Lawrence Gushee, "New Orleans-Area Musicians on the West Coast, 1908 1925," *Black Music Research Journal* pp. 1–17; Richard Wang, "Researching the New Orleans-Chicago Jazz Connection: Tools and Methods," *Black Music Research Journal* pp. 101–111.
23. James L. Collier, *The Making of Jazz*, p. 79; Leroy Ostransky, *Jazz City*, pp. 1, 33–39, 58–59; Charles Edward Smith, booklet to *History of Classic Jazz* (Riverside RB-005), p. 7.
24. Samuel Charters, *Jazz New Orleans*, pp. 7–9, 26, 33, 36, 46–48; Leroy Ostransky, *Jazz City*, pp. 62–63. The work of Wang and Gushee referred to above has emphasized the earlier period of the New Orleans migration.
25. Samuel Charters, *Jazz New Orleans*, pp. 18–109 give the overall picture of this period, specific biographies that illustrate these points include pp. 7, 23–24, 27, 28, 33, 34, 36, 39, 42, 43–51, 61, 93–95.

26. Goldfield and Browness, *Urban America*, pp. 222–223; Allan Spear, *Black Chicago*, pp. 138–146.

27. *Chicago Defender*, Jan. 9, 1915, p. 6; Jan. 17, 1917, p. 6; April 7, 1917, p. 6; Feb. 22, 1919, p. 16; April 12, 1919, p. 8; May 10, 1919, p. 17; Tom Hennessey, "Chicago's Black Establishment," *Journal of Jazz Studies*, 2, 1 (Dec, 1974) pp.23, 26; Louise Henry, "History of Negro Music and Negro Musicians," Dr. Robert A. Giles file, (WPA files) on the Negro in Illinois, Chicago Public Library; Edward Joseph interview with Louella Joseph, Louella Joseph file, WPA files.

28. *Chicago Defender*, Feb. 6, 1915, p. 6.

29. Lawrence Gushee, "How the Creole Band," pp. 97–100.

30. *Chicago Defender*, Aug. 1, 1914, p. 6; Aug. 17, 1914, p. 6; Aug., 29, 1914, p. 6; Sept. 5, 1914, p. 6; John Steiner, "Chicago," pp. 140–147.

31. *Chicago Defender*, Feb. 9, 1918, p. 9; March 9, 1918, p. 9; March 18, 1918, p. 6; March 30, 1918, p. 8; April 27, 1918, p. 6; July 27, 1918, p. 7; Nov. 2, 1918, p. 6; Nov. 9, 1918, p. 6; Samuel Charters, *Jazz New Orleans*, pp. 25, 27.

32. *Chicago Defender*, March 18, 1918, p. 1; April 6, 1918, p. 16; Samuel Charters, *Jazz New Orleans*, pp. 25, 27; Lawrence Gushee, "New Orleans Area Musicians on the West Coast, 1908–1925," pp. 3, 14, 15.

33. *Chicago Defender*, May 10, 1918, p. 8; June 1, 1918, p. 4; May 14, 1927, p. 8; Tom Hennessey, "Chicago's Black Establishment," p. 31.

34. Edmond Souchon, "King Oliver: A Very Personal Memoir," in Martin Williams, ed., *Jazz Panorama*, pp. 28–29.

35. Warren "Baby" Dodds with Larry Gara, "The Baby Dodds Story," part 3, *Jazz Journal* 8,7 (July, 1955) p. 8.

36. James L. Collier, *Louis Armstrong*, pp. 98–99.

37. For an idea of the importance of this compare any Oliver recording with the compact disc reissue Johnny Dodds, *Blue Clarinet Stomp* (BMG 2293-2-RB) which clearly shows the impact of Johnson's string bass in a ensemble.

38. James L. Collier, *Louis Armstrong*, pp. 100–109; Gunther Schuller, *Early Jazz*, (New York: Oxford University Press, 1968) pp. 77–88; Lawrence Gushee, "King Oliver" in Martin Williams, *Jazz Panorama*, pp. 39–43; Lawrence Gushee, "King Oliver," in *New Grove Dictionary of Jazz*.

39. Nat Shapiro and Nat Hentoff, *Hear Me Talkin' To Ya*, pp. 97, 192; Jimmy Rushing with Frank Driggs, "Jimmy Rushing's Story,"*Evergreen Review* (April, 1966) pp. 66.

40. James L. Collier, *The Making of Jazz*, pp. 123–131; Frank Tirro, *Jazz: A History*, pp. 201–206; Gunther Schuller, *Early Jazz*, pp. 186–194; Nat Shapiro and Nat Hentoff, *Hear Me Talkin' To Ya*, pp. 115–121, 124–135; Richard Hadlock, *Jazz Masters of the Twenties*, pp. 76–105.

41. Tom Hennessey, "Chicago's Black Establishment," *Journal of Jazz Studies* 2, 1 (Dec. 1974) pp. 31–35; *Chicago Defender*, Dec. 16, 1922, p. 2; Brian Rust, *Jazz Records, 1897–1942*, pp. 337, 1529, 1614.

42. David A. Goldfield and Blaine A. Brownell, *Urban America*, pp. 222–223; Jervis Anderson, *Harlem: The Great Black Way*, pp. 49–71, 204–231.

43. *Chicago Defender*, March 7, 1914, p. 6.

44. Samuel Charters and Leonard Kunstadt, *Jazz: New York*, pp. 32–40; Albert J. McCarthy, *Big Band Jazz*, p. 12; J. Reid Badger, "James Reese Europe," pp. 51–56; Brian Rust, *Jazz Records, 1897-1942*, p. 512. Six Brown Brothers and Jim Europe's bands are both on *Steppin' On The Gas* (NW 269). Europe's version of "Down Home Rag" is on *Jazz: Some Beginnings*, Folkways Records (RF 31).

45. Samuel Charters and Leonard Kunstadt, *Jazz: New York*, p. 54; Leonard Kunstadt, "Ford Dabney Discography," *Record Research* 2 (April, 1955) pp. 5–7; Brian Rust, *Jazz Records, 1897–1942*, pp. 378–380; Albert J. McCarthy, *Big Band Jazz*, pp. 12–13.

46. Samuel Charters and Leonard Kunstadt, *Jazz: New York*, pp. 64–74, 110–111; R. Reid Badger, "James Reese Europe," *American Music* (Spring, 1989) pp. 58–67; Albert J. McCarthy, *Big Band Jazz*, p. 12; Brian Rust, *Jazz Records*, pp. 512–513; *Chicago Defender*, May 10, 1919, p. 15; May 17, 1919, p. 1, a detailed obituary; May 24, 1919, p. 17; June 14, 1919, p. 1.

47. Nat Hentoff, "Jazz in the Twenties: Garvin Bushell" in Martin Williams ed., *Jazz Panorama*, pp. 72–73; Samuel Charters and Leonard Kunstadt, *Jazz: New York*, pp. 73–75; Tom Riis, *Just Before Jazz*, pp. 40–43, 143–144; Albert J. McCarthy, *Big Band Jazz*, pp. 12–13; *Chicago Defender*, Sept. 28, 1918, p. 6; Nov. 2, 1918, p. 5; June 7, 1919, p. 6; Dec. 20, 1919, p. 8; Dec. 27, 1919, p. 3; Jan. 3, 1920, pp. 2, 3; March 20, 1920, p. 6.

48. W. C. Handy, *Father of the Blues*, pp. 96–117, 122–136, 171–177, 186–203; *Chicago Defender*, Dec. 30, 1916, p. 6; Feb. 22, 1919, p. 14; May 10, 1919, pp. 9, 15; July 7, 1919, p. 9; Dec. 27, 1919, p. 8; March 6, 1920, p. 8; May 15, 1920, p. 7; For information on blues compositions see the following: Jan. 3, 1920, p. 7; Jan. 10, 1920, p. 7; Jan. 17, 1920, p. 6; Jan. 31, 1920, p. 7; Feb. 7, 1920, p. 9; Feb. 21, 1920, p. 6, 7; Feb. 28, 1920, p. 8.

49. Samuel Charters and Leonard Kunstadt, *Jazz: New York*, pp. 56–61, 109–118; Author's interview with Eubie Blake; James Weldon Johnson, *Black Manhattan*, New ed., (New York: Atheneum, 1969) pp. 186–189; Eileen Southern, *The Music of Black Americans*, pp. 436–440; Roger D. Kinkle, *The Complete Encyclopedia of Popular Music and Jazz, 1900–1950*, (New Rochelle: Arlington House, 1974) p. 121.

50. Samuel Charters and Leonard Kunstadt, *Jazz: New York*, pp. 56–61; James L. Collier, *The Making of Jazz*, pp. 72–75; Frank Tirro, *Jazz: A History*, pp. 167–169, 175–179; Gunther Schuller, *Early Jazz*, pp. 175–182; Garvin Bushell with Mark Tucker, *Jazz From the Beginning*, p. 18; Brian Rust, *Jazz Records, 1897–1942*, pp 1175–1177. For a detailed but not critical biography of the band see H. O. Brunn, *The Story of the Original Dixieland Jazz Band*, (Baton Rouge: Louisiana State University Press, 1960).

51. Walter C. Allen, "Freddie Keppard, Jazz Giant," Freddie Keppard file, I.J.S.;

James L. Collier, *The Making of Jazz*, p. 72; Gunther Schuller, *Early Jazz*, pp. 175–177, 179–182.

52. Brian Rust, *Jazz Records*, pp. 1515–1518; Samuel Charters and Leonard Kunstadt, *Jazz: New York*, p. 81; Unsigned, undated clippings, Wilber Sweatman file, I.J.S.; Albert J. McCarthy, *Big Band Jazz*, pp. 13–14.

53. Frank Tirro, *Jazz: A History*, pp. 177, 179; Gunther Schuller, *Early Jazz*, pp. 182–186; James L. Collier, *The Making of Jazz*, p. 125.

54. Gunther Schuller, *Early Jazz*, pp. 69–70; Brian Rust, *Jazz Records*, pp. 748, 1680; Brian Priestly, *Jazz On Record*, p. 23.

55. Perry Bradford, *Born With The Blues*, (New York: Oak Publications, 1965) has the fullest treatment of this. Samuel Charters and Leonard Kunstadt, *Jazz: New York*, pp. 62–108; are more concise, and George Hoefer, booklet of notes for *The Sound of Harlem*, Columbia Records (C3L 33) pp. 7–10 even more so. *Chicago Defender*, March 13, 1920, p. 6; July 31, 1920, p. 4, show her Feb. side, "That Thing Called Love" got attention in the black community as well.

56. Garvin Bushell with Mark Tucker, *Jazz From The Beginning*, pp. 17–20; George Hoefer, booklet for *Sound of Harlem*, pp. 9–13, 23–31; Frank Tirro, *Jazz: A History*, p. 160; Gunther Schuller, *Early Jazz*, pp. 214–222; Walter C. Allen, *Hendersonia*, pp. 12–14, 24–26; Leonard Kunstadt, letter to *Jazz Journal* 6, 8 (Aug., 1953) p. 25; Marshall Stearns draft article and questionnaire on June Clark, June Clark file, I.J.S.; Rex Stewart, "Coleman Hawkins," *Downbeat* May 19, 1966 p. 23; George Hoefer, notes on Coleman Hawkins, Coleman Hawkins file, I.J.S.; Lucille Hegamin and Leonard Kunstadt, "The Lucille Hegamin Story," *Record Research* 39 (Nov., 1961) pp. 5–7; Mike Lipskin and Leonard Kunstadt, "This Is William D. Gant," *Record Research* 30 (Oct., 1960) p. 3; Brian Rust, *Jazz Records*, pp. 357, 1008, 1617–1618, 1698–1699.

57. Brian Priestly, *Jazz On Record*, p. 21.; George "Pops" Foster with Tom Stoddard, *Pops Foster, The Autobiography of a New Orleans Jazzman*, (Berkley: University of California Press, 1971) pp. 6, 98, 100–101, 118, 126; *Chicago Defender*, May 12, 1917, p. 6; Dec. 7, 1918, p. 6; Jan. 3, 1920, p. 7; Jan. 10, 1920, p. 7; Jan. 31, 1920, p. 7; Feb. 14, 1920, p. 9; Feb. 21, 1920, p. 6; March 27, 1920, p. 5; April 24, 1920, p. 7; May 1, 1920, p. 7; Samuel Charters, *Jazz New Orleans*, p. 51; Brian Rust, *Jazz Records*, pp. 1009–1014; 1531–1535, 1698–1709.

58. Walter C. Allen, *Hendersonia*, pp. 1–75; Samuel Charters and Leonard Kunstadt, *Jazz: New York*, pp. 166–172; Albert J. McCarthy, *Big Band Jazz*, p. 64; James Collier, *The Making of Jazz*, p. 178; Gunther Schuller, *Early Jazz*, pp. 244, 251–256.

Chapter 3

1. Author's interviews with Eubie Blake and Willie "the Lion" Smith; Mark Tucker, *Ellington: The Early Years* (Urbana: University of Illinois Press, 1991) pp. 28–34; Stanley Dance, *The World of Swing*, (New York: DaCapo, 1979)

pp. 31–32, 46–49; Count Basie with Murray, *Good Morning Blues*, pp. 36–48. Tom Davin, "Conversation with James P. Johnson," in Martin Williams, *Jazz Panorama*, pp. 54–56, 59; Frank Tirro, *Jazz: A History*, p.112; *Chicago Defender*, Feb. 5, 1916, p. 2; Sept. 7, 1918, p. 5; May 17, 1919, p. 3; June 14, 1919, p. 18; Oct. 4, 1919, p. 3; Feb. 14, 1920, p. 5; May 29, 1920, p. 7; July 15, 1922, p. 7; Russ Shor, "Charlie Gaines," *Storyville* (Dec. 76–Jan. 77) pp. 45–46; George Hoefer, "Jimmie Harrison, Forgotten Giant," *Jazz* 2, 5 (June, 1963) p. 8; John Bentley and Ralph W. Miller, "West Coast Jazz in the Twenties," *Jazz Monthly* 7, 3 (May, 1961) pp. 4–5.

2. *Chicago Defender*, Oct. 18, 1913, p. 6; Nov. 22, 1913, p. 6; Jan. 2, 1915, p. 6; Mark Tucker, *Ellington: The Early Years*, pp. 11–15.

3. Tom Riis, *Just Before Jazz*, pp. 24–28, 141–149; Mark Tucker, *Ellington: The Early Years*, p. 12; *Chicago Defender*, Dec. 5, 1914, p. 6; Oct. 2, 1915, p. 6; Sept. 16, 1916, p. 6; June 2, 1917, p. 6; Sept. 8, 1917, pp. 6, 7; Oct. 6, 1917, p. 6; April 20, 1918, p. 5; Sept. 28, 1918, p. 7; March 6, 1920, p. 8; April 3, 1920, p 6; May 29, 1920, p. 7; Bruce King, "Albert Nicholas: Artist in Exile,"Albert Nicholas file, I.J.S.

4. Edward K. "Duke" Ellington, "Jazz As I Have Seen It" part 4, *Swing*, (June, 1940) pp. 10, 22; Mark Tucker, *Ellington: The Early Years*, pp. 47–75; Barry Ulanov, *Duke Ellington* (New York: Creative Age Press, 1946) pp. 1–25; Stanley Dance, *The World of Duke Ellington*, (New York: Scribner's 1970) pp. 55–56, 62–63; Charters and Kunstadt, *Jazz: New York*, p. 210; James Collier, *Duke Ellington* (New York: Oxford University Press, 1987) pp. 4–30.

5. Russ Shor, "Charlie Gaines," pp. 45–46; *Chicago Defender*, Sept. 20, 1919, p. 9; Feb. 14, 1920, p. 9; May 29, 1920, p. 7; June 26, 1920, p. 6; Aug. 7, 1920, p. 4; Aug. 21, 1920, p. 4; Jan. 22, 1921 p. 1.

6. Samuel Charters, *Jazz: New Orleans*, pp. 18–109; Nat Shapiro and Nat Hentoff, *Hear Me Talkin' To Ya*, pp. 55–61; "Pops" Foster with Tom Stoddard, *The Autobiography of a New Orleans Jazzman*, pp. 105–113, 119.

7. W. C. Handy, *Father of the Blues*, pp. 94–98, 100–111, 178–185, Nat Shapiro and Nat Hentoff, *Hear Me Talkin' To Ya*, pp. 15–17, Stanley R. "Fess" Williams with Harrison Smith, "The Fess Williams Story," *Record Research*, 15 (Oct.–Nov., 1958) pp. 1–3; *Chicago Defender*, Aug. 12, 1916, p. 6; Sept. 15, 1917, p. 6; Oct. 20, 1917, p. 4; May 15, 1920, p. 7.

8. W. C. Handy, *Father of the Blues*, pp. 178–185; Nat Shapiro and Nat Hentoff, *Hear Me Talkin' To Ya*, pp. 75–77; *Chicago Defender*, Feb. 22, 1919, p. 14; April 19, 1919, p. 8; May 20, 1919, p. 9; Sept. 1, 1917, p. 6; May 10, 1919, p. 8; John Chilton, *Who's Who of Jazz*, pp. 8, 13, 371.

9. Dickie Wells with Stanley Dance, *The Night People*, (Boston: Crescendo Publishing, 1971) p. 8.

10. Dickie Wells with Stanley Dance, *Night People*, pp. 5, 3.

11. *Chicago Defender*, Oct. 20, 1917, p. 5; Stanley R. Williams with Harrison Smith, "Fess Williams Story," pp. 4–5.

12. W. C. Handy, *Father of the Blues*, p. 65; *Chicago Defender*, Feb. 11, 1911, p. 1; July 12, 1913, p. 5; Jan. 19, 1918, p. 3; May 22, 1920, p. 10; Milt Hinton and David G. Berger, *Bass Line: The Stories and Photographs of Milt Hinton*, (Philadelphia: Temple University Press, 1988) pp. 22–24, 31–32.

13. Albert J. McCarthy, *Big Band Jazz*, p. 88.

14. John Chilton, *A Jazz Nursery: The Story of the Jenkins' Orphanage Jazz Bands*, pp. 13–59; *Chicago Defender*, May 22, 1920, p. 7; John Chilton, *Who's Who of Jazz*, pp. 1, 26; Garvin Bushell with Mark Tucker, *Jazz From The Beginning* pp. 17–20, 33; Nat Hentoff, "Jazz in the Twenties: Garvin Bushell" in Martin Williams, *Jazz Panorama*, p. 77; Brian Rust, *Jazz Records*, pp. 164, 187, 645, 810, 940, 1008, 1306, 1576, 1649, 1692, 1727.

15. Athelia Knight, "In Retrospect, Sherman H. Dudley," *The Black Perspective In Music*, 15, 2 (Spring, 1987) pp. 153–181; *Chicago Defender*, Sept. 15, 1917, p. 6; Jan. 29, 1921, p. 5; Feb. 12, 1921, p. 5.

16. Paul Oliver, *The Story of the Blues*, pp. 17–35, 42–57.

17. Emerson "Geechie" Harper with Bertrand DeMeusy, "Leroy Smith and his Band," *Jazz Monthly*, 170 p. 5.

18. *Chicago Defender*, June 1, 1918, p. 4; Emerson Harper with Bertrand De-Meusy, "Leroy Smith and His Band," pp. 5–6; Albert J. McCarthy, *Big Band Jazz*, pp. 53.

19. Emerson Harper with Bertrand DeMeusy, "Leroy Smith and His Band," p. 7.

20. Ibid.; Albert J. McCarthy, *Big Band Jazz*, p. 53; Brian Rust, *Jazz Records*, p. 1459. I have not heard Leroy Smith's 1921 records that might answer this question.

21. Ralph Gulliver, "The Band From Columbus: Sammy Stewart and His Orchestra," *Storyville* 48 (Aug.–Sept., 1973) pp. 213–217. *Chicago Defender*, May 8, 1920, p. 7; This is, of course, not the Charlie Parker of bop fame, and apparently no relation at all.

22. Duncan Scheidt, *The Jazz State of Indiana*, (Pittsboro, Indiana: Duncan Sheidt, 1977) pp. 3–16, 26.

23. *Chicago Defender*, April 25, 1919, p. 3; May 17, 1919, p. 3; Aug. 2, 1919, p. 13; Sept. 6, 1919, p. 10; Ralph Gulliver, "The Band From Columbus," pp. 214–216; Onah L. Spencer and Amy Lee, "The Purest Trumpet Tone of All," *Downbeat* (Aug. 1, 1943), p. 13; Bernard Houghton, "Joe Smith: A Biography and Appreciation," *Jazz Journal* 18, 12 (Dec., 1965) p. 18; George Hoefer, "Jimmy Harrison" *Jazz* 2, 5 (June, 1963) pp. 8–9.

24. George W. Kay, "The Springfield Story" in McKinney's Cotton Pickers file I.J.S. ; Todd Rhodes with Thurman and Mary Grove, "Todd Rhodes—Then and Now," *Jazz Journal* 6, 2 (Feb., 1953) pp. 18–20; H. B. M. "Everybody Loves Cecil," in Art Hodes and Chadwick Hansen, eds. *Selections From the Gutter* (Berkley: University of California Press, 1977) p. 215; Richard Congdon, "Great Scott," *Record Changer* (Sept., 1953) pp. 6–7; Thurman and Mary Grove, "Cecil Scott and His Bright Boys," *Jazz Journal* 6, 12 (Dec., 1953) pp. 29–30; Claude Jones with David Ives, "Claude Jones," *Jazz Journal* 15,

6 (June, 1962) pp. 13–14; Claude Jones with John E. Mann, "Claude Jones, Fragment of an Autobiography," *Jazz Monthly* 8,1 (March, 1962) pp. 3–4.

25. Claude Jones with John E. Mann, "Fragment of an Autobiography," pp. 3–4.

26. Ibid.; George W. Kay, "The Springfield Story," McKinney's Cotton Pickers file I.J.S.; Todd Rhodes with Thurman Grove and Mary Grove, "Todd Rhodes," *Jazz Journal* 6, 12 (Dec., 1953) p. 19; Thurman and Mary Grove, "Cecil Scott and His Bright Boys," *Jazz Journal* 6, 12 (Dec., 1953) pp. 29–30; Claude Jones with David Ives, "Claude Jones," *Jazz Journal* 15, 6 (June, 1962) pp. 13–14; Albert J. McCarthy, *Big Band Jazz*, pp. 43–45, 75–79.

27. Preston Love, "Chords and Dischords," *Sounds and Fury* 1,1 (July–Aug., 1965) p. 28.

28. W. C. Handy, *Father of the Blues*, pp 63–67; Brian Rust, *Jazz Records*, p. 1515; Albert J. McCarthy, *Big Band Jazz*, p. 13.

29. *Chicago Defender*, July 15, 1916, p. 6; July 22, 1916, p. 6; Nov. 11, 1916, p. 6 Nov, 18, 1916, p. 6; Feb. 11, 1917, p. 6; March 23, 1918, p. 6; Frank Driggs, "Red Perkins and His Dixie Ramblers," *Jazz Journal* 17, 11 (Nov. 1964) p. 15.

30. *Chicago Defender*. June 17, 1916, p. 4; July 15, 1916, p. 6; March 17, 1917, p. 2; June 2, 1917, p. 6; Aug. 8, 1917, p. 1.

31. *Chicago Defender*, Dec. 5. 1914, p. 6; Sept. 10, 1921, p. 8; Frank Driggs, "Red Perkins and His Dixie Ramblers," *Jazz Journal* 17, 11 (Nov., 1964) pp. 14–16.

32. Frank Driggs, "Red Perkins and His Dixie Ramblers," p. 14–16; Albert J. McCarthy, *Big Band Jazz*, p. 126.

33. *Chicago Defender*, May 12, 1917, p. 6; March 30, 1918, p. 7; May 11, 1918, p. 5; Nov. 23, 1918, p. 7; Sept. 6, 1919, p. 9; Oct. 4, 1919, p. 9; Nov. 1, 1919, p. 8; March 20, 1920, p. 6; Aug. 14, 1920, p. 4; Aug. 19, 1922, p. 7; Leonard Kunstadt, Mike Montgomery, John Baker, and Jimmy Dudley, "Everett 'Happy' Robbins," *Record Research* 61 (July, 1964) pp. 15–16.

34 Jimmy Rushing with Frank Driggs, "Jimmy Rushing's Story," *Evergreen Review* (April, 1966) p. 66.

35. See *Chicago Defender*, March 13, 1920, p. 7; July 31, 1920, p. 4; Aug. 14, 1920, p. 4, Sept. 22, 1922, p. on Portland.

36. Lawrence Gushee, "How The Creole Band Came To Be," *Black Music Research Journal*, 8, 1 (1988) pp. 83–100; Lawrence Gushes, "New Orleans-Area Musicians on the West Coast, 1908–1925" *Black Music Research Journal*, 9, 1 (1989) pp. 1–17; *Chicago Defender*, Aug. 26, 1916, p. 6; Sept. 2, 1916, p. 6; Oct, 28, 1916, p. 6; Nov. 11, 1916, p. 6; Nov. 18, 1916, p. 6.

37. Floyd Levin, "The Spikes Brothers—A Los Angeles Saga," *Jazz Journal* 4, 12 (Dec., 1951) pp. 12–15; John Bentley and Ralph Miller, "West Coast Jazz in the Twenties," *Jazz Monthly* 7, 3 (May 1961) pp. 4–5; John Bentley and Ralph W. Miller, Andrae Nordskog: Record Man," *Jazz Monthly* 5, 3 (May, 1959) pp. 8–9; Albert J. McCarthy, *Big Band Jazz*, pp. 168–169; *Chicago Defender* March 9, 1918, p. 7; July 10, 1920, p. 7; Jan. 1, 1921, p. 5; July

9, 1921, p. 7; Aug. 13, 1921, p. 6; The *Chicago Defender* covered the West Coast scene extensively in the 1920–1923 period in Ragtime Billy Tucker's column, "Coast Dope."

38. Paul L. Howard and Berta Wood, "Paul Leroy Howard," part 1, *Jazz Journal* 10, 11 (Nov., 1957) pp. 6–7. *Chicago Defender* March 23, 1918, p. 7; April 3, 1920, p. 6; July 23, 1921, p. 6; Aug. 27, 1921, p. 6; July 15, 1922, p. 6; Aug. 26, 1922, p. 8; Sept. 2, 1922, p. 6; Oct. 29, 1922, p. 6; Dec. 23, 1922, p. 8; July 1, 1923, p. 6; Albert J. McCarthy, *Big Band Jazz*, pp. 168–170; "Pops" Foster with Tom Stoddard, *The Autobiography of a New Orleans Jazzman*, p. 122.

39. John Bentley and Ralph W. Miller, "West Coast Jazz in the Twenties," *Jazz Monthly* 7, 3 (May, 1961) pp. 4–5; *Chicago Defender* July 29, 1922, p. 6; Sept. 2, 1922, p. 6; Oct. 7, 1922, p. 8; July 7, 1923, p. 6; Albert McCarthy, *Big Band Jazz*, pp. 172–174.

40. Lawrence Gushee, "New Orleans-Area Musicians on the West Coast, 1908–1925," *Black Music Research Journal*, 9, 1 (1989) pp. 1–17; "Pops" Foster with Tom Stoddard, *The Autobiography of a New Orleans Jazzman*, pp. 120–122' Eugene Williams and Marili Stuart, "Papa Mutt Carey," *Jazz*, (March, 1943) p. 7; *Chicago Defender*, Feb. 23, 1918, p. 4; May 11, 1918, p. 5; Feb. 22, 1919, p. 14; April 24, 1920, p. 6; Aug. 28, 1920, p. 5; Jan. 1, 1921, p. 5; April 3, 1921, p. 6; July 23, 1921, p. 6; July 15, 1922, p. 6; July 22, 1922, p. 6; July 29, 1922, p. 6; Aug. 5, 1922, p. 7; Aug. 12, 1922, p. 6; Aug. 26, 1922, p. 8.

41. Floyd Levin, "The Spikes Brothers—A Los Angeles Saga," *Jazz Journal* 4, 12 (Dec., 1951) pp. 12–15; John Bentley and Ralph Miller, "West Coast Jazz in the Twenties," *Jazz Monthly* 7, 3 (May, 1961) pp. 4–5; John Bentley and Ralph W. Miller, "Andrae Nordskog: Record Man," *Jazz Monthly* 5, 3 (May, 1959) pp. 8–9; Albert J. McCarthy, *Big Band Jazz*, pp. 4–5; 168–169; Dick Raichelson, notes to *West Coast Jazz—v. 1* (Arcadia 2001).

42. Brian Rust, *Jazz Records*, p. 1485. The Ory sides as issued by Spikes Seven Pods of Pepper Orchestra, were "Ory's Creole Trombone," and "Society Blues" on Nordskog label, 3009 reissued on *West Coast Jazz—v. 1*. "Slidus Trombonus" by Sodero's Military Band is on the *Riverside History of Classic Jazz*.

43. Brian Rust, *Jazz Records*, p. 218; The Sonny Clay sides as issued by the California Poppies, were "What a Wonderful Time," and "Lou" on Sunset label, S-507.

44. David Chevan, "Riverboat Music from St. Louis and the Streckfus Steamboat Line," *Black Music Research Journal*, 9, 2 (Fall, 1989) pp. 153–155, 160–162; Bartlett D. Simms "Jazz In St. Louis," *Record Changer* (Nov., 1945) p. 4.

45. David Chevan, "Riverboat Music from St. Louis," pp. 155–158; George "Pops" Foster with Tom Stoddard, *The Autobiography of a New Orleans Jazzman*, pp. 107–108.

46. Tony Catalano and Fate Marable, "Tony Catalano Talks to Fate Marable," *Downbeat* 5, 6 (June, 1938) p. 8; Beulah Schact, "The Story of Fate Marable,"

Jazz Record (March, 1946) p. 5; Robert B. Sales, "Fate Marable," *Jazz Information* 2.2 (Aug., 9, 1940) pp. 7–8; David Chevan, "Riverboat Music from St. Louis," *Black Music Research Journal* (Fall, 1989) pp. 161–164.

47. Nat Shapiro and Nat Hentoff, eds, *Hear Me Talkin' To Ya*, pp. 75–77; James Lincoln Collier, *Louis Armstrong*, pp. 76–81; Albert J. McCarthy, *Big Band Jazz*, pp. 116–117; Max Jones and John Chilton, *Louis: The Louis Armstrong Story*, (Boston: Little, Brown and Co., 1971) pp. 57–58, 210; George "Pops" Foster with Tom Stoddard, *The Autobiography of a New Orleans Jazzman*, pp. 109–114; Johnny St. Cyr, "Jazz As I Remember It," part 3, the Riverboats, *Jazz Journal* 19, 11 (Nov. 1966) pp. 6–7, 9; Warren "Baby" Dodds with Larry Gara "The Baby Dodds Story" part 2, *Jazz Journal*, 8, 6 (June, 1955) pp. 4–5; Jerome Don Pasquall with Frank Driggs and Thornton Hagert, "Jerome Don Pasquall," part 1 *Jazz Journal* 17, 5 (May, 1964) p. 24.

48. David Chevan, "Riverboat Music from St. Louis," *Black Music Research Journal* 9, 2 (Fall, 1989) pp. 158–166, 174–175; Baby Dodds with Larry Gara, "The Baby Dodds Story," part 2, *Jazz Journal* 8, 6 (June, 1955) pp. 4–6; George "Pops" Foster with Tom Stoddard, *The Autobiography of a New Orleans Jazzman*, pp. 109–111.

49. George "Pops" Foster with Tom Stoddard, *The Autobiography of a New Orleans Jazzman*, pp. 106–107, 111–112; David Chevan, "Riverboat Music from St. Louis," *Black Music Journal* 9, 2 (Fall, 1989) pp. 158–159; Baby Dodds with Larry Gara, "The Baby Dodds Story," part 2, *Jazz Journal* 8, 6 (June, 1955) pp. 4–6; Ed Crowder and A. F. Niemoeller, "Dewey Jackson, St. Louis Jazzman" in Art Hodes and Chadwick Hansen, *Selections From the Gutter*, pp. 210–211.

50. Johnny St. Cyr. "Jazz As I Remember It," part 3, *Jazz Journal* 19, 11 (Nov. 1966) p. 7.

51. Douglas Hague, "Ed Allen," *Jazz Journal* 11, 1 (Jan., 1958) pp. 11–14; Frank Driggs, "Jazz In Kansas City and the Southwest," in Nat Hentoff and Al McCarthy, eds *Jazz*, pp. 217–219; Ed Crowder and A. F. Niemoeller, "Dewey Jackson St. Louis Jazzman, in Art Hodes and Chadwick Hansen, *Selections From the Gutter*, pp. 208–211; Bartlett D. Simms, "Jazz In St Louis," *Record Changer* (Nov., 1945) pp. 4–6; Albert J. McCarthy, *Big Band Jazz*, pp. 113–118.

52. Jerome Don Pasquall, Frank Driggs, and Thornton Hagert, "Jerome Don Pasquall," part 1, *Jazz Journal* 17, 5 (May, 1964) p. 23.

53. Ibid.; Harry Dial, "Drums on the Mississippi," in Art Hodes and Chadwick Hansen, *Selections from the Gutter*, pp. 211–212; Louis Metcalf with Derrick Stewart-Baker, "Louis Metcalf," part 1, *Jazz Journal* 19,11 (Nov., 1966) p. 15; John Chilton, *Who's Who of Jazz*, pp. 88, 105, 244, 300, 375–376.

54. "Pops" Foster with Tom Stoddard, *The Autobiography of a New Orleans Jazzman*, pp. 116–125; Jerome Don Pasquall, Frank Driggs, and Thornton Hagert, "Jerome Don Pasquall," part 1, p. 23; Douglas Hague "Ed Allen," *Jazz Journal* 11, 1 (Jan., 1958), pp. 11–14; Bartlett D. Simms, "Jazz In St. Louis," *Record Changer* (Nov., 1945) p. 4; Leonard Kunstadt, "Eugene

Sedric—Gentleman Musician," *Record Research* 53 (Sept., 1963) pp. 3–5; Jack Bradley, "Honey Bear, Gene Sedric 1907–1963," *Coda* 5, 10 (May, 1963) p. 21; Ed Crowder and A. F. Niemoeller, "Dewey Jackson, St. Louis Jazzman," in Art Hodes and Chadwick Hansen, *Selections From the Gutter*, pp. 208–211; Albert McCarthy, *Big Band Jazz*, p. 113–118.

55. George "Pops" Foster, "Talks About Jazz," *Coda* 7, 11 (Dec., 1965–Jan., 1966) pp. 4–5.

56. Buster Smith with Don Gazzaway, "Conversations with Buster Smith," part 1 *Jazz Review* 2, 12 (Dec., 1959) p. 20.

57. Ross Russell, *Jazz Style in Kansas City and the Southwest*, (Berkley: University of California Press, 1971) p. 79; Frank Driggs, "Andy Kirk's Story," in Martin Williams, *Jazz Panorama*, pp. 119–120; Frank Driggs, "Kansas City and the Southwest," in Nat Hentoff and Al McCarthy, *Jazz*, pp. 197, 200, 202; Albert J. McCarthy, *Big Band Jazz*, p. 99.

58. Buster Smith with Don Gazzaway, "Conversations with Buster Smith," part 1 *Jazz Review* 2, 12 (Dec., 1959) p. 20; Booker Pittman with Frank Driggs, "Booker Pittman," *Coda*, 6, 3 (Oct., 1963) p. 8; George Hoefer, notes on Budd Johnson, Budd Johnson file, I.J.S.; Keg Johnson, questionnaire for *Encyclopedia of Jazz*, Keg Johnson file, I.J.S.

59. Nathan W. Pearson, Jr., "Political and Musical Forces . . . Kansas City," *Black Music Research Journal* 9, 2 (Fall, 1989) pp. 183–186; Paul Banks with Frank Driggs, "Paul Banks Tells His Story," *Jazz Journal* 11, 8 (Aug., 1958) pp. 4–5; Ross Russell, *Jazz Style in Kansas City*, pp. 113–115; Albert J. McCarthy, *Big Band Jazz*, pp 140, 138; Gunther Schuller, *The Swing Era* (New York: Oxford University Press, 1989) p. 781.

60. Frank Driggs, "Kansas City and The Southwest," in Nat Hentoff and Al McCarthy, *Jazz*, pp. 192–193; Paul Oliver, *Story of the Blues*, pp. 36–41, 66–67; Ross Russell, *Jazz Style in Kansas City*, pp. 32–40, 59–60, 74–77; Samuel Charters, *Country Blues*, (New York: Reinhart, 1959) pp. 57–72, 87–88, 155–165.

61. Ross Russell, *Jazz Style in Kansas City*, p. 49.

62. Gunther Schuller, *Early Jazz*, pp. 282–285; Ross Russell, *Jazz Style in Kansas City*, pp. 88–89, 113–115, 92–97, 39–40, 48–52; Albert J. McCarthy, *Big Band Jazz*, pp. 134–135; Brian Rust, *Jazz Records*, p. 1109; Bennie Moten Orchestra, "Elephant's Wobble," "Crawford Blues" Okeh 8100. The early Moten recordings have not been frequently reissued unlike his 1929–1932 output.

Chapter 4

1. *Chicago Defender*, June 12, 1926, four-page promotional insert for Okeh-Local 208 ball.

2. Ibid.; *Chicago Defender* June 19, 1926, p. 7; Max Jones and John Chilton, *Louis*, pp. 90–104; John L. Collier, *Louis Armstrong*, pp. 151–191; Brian Rust, *Jazz Records*, pp. 40–44.

3. John Chilton, *Who's Who of Jazz*, pp. 9, 107, 116, 268, 279, 280, 287, 366, 162, 269, 282, 313, 391.

4. Leroy Ostransky, *Jazz City*, pp. 92–99; Alan H. Spear, *Black Chicago*, pp. 201– 229; St. Clair Drake and Horace R. Clayton, *Black Metropolis*, pp. 65–83, 108–111, 346–351; Lloyd Wendt and Herman Kogan, *Big Bill of Chicago*, (Indianapolis: Bobbs-Merrill, 1953) pp. 234–277; William H. Stuart, *The Twenty Incredible Years*, (New York: M.A. Donohue, 1935) pp. 301–318.

5. St. Clair Drake and Horace R. Cayton, *Black Metropolis*, pp. 115–127, 399– 754.

6. *Chicago Defender*, Feb. 12, 1927, p. 8; Tom Hennessey, "Chicago's Black Establishment," *Journal of Jazz Studies* 2, 1 (Dec. 1974) pp. 31–34; Clark Halker, "A History of Local 208 and the Struggle for Racial Equality," *Black Music Research Journal* 8, 2 (Fall, 1988) pp. 211–215; Robert D. Leiter, *The Musicians and Petrillo*, (New York: Bookman Associates, 1953) pp. 42–47; Albert McCarthy, *Big Band Jazz*, pp. 20–21, 22–25.

7. Tom Hennessey, "Chicago's Black Establishment," *Journal of Jazz Studies* 2, 1 (Dec., 1974) pp. 21–38.

8. Ibid., pp. 15–21; *Chicago Defender*, Oct. 10, 1925, p. 6; Oct. 24, 1925, p. 6; July 3, 1926, p. 6; Dec. 25, 1926, p. 6; Sept. 11, 1926, p. 6; Nov. 6, 1926, p. 6; Chadwick C. Hansen, "Social Influences on Jazz Style: Chicago, 1920–1930," *American Quarterly*, 12, 4 (Winter, 1960), pp. 493–499.

9. *Chicago Defender*, July 10, 1920, p. 1.

10. *Chicago Defender*, Sept. 24, 1927, p. 8; Oct. 1, 1927, p. 8; Nov. 19, 1927, p. 11; Dec. 10, 1927, p. 11; Dec. 17, 1927, p. 10; Dec. 31, 1927, p. 6; Nat Shapiro and Nat Hentoff, *Hear Me Talkin' To Ya*, pp. 130–131; Milt Hinton and David G. Berger, *Bass Line*, p. 31.

11. Walter C. Allen and Brian Rust, *King Joe Oliver*, (London: Jazz Book Club, 1957) pp. 14–21; *Chicago Defender*, March 12, 1927, p. 8; April 2, 1927, p. 8; April 23, 1927, p. 8, June 1, 1927, p 8; July 2, 1927, p. 1; March 24, 1928, p. 10; Nat Shapiro and Nat Hentoff, *Hear Me Talkin' To Ya*, pp. 130–131.

12. Nat Shapiro and Nat Hentoff, *Hear Me Talkin' To Ya*, pp. 96–100, 115–121; *Chicago Defender* Jan. 23, 1926 p. 6.

13. Dempsey J. Travis, *An Autobiography of Black Jazz*, pp. 11–18.

14. Tom Hennessey, "Chicago's Black Establishment," *Journal of Jazz Studies* 2, 1 (Dec., 1974) pp. 21–29; Ralph Gulliver, "The Band From Columbus, Sammy Stewart and His Orchestra," p. 217–223; *Chicago Defender*, April 2, 1927, p. 11; Feb. 10, 1923, p. 6; April 3, 1926, p. 6; Feb. 12, 1927, p. 8; Jan. 7, 1928, p. 8; Jan. 14, 1928, p. 8; Jan. 21, 1928, p. 8; Feb. 4, 1928, pp. 5, 8; March 17, 1928, p. 10. Milt Hinton and David G. Berger, *Bass Line*, p. 27.

15. Tom Hennessey, "Chicago's Black Establishment," *Journal of Jazz Studies* 2, 1 (Dec., 1974) pp. 23–26; *Chicago Defender*, April 17, 1926, p. 7; June 4, 1927, p. 3; June 11, 1927, p. 4; Sept. 24, 1927, p. 8.

16. None of Dave Peyton's groups ever recorded. Erskine Tate's band only made four sides, two in 1923 including Freddie Keppard and two in 1926 featuring

Louis Armstrong. An asterisk might be added for Reuben Reeves's 1933 date of four sides which included several Tate alumni including Reeves, James and Cicero Tate, and Norval Morton. Ralph Gulliver, "The Band From Columbus, Sammy Stewart and His Orchestra," *Storyville* 48 (Aug.–Sept., 1973) pp. 222–225, 229–230; Dick Raichelson, notes to *Chicago in the Twenties, v. 1, 1926–1928*, (Arcadia, 2011) which includes all four Stewart 1928 records; Tom Hennessey, "Chicago's Black Establishment," *Journal of Jazz Studies* 2, 1 (Dec., 1974) pp. 22–26; Brian Rust, *Jazz Records*, pp. 1282, 1501, 1529.

17. Nat Shapiro and Nat Hentoff, *Hear Me Talkin'To Ya*, pp. 106–112; *Chicago Defender*, Nov. 7, 1925, p.8; Nov. 21, 1925, p. 6; Nov. 28, 1925, p. 6; Jan. 23, 1926, p. 6.

18. Tom Hennessey, "Chicago's Black Establishment," *Journal of Jazz Studies*, 2, 1 (Dec., 1974) pp. 31–33; *Chicago Defender*, Aug, 28, 1926, p. 6; May 7, 1927, p. 8; Albert J. McCarthy, *Big Band Jazz*, pp. 20–21, 23–25; Brian Rust, *Jazz Records*, pp. 337–341.

19. Ralph Gulliver, "Jimmy Wade," *Storyville*, 56 (Dec. 1974–Jan. 1975) pp. 55–68; Tom Hennessey, "Chicago's Black Establishment," *Journal of Jazz Studies* 2, 1 (Dec., 1974) pp. 34–35; *Chicago Defender*, Dec. 16, 1922, p. 10; May 15, 1926, p. 6; Brian Rust, *Jazz Records*, pp. 337–341.

20. Dempsey J. Travis, *An Autobiography of Black Jazz*, pp. 52–58; St. Clair Drake and Horace R. Cayton, *Black Metropolis*, pp. 608–611; Paul Oliver, *The Story of the Blues*, pp. 68–69, 82–86, 100–101, 103–115.

21. *Chicago Defender*, Aug. 7, 1926, p. 7; Dec. 15, 1928, p. 10; Dec. 19, 1925, p. 8; Feb. 13, 1926, p. 6; Dec. 17, 1927, p. 10; Feb. 18, 1928, p. 8; insert to *Chicago Defender*, June 12, 1926, for Okeh-208 ball, pp. 1, 2; Nat Shapiro and Nat Hentoff, *Hear Me Talkin' To Ya*, p. 80; Malcom E. Bessom, "Earl Hines and His Trumpet-Style Piano," *Jazz and Pop* 7, 1 (Jan., 1968) p. 32; Johnny St. Cyr, "Jazz As I Remember It," part 4 *Jazz Journal*, 20, 1 (Jan., 1967) p. 16; Onah Spencer, "Preston Jackson Recalls His First Gig," *Downbeat*, 9, 21 (Nov. 1, 1942) p. 23; Drake and Cayton, *Black Metropolis*, pp. 691–694; Dempsey J. Travis, *An Autobiography of Black Jazz*, pp. 84–90; Max Jones and John Chilton, *Louis*, pp. 99–100, Dick Raichelson, notes to *Chicago in the Twenties, v. 1, 1926–1928*, (Arcadia, 2011).

22. *Chicago Defender*, Nov. 5, 1927, p. 2; Nov. 19, 1927, p. 3; Jan. 28, 1928, p. 9; Feb. 25, 1928, p. 8; April 14, 1928, p. 10; May 4, 1929, p. 8; Dempsey J. Travis, *An Autobiography of Black Jazz*, pp. 77–84, 98–109; John Steiner notes on the Carroll Dickerson sides, "Shades of McKinney, Henderson and Goldkette! The arranging style of Redman and Fud Livingston . . . had captivated Chicago's biggest hot band. . . . Big ballrooms had necessitated this development," booklet to *The Sound of Chicago* (Columbia, C3L32) p. 17.

23. *Chicago Defender*, Nov. 5, 1927, p. 2; Nov. 26, 1927, p. 10; Feb. 25, 1928, p. 10; Sept. 22, 1928, p. 8; Nov. 24, 1928, p. 10; Dec. 1, 1928, p. 8; May 4, 1929, p. 9; May 18, 1929, p. 11; June 15, 1929, p. 10; July 6, 1929, p. 4;

Aug. 10, 1929, p. 9; Aug. 24, 1929, p. 9; Tom Hennessey, "Chicago's Black Establishment," *Journal of Jazz Studies* 2, 1 (Dec., 1974) pp. 33–34.

24. *Chicago Defender*, Aug. 19, 1922, p. 3.

25. *Chicago Defender*, Aug. 7, 1926, p. 7; Feb. 12, 1927, p. 8; Feb. 28, 1925, p. 6; May 23, 1925, p. 7; May 30, 1925, p. 7, 8; June 6, 1925, p. 6.

26. Warren "Baby" Dodds with Larry Gara, "The Baby Dodds Story," part 4, *Jazz Journal* 8, 8 (Aug., 1955) pp. 4–5; Nat Shapiro and Nat Hentoff, *Hear Me Talkin' To Ya*, p. 113; Art Hodes, "Baby Dodds," in Art Hodes and Chadwick Hansen, eds., *Selections From the Gutter*, p. 97; Brian Rust, *Jazz Records*, p. 65.

27. *Chicago Defender*, July 2, 1928, p. 8; Aug. 27, 1927, p. 8; March 2, 1928, p. 8; William H. Kenney, III, "Jimmie Noone: Chicago's Classic Jazz Clarinetist," *American Music*, 4, 2 (Summer, 1986) pp. 145–158; Wesley M. Neff, "New Orleans Clarinets, 5: Jimmie Noone," *Jazz Information* 2, 6 (Nov., 1941) pp. 6–9; Hagues Panassie, notes to *Jimmie Noone and Earl Hines, At The Apex Club*, (Decca DL 79235); Nat Shapiro and Nat Hentoff, *Hear Me Talkin' To Ya*, pp. 106, 114; Brian Rust, *Jazz Records*, pp. 1151–1154. Noone recorded more than sixty sides under his own name between 1928 and 1931 and only ten have a trumpet and trombone on them.

28. Walter C. Allen and Brian Rust, *King Joe Oliver*, pp. 14–21; *Chicago Defender*, March 12, 1927, p. 8; April 2, 1927, p. 8; April 23, 1927, p. 8; June 1, 1927, p. 8; July 2, 1927, p. 1; Hugues Panassie, notes to *King Oliver and His Dixie Syncopators, Papa Joe*, (Decca DL 79246); Richard Hadlock, notes to King Oliver, *Sugar Foot Stomp*, (GRP GRD-616). This includes fourteen sides recorded by this band in Chicago in 1926–1927 which show increasing elements of the Fletcher Henderson arranged style and Louis Armstrong string of solos and little of the old Creole Jazz Band style. Brian Rust, *Jazz Records*, pp. 1167–1168.

29. *Chicago Defender*, Oct. 1, 1927, p. 8; Walter C. Allen and Brian Rust, *King Joe Oliver*; Clyde Bernhardt, *I Remember: Eighty Years in Black Entertainment, Big Bands and Blues*, (Philadelphia: University of Pennsylvania Press, 1986) pp. 90–102; Fred Moore, "King Oliver's Last Tour" in Art Hodes and Chadwick Hanson, eds. *Selections From the Gutter*, pp. 86–89; Nat Shapiro and Nat Hentoff, *Hear Me Talkin' To Ya*, pp. 183–187.

30. *Chicago Defender*, Feb. 12, 1927, p. 8.

31. *Chicago Defender* Sept. 17, 1927, p. 10; Oct. 1, 1927, p. 8; Oct. 8, 1927, p. 8; Oct. 15, 1928, p. 9; Nov. 19, 1927, p. 11; Dec. 10, 1927, p. 11; Dec. 17, 1927, p. 10; Dec. 31, 1927, p. 6; Jan. 28, 1928, p. 9; Feb. 18, 1928, p. 8; March 17, 1928, p. 1, 10, 12; April 21, 1928, p. 8; May 12, 1928, p. 10; Sept. 1, 1928, p. 8; Sept. 29, 1928, p. 10; Oct. 13, 1928, p. 9; Nov. 10, 1928, p. 10; Ralph Gulliver, "The Band From Columbus, Sammy Stewart and His Orchestra," *Storyville* 48 (Aug.–Sept., 1973) pp. 224, 229; Dick Raichelson, notes to *Chicago in the Twenties, v. 1, 1926–1928*, (Arcadia, 2011).

32. *Chicago Defender*, Sept. 17, 1927, p. 10; Oct. 1, 1927, p. 10; April 21, 1928,

p. 8; May 12, 1928, p. 10; June 2, 1928, p. 8; June 16, 1928, p. 10; Nov. 10, 1928, p. 10; Dec. 15, 1928, p. 10; Albert J. McCarthy, *Big Band Jazz*, pp. 48–49, 79–80; Gunther Schuller, *The Swing Era*, pp. 326–329; Cab Calloway and Bryant Rollins, *Of Minnie The Moocher and Me*, (New York: Thomas Y. Crowell, 1976) pp. 62–82.

33. *Chicago Defender*, Sept. 3, 1928, p. 8; Sept. 17, 1928, p. 8; Nov. 19, 1927, p. 11; Dec. 10, 1927, p. 11; March 10, 1928, p. 8; May 12, 1928, p. 10; John Chilton, *Who's Who of Jazz*, pp. 9–10, 107, 280–281; Nat Shapiro and Nat Hentoff, *Hear Me Talkin' To Ya*, p. 109.

34. Brian Rust, *Jazz Records*, pp. 1100–1102; John Chilton, *Who's Who of Jazz*, pp. 29–30, 172, 261, 337; Nat Shapiro and Nat Hentoff, *Hear Me Talkin' To Ya*, pp. 180–183; Alan Lomax, *Mr. Jelly Lord*, pp. 173–182, 185–186.

35. Robert M. W. Dixon and John Goodrich, *Recording The Blues*, (London: Studio Vista, 1970) pp. 6–64; Paul Oliver, *The Story of the Blues*, pp. 95–97; Brian Priestly, *Jazz On Record*, (New York: Billboard Books, 1991) pp. 1–3, 11–17, 20–22, 26–29, 34–37.

36. *Chicago Defender*, Oct. 31, 1925, p. 6.

37. *Chicago Defender*, Nov. 7, 1926, p. 8; Nov. 14, 1926, p. 7; Nov. 21, 1926, p. 6; Max Jones and John Chilton, *Louis*, p. 90.

38. Max Jones and John Chilton, *Louis*, pp. 96–97; John L. Collier, *Louis Armstrong*, pp. 169–173; Brian Rust, *Jazz Records*, pp. 40–41. In a WPA interview with Onah Spencer, Richard Jones, claimed the credit for the idea of the Hot Five but he also claimed credit for starting the career of virtually every New Orleans-in-Chicago musician, so it probably needs to be taken with a grain of salt. Onah L. Spencer, "Chicago Jazz Composers—Richard M. Jones, Composer and Trailblazer," Richard M. Jones files, W.P.A. files, Chicago Public Library.

39. Nat Shapiro and Nat Hentoff, *Hear Me Talkin' To Ya*, p. 109; Baby Dodds also stressed that Armstrong rehearsals were informal, mostly just talking things out, but he does say that Lil Armstrong wrote out some parts. Warren "Baby" Dodds with Larry Gara, "The Baby Dodds Story," part 6, *Jazz Journal* 8, 10 (Oct., 1955) p. 26.

40. Gunther Schuller, *Early Jazz*, pp. 89–127; John L. Collier, *Louis Armstrong: An American Genius*, pp. 167–198; Andre Hodier, *Jazz: Its Evolution and Essence*, (New York: Grove Press, 1956) pp. 49–62.

41. Gunther Schuller, *Early Jazz*, pp. 89–127.

42. Gunther Schuller, *Early Jazz*, pp. 135–136.

43. Gunther Schuller, *Early Jazz*, pp. 134–169. Jelly Roll Morton is one of the 1920s figures who most profits from digital remastering since it shows the full range of the interplays in his arrangements. See the 1988 reissue, *The Pearls* (BMG, 6588-1-RB).

44. Omer Simeon, "Mostly About Morton," in Art Hodes and Chadwick Hansen, eds. *Selections From the Gutter*, pp. 92–93; Alan Lomas, *Mr. Jelly Lord*, pp. 182–185; Nat Shapiro and Nat Hentoff, *Hear Me Talkin' to Ya*, pp. 181–182; Warren "Baby" Dodds with Larry Gara, "The Baby Dodds Story," part

6, *Jazz Journal* 8, 10 (Oct., 1955) p. 26; James L. Collier, *The Making of Jazz*, pp. 99–105; Martin Williams, "Jelly Roll Morton," in Nat Hentoff and Albert J. McCarthy, eds. *Jazz*, pp. 74–79; Wesley M. Neff, "Little Mitch," *Jazz Information*, 2, 16 (Nov., 1941) pp. 32–36.

45. Gunther Schuller, *Early Jazz*, p 166; on *Mr. Jelly Lord*, (Victor, LPV 546).
46. *Chicago Defender*, July 30, 1927, p. 8; Aug. 20, 1927, p. 8; Omer Simeon, "Mostly About Morton," in Art Hodes and Chadwick Hansen, *Selections From the Gutter*, pp. 92–93; Alan Lomax, *Mr. Jelly Lord*, pp. 182-185.
47. Albert J. McCarthy, *Big Band Jazz*, pp. 237–239; Gunther Schuller, *The Swing Era*, pp. 263–267, 272–288.
48. *Chicago Defender*, Aug. 10, 1929, p. 8; Aug. 17, 1929, p. 8; Aug. 24, 1929, p. 8, 9; Aug. 31, 1929, p. 8; Sept 28, 1929, p. 10; Oct. 5, 1929, p. 10; George Hoefer, notes on Walter Barnes, Walter Barnes file, I.J.S.
49. Clark Halker, "A History of Local 208 and the Struggle for Racial Equality," *Black Music Research Journal* 8, 2 (Fall, 1988) pp. 211-215.

Chapter 5

1. Frank Driggs, "Don Redman, Jazz Composer-Arranger" in Martin Williams, *Jazz Panorama*, p. 95. Walter C. Allen goes into the details of the Club Alabam audition at length in *Hendersonia*, pp. 84–88. Don Redman in interviews with Frank Driggs and Felix Manskleid, "Passing Notes on Fletcher Henderson," *Jazz Monthly* 3, 10 (Dec., 1957) p. 27, is the main source for this version of the story, which can also be found in Samuel Charters and Leonard Kunstadt, *Jazz: New York*, pp. 168–171; Gunther Schuller, *Early Jazz*, pp. 253–254; and James L. Collier, *Making of Jazz*, p. 179. It plays up Redman's role in the band, but it does fit with some other pictures of Henderson's business practices and personality. Allen on pp.86–87 presents Henderson's own version that the club manager called and offered him the job based on the band's recordings and that after trying to convince the manager that the band only existed in the studio, Henderson gave in and accepted the job. The year 1923 is very early for a manager to book a band only on recordings, and Henderson was trying to counter criticism of not being aggressive enough as a businessman. It is likely that the truth lies somewhere between the two stories. The audition probably clinched the gig while their recordings were another plus factor. Even in his story, Henderson is responding to someone else's initiative. The key fact was that the Henderson band became a live group after it has been a recording gang. Allen dates the Club Alabam as being in business by January 4, 1924 (p. 86). The club business having certain basic realities, it is very likely that the place had actually opened in very late December in order to catch the New Year's Eve crowd.
2. St. Clair Drake and Horace Cayton, *Black Metropolis*, pp. 661–662.
3. Hsio Wen Shih, "The Spread of Jazz and the Big Bands," in Nat Hentoff and Al McCarthy, eds. *Jazz*, pp. 173–174.

4. Margery P. Dews, "F. H. Henderson and the Howard Normal School," *Georgia Historical Quarterly* 63, 2 (Summer, 1979) pp. 252–263; Walter C. Allen, *Hendersonia*, pp. 2–7; Samuel Charters and Leonard Kunstadt, *Jazz: New York*, pp. 165–166.

5. Eileen Southern, *Music of Black Americans*, pp. 438-443; Author's interview with Eubie Blake; Walter C. Allen, *Hendersonia*, p. 571; James Weldon Johnson, *Black Manhattan*, pp 186–190. 196–201, 209–210, 212–218, 224–225; Roger D. Kinkle, *Encyclopedia of Popular Music*, p. 121, 129, 130, 136–137, 143–144, 173, 176–177, 185–187, 198–199; Samuel Charters and Leonard Kunstadt, *Jazz: New York*, pp. 109–118

6. David Levering Lewis, *When Harlem Was In Vogue*, (New York: Knopf, 1981) pp. 28–49, 89–155; Jervis Anderson, *Harlem, Great Black Way*, pp. 137–224; Harold Cruse, *The Crisis of the Negro Intellectual*, (New York: Morrow, 1967) pp. 3–111; Jim Haskins, *The Cotton Club*, (New York: Random House, 1977) pp. 15–26.

7. James L. Collier, *Making of Jazz*, p. 179.

8. David Levering Lewis, *When Harlem Was In Vogue*, p. 48.

9. Jervis Anderson, *Harlem, Great Black Way*, pp. 145-148; 168–180; Lewis Ehrenberg, *Steppin' Out*, pp. 146–175; Kathy J. Ogren, *The Jazz Revolution* p. 57; Paula Fass, *The Damned and the Beautiful*, pp. 260–326.

10. Morroe Berger, Edward Berger, and James Patrick, *Benny Carter*, p. 17; Florette Henri, *Black Migration*, pp. 174–182; Gary Nash et al., *The American People: Creating a Nation and a Society*, (New York: Harper and Row, 1990) pp. 778–780.

11. David Levering Lewis, *When Harlem Was In Vogue*, p. 48.

12. Erik Barnouw, *A Tower In Babel*, (New York: Oxford Press, 1966) pp. 125–135: Harvey Rettberg, "Coon-Sanders: a Study in Nostalgia," *The Second Line*, 13, 1–2 (Jan.–Feb., 1962) pp. 5, 22: Phillip K. Eberly, *Music in the Air: America's Changing Tastes in Popular Music, 1920–1980* (New York: Hastings House, 1982) pp. 4–6, 11–12, 14–26.

13. Rudy Powell with Ernie Smith, "Sideman" *Record Research* 20 (Nov.–Dec., 1958) p. 4.

14. Buck Clayton with Nancy Miller Elliott, *Buck Clayton's Jazz World*, (New York: Oxford University Press, 1987) pp. 22–23.

15. Brian Rust, *Jazz Records*, pp. 710–731. Smaller versions of the group are listed as the Hot Six and Henderson and His Sawin' Six and the Henderson band does show up on record under such stereotyped labels as the Seven Brown Babies, p. 711, Six Black Diamonds p. 715, and particularly the Dixie Stompers, p. 719–723. However, these are often either pirated versions, foreign issues, or moonlighting while under contract to another company where the object of the label was to hide the identity of the band. Many of these secondary label versions use titles such as Eldon's Dance Orchestra, Casino Dance Orchestra, New Jersey Dance Orchestra which may have suggested that this was a white band. It is also interesting that Fletcher Henderson did not participate in the Chocolate Dandies recordings that included members and alumni of his band.

This stereotypical label has grated on some participants and critics to the present.

16. Morroe Berger, Edward Berger, and James Patrick, *Benny Carter*, pp. 70–72; Walter C. Allen, *Hendersonia*, pp. 63–64, 76–92.

17. Frank Driggs, "Don Redman, Jazz Composer-Arranger," in Martin Williams, ed. *Panorama*, pp. 91–98; Harold Grut, "Don Redman," *Jazz Music* 33, pp. 8–10; David Innes, "A View of Don Redman," *Jazz Journal* 21, 7 (July, 1968) pp. 14–15; Barry Ulanov, "Thanks, Mr. Redman, For Modern Style," *Metronome* 57, 6 (June, 1941) p. 20; Gunther Schuller, *Early Jazz*, pp. 256–266; Morroe Berger, Edward Berger, and James Patrick, *Benny Carter*, pp. 75–81; Walter C. Allen, *Hendersonia*, pp. 43–44; Gunther Schuller, *Swing Era*, pp. 9, 368; James Collier, *Making of Jazz*, pp. 177-182.

18. Brian Rust, *Jazz Records*, pp. 710–715. The Henderson orchestra recorded well over thirty sides before its Club Alabam opening; unfortunately, they have not been often reissued. Those mentioned here come from three reissues each entitled *Fletcher Henderson and his orchestra*, Historical Records, HLP 13, HLP 18, and Biograph BLP 12039. The post-Club Alabam band is well-documented on *Fletcher Henderson: The Making of an American Orchestra* (Smithsonian) and *The Fletcher Henderson Story: A Study in Frustration* (Columbia C4L 19; now on compact disk as C3K 57596).

19. Brian Rust, *Jazz Records*, p. 712. Ajax 17016 and Edison 51277 recorded within a month of each other in late 1923 (Biograph BLP 12039).

20. Brian Rust, *Jazz Records*, p. 711; Columbia A-3995(C4L19), Ajax 17011 (HLP 13).

21. Gunther Schuller, *Early Jazz*, pp. 254-256, James L. Collier, *Making of Jazz*, pp. 78–79; James L. Collier, *Duke Ellington*, pp. 72–74, 107.

22. Brian Rust, *Jazz Records*, p. 713; Gennett 8205, according to Walter C. Allen in notes to (Biograph BLP 12039) Rust gives releases on Banner, Regal, and Apex for that matrix, none with that release number. Paramount 20339 (Biograph BLP 12039).

23. Frank Tirro, *Jazz: A History*, p. 218.

24. Walter C. Allen, *Hendersonia*, pp. 43–44, 51–57, 65–77, 80–83; 558–560, 570; Brian Rust, *Jazz Records*, pp. 710–712.

25. Walter C. Allen, *Hendersonia*, pp. 1, 12, 26, 28, 33–34, 41, 44, 47, 65, 570; Onah L. Spencer and Amy Lee, "The Purest Trumpet Tone of All," *Downbeat* 10, 13 (Aug. 1, 1943) p. 13; Bernard Houghton, "Joe Smith, A Biography and Appreciation," *Jazz Journal* 18, 12 (Dec., 1965) p. 18; Russell Smith with Anne Judd, "A Portrait of Russell Smith," *Jazz Journal* 20, 4 (April, 1967) pp. 5–7.

26. Walter C. Allen, *Hendersonia*, pp. 42, 44, 62–63, 67, 563; George Hoefer, notes on Coleman Hawkins, Coleman Hawkins file, I.J.S.; Gunther Schuller, *Early Jazz*, pp. 253–256; James L. Collier, *Making of Jazz*, p. 221.

27. Walter C. Allen, *Hendersonia*, pp. 1, 13, 34, 44, 63, 70, 71, 561, 567; Author's interviews with Eubie Blake and Willie "The Lion" Smith; Samuel Charters

and Leonard Kunstadt, *Jazz: New York*, pp. 167–170; obituaries in Kaiser Marshall file, I.J.S.

28. Walter C. Allen, *Hendersonia*, pp. 27, 42, 44, 64, 111, 113, 126–129, 557, 562.

29. Gunther Schuller, *Early Jazz*, pp. 257–258; Walter C. Allen, *Hendersonia*, p. 124; Max Jones and John Chilton, *Louis*, pp. 77–82, 211; James L. Collier, *Louis Armstrong*, pp. 111–114, 117.

30. Quoted in James L. Collier, *Louis Armstrong*, p. 125, Sam Wooding's 1925 recording of the piece, Vox 01882 shows its complexity, on *Sam Wooding* (Biograph BLP 12025).

31. Quoted by George Hoefer in liner notes to *Coleman Hawkins, Body and Soul*, (RCA Victor, LPV 501).

32. Brian Rust, *Jazz Records*, pp. 715–718. Armstrong's sides with Henderson have been reissued in a wide variety of places. The most easily available today are those on the Smithsonian collection *Fletcher Henderson, The Making of An American Orchestra*, (Smithsonian) Gunther Schuller, *Early Jazz*, p. 257; James L. Collier, *Louis Armstrong*, pp. 128–134.

33. Frank Driggs, booklet to *The Fletcher Henderson Story: A Study In Frustration* Columbia C4L19 p. 8; Kaiser Marshall, "When Armstrong Came to New York," in Art Hodes and Chadwick Hansen, *Selections from the Gutter* pp. 83–85.

34. Rex Stewart, *Jazz Masters of the Thirties*, (New York: Macmillan, 1972) p. 11.

35. Morroe Berger, Edward Berger, and James Patrick, *Benny Carter*, pp. 80–82; Walter C. Allen, *Hendersonia*, pp. 498–500; Gunther Schuller, *Early Jazz*, pp. 192, 262–268.

36. Reviews of *The Fletcher Henderson Story: A Study In Frustration*, Tony Standish, *Jazz Journal* 15, 8 (Aug., 1962) pp. 9–11 and Ron Auger, *Coda* 4, 8 (Dec., 1961) pp. 22–26.

37. David Levering Lewis, *When Harlem Was In Vogue*, pp. 169–170.

38. Ibid., p. 178.

39. Morroe Berger, Edward Berger, and James Patrick, *Benny Carter*, pp. 80–82; Walter C. Allen, *Hendersonia*, pp. 498–500.

40. Walter C. Allen, *Hendersonia*, p. 142; David Levering Lewis, *When Harlem Was In Vogue*, pp. 170–171, 173; Samuel Charters and Leonard Kunstadt, *Jazz: New York*, pp. 173–180; *Amsterdam News* Feb. 18, 1925 p. 18; *New York Age*, April 4, 1925 p. 5.

41. *Chicago Defender*, Feb. 27, 1926, p. 6.

42. Frank Driggs, notes to *Fletcher Henderson Story*, p. 8.

43. Samuel Charters and Leonard Kunstadt, *Jazz: New York*, p. 177.

44. Frank Driggs, notes to *Fletcher Henderson Story*, p. 8; Ernest W. Mandeville, "Roger Wolfe Kahn," *Outlook* (May 5, 1926) p. 34; Anonymous, "Strickfadden Quits As Whiteman Treasurer," *Metronome*, 51, 2 (Feb., 1935) p. 14.

45. Kaiser Marshall, "When Armstrong Came to New York," p. 85.

46. Russell Smith with Anne Judd, "A Portrait of Russell Smith," *Jazz Journal* 20, 4 (April, 1967) pp. 5–7; Claude Jones with David Ives, "Claude Jones,"

Jazz Journal 15, 6 (June, 1962) pp. 13-14; Claude Jones with John E. Mann, "Fragment of an Autobiography," *Jazz Monthly* 8, 1 (March, 1962) pp. 3–4; Jerome Don Pasqual, Frank Driggs, and Thornton Hagert, "Jerome Don Pasqual," part 1, p. 24; Walter C. Allen, *Hendersonia*, pp. 1, 12, 44, 168–172, 559, 566, 568, 571.

47. Walter C. Allen, *Hendersonia*, pp. 571, 568, 563, 559. Just as later during the bop era, only a couple of years younger moves a musician into the "second line" or "second generation" here. All that is needed is that the musician could have heard the originator of a certain style either before becoming a professional, or early in his career.

48. Rex Stewart quoted in Nat Shapiro and Nat Hentoff, ed. *Hear Me Talkin' To Ya*, p. 221.

49. Brian Rust, *Jazz Records*, pp. 718, 720; Columbia 509, Columbia 654, both on *Fletcher Henderson Story*. Louis Armstrong has the first two cornet solos on "T.N.T." and Rex Stewart has the first and last solos on "The Stampede." The very different sound of Joe Smith can be heard in the final solo on "T.N.T." and the second on "The Stampede."

50. Benny Carter, quoted in Morroe Berger, Edward Berger, and James Patrick, *Benny Carter*, p. 76.

51. Ibid., p. 17.

52. Stanley Dance, "Russell Procope," part 1, *Jazz Journal*, 16, 1 (Jan., 1963) p. 15.

53. Ibid., p. 16; John Chilton, *Who's Who in Jazz*, p. 245.

54. George Hoefer, notes on Louis Metcalf, Louis Metcalf file, I.J.S.

55. Quoted in Morroe Berger, Edward Berger, and James Patrick, *Benny Carter*, p. 81.

56. Author's interviews with Eubie Blake and Willie "The Lion" Smith; George Hoefer notes to *The Sound of Harlem*, (Columbia C3L 33), pp. 7–8.

57. George Hoefer, notes to *Sound of Harlem*, pp. 17, 32–34; Barry McRae, "June Clark," *Jazz Journal*, (May, 1963) pp. 17–18; Marshall Stearns, draft material on June Clark in June Clark file, I.J.S.

58. Albert J. McCarthy, *Big Band Jazz*, p. 61; Herman Rosenberg and Eugene Williams, "Omer Simeon," *Jazz Information* 2, 1 (July 26, 1940) pp. 8–9; Stanley Dance, *The World of Swing*, (New York: DaCapo, 1979) p. 36; Stanley Dance, "Russell Procope," part 2, *Jazz Journal*, 16, 2 (Feb., 1963) p. 6; Brian Rust, *Jazz Records*, pp. 1103–1104.

59. Albert J. McCarthy, *Big Band Jazz*, p. 49; Bingie Madison with Bertrand DeMeusy, "Biography of a Career," *Jazz Monthly* 10, 7 (Sept., 1963) p. 9.

60. George Hoefer, notes to *Sound of Harlem*, p. 32; Samuel Charters and Leonard Kunstadt, *Jazz: New York*, p. 185–187.

61. Samuel Charters and Leonard Kunstadt, *Jazz: New York*, pp. 185–190; *New York Age*, March 6, 1926, p. 8; *The Savoy Story*, 1951 souvenir book, in Savoy ballroom file, I.J.S.; Stanley R. Williams with Harrison Smith, "Fess Williams Story," pp. 2–5; Albert McCarthy, *Big Band Jazz*, pp. 51–53.

62. Albert J. McCarthy, *Big Band Jazz*, p. 41; Samuel Charters and Leonard Kunstadt, *Jazz: New York*, pp. 190–191; Gene Fernett, *Swing Out: Great Negro Dance Bands*, (Midland, Mich.: Pendell Publishing, 1970) pp. 125–126, 160; Daniel Nevers, notes to *The Savoy Bands* (RCA-France PM 42044) which has all six of the bands issued sides and six alternate takes; Brian Rust, *Jazz Records*, p. 1362.

63. George Hoefer, notes to *Sound of Harlem* p. 32; Samuel Charters and Leonard Kunstadt, *Jazz: New York*, pp. 198–202, 232–234; *Chicago Defender*, March 12, 1927, p. 8; March 26, 1927, p. 8; April 16, 1927, p. 8; Brian Rust and Walter Allen, *King Joe Oliver*, pp. 21–24.

64. Thurman Grove and Mary Grove, "Cecil Scott and His Bright Boys," part 2, *Jazz Journal* 7, 1 (Jan., 1953) pp. 3–4; Albert J. McCarthy, *Big Band Jazz*, pp. 43–45.

65. Albert J. McCarthy, *Big Band Jazz*, p. 265; Samuel Charters and Leonard Kunstadt, *Jazz: New York*, pp. 190–192; Gunther Schuller, *Swing Era*, pp. 292–294; Stanley Dance, *World of Swing*, pp. 251–254, 384–386.

66. George Hoefer, notes to *Sound of Harlem*, pp. 31–32; Nat Shapiro and Nat Hentoff, eds., *Hear Me*, pp. 167–168; Louis Metcalf with Derrick Stewart-Baker, "Louis Metcalf," *Jazz Journal*, 19, 11 (Nov., 1966) pp. 15–16.

67. George Hoefer, notes to *Sound of Harlem*, pp. 23–35; Stanley Dance, *World of Swing*, pp. 45–62; George Hoefer, "Jimmy Harrison, Forgotten Giant," part 2, *Jazz*, 2, 6 (July–Aug., 1963) pp. 12–13; Walter C. Allen, "Jimmy Archey," Jimmy Archey file, I.J.S.; Albert J. McCarthy, "Ward Pinkett," *Jazz Forum* 2 (n.d.) pp. 24–26; Thurman Grove and Mary Grove, "Cecil Scott and His Bright Boys," part 2, *Jazz Journal* 7, 1 (Jan., 1954) pp. 3–4.

68. George Hoefer, notes to *Sound of Harlem*, p. 26; Emerson "Geechie" Harper, "Leroy Smith and His Band," *Jazz Monthly* (170) p. 6; Albert McCarthy, *Big Band Jazz*, pp. 53–54.

69. George Hoefer, notes to *Sound of Harlem*, p. 26; James L. Collier, *Louis Armstrong*, pp. 211–214.

70. George Hoefer, notes to *Sound of Harlem*, p. 32; Albert J. McCarthy, *Big Band Jazz*, pp. 41–43; Gunther Schuller, *Early Jazz*, p. 270; Brian Rust, *Jazz Records*, p. 833; "The Boy in the Boat" is on *Sweet and Low Blues* New World Records (NW 256).

71. Jim Haskins, *Cotton Club*, pp. 29–41; George Hoefer, notes to *Harlem*, p. 27; Cab Calloway and Bryant Rollins, *Of Minnie the Moocher and Me*, (New York: Crowell, 1976) pp. 62–64, 73–74, 77–81; Albert J. McCarthy, *Big Band Jazz*, pp. 79–80, 210–211; Gunther Schuller, *Swing Era*, pp. 326–331. "Market St. Stomp" Victor V-38067 (June 3, 1929) is on *Big Band Jazz* Smithsonian (R 030 DMM-0610).

Chapter 6

1. Albert J. McCarthy, *Big Band Jazz* pulls much of this documentation together. Almost 100 of his 350 pages are on the territories, much of it from the

1923–1929 period. My definitions of individual territories differ somewhat from McCarthy's and Gunther Schuller's, *Early Jazz*, pp. 279–283; and *Swing Era*, pp. 771–775. My choices reflect musical styles, geographic contact between bands and musicians, similarities in social and racial structures including legal segregation, and the size of the black population.

2. Neil Leonard, *Jazz and the White Americans*, (Chicago: University of Chicago Press, 1962) and Kathy J. Ogren, *The Jazz Revolution* both cover this issue at length. One possible problem with both of their treatments is that they focus on evidence from New York rather than the territories. Robert and Helen Lynd, *Middletown: A Study in Modern American Culture* (New York: Harcourt, 1929) and Paula S. Fass, *The Damned and the Beautiful: American Youth in the 1920s* (New York: Oxford University Press, 1977) both showed clearly that this change in lifestyle was occurring on a national scale particularly in middle-sized Middle American communities which were precisely the home turf of the territory bands. For a general treatment of the conflict of cultures in the 1920s see Robert Divine, et. al., *America: Past and Present*, 3d ed., (New York: HarperCollins, 1991) pp. 744–759.

3. Robert Lynd and Helen Lynd, *Middletown*, p. 281.

4. *Chicago Defender*, Aug. 27, 1927, p. 8; May 5, 1928, p. 10; May 12, 1928, p. 11; June 23, 1928, p. 11; Sept. 8, 1928, p. 8; Oct. 6, 1928, p. 10; Mark Tucker, *Ellington: The Early Years*, pp. 182–193; James L. Collier, *Duke Ellington*, pp. 55, 62; Russ Shor, "Charlie Gaines," *Storyville* (Dec., 1976–Jan., 1977) pp. 46–47; Emerson Harper with Bertrand DeMeusy, "Leroy Smith and His Band," *Jazz Monthly* (170), pp. 6–7.

5. John Chilton, *Who's Who of Jazz*, pp. 65, 71, 90, 128, 136, 168, 170, 171, 365, 379, 390; *Chicago Defender* Jan. 14, 1928, p. 8; Stanley Dance, *The World of Swing*, pp. 36, 241–245, 249–254, 384–386; Samuel Charters and Leonard Kunstadt, *Jazz, New York*, p. 253–255.

6. Albert J. McCarthy, *Big Band Jazz*, pp. 155–156, 159, 166, 55; undated clippings. "The Father of Swing Trombone," Rex Stewart file, I.J.S.; *Chicago Defender*, July 31, 1926, p. 6; Aug. 20, 1927, p. 8; Aug. 31, 1929, p. 8; Stanley Dance, *The World of Swing*, pp. 31–38, 242.

7. Paul Oliver, *Story of the Blues*, pp. 8–72.

8. *Chicago Defender*, Jan. 27, 1927, p. 7.

9. Dick Raichelson, liner notes to *The Territories, vol. III—The South 1926–1936*, Arcadia 2010, which includes two sides by Heywood and four by Williamson. Heywood's "Let's Start Over" uses a New Orleans-style ensemble with the alto sax and tuba taking the roles of the clarinet and trombone. *Chicago Defender*, Jan. 14, 1928, pp. 8.

10. This would include groups like the Kentucky Jazz Syncopators, Carolina Stompers, Kelly's Jazz Band, the Alger Bass Band, North Carolina Ramblers, and the Jim Love Orchestra; *Chicago Defender*, May 8, 1926, p. 6; Oct. 6, 1928, p. 10; Jan. 12, 1929, p. 8; March 23, 1929, p. 10; June 8, 1929, p. 10; July 20, 1929, p. 10.

11. Paul Oliver, *The Story of the Blues*, pp. 53–55; *Chicago Defender* July 2, 1927, p. 8.

12. Albert J. McCarthy, *Big Band Jazz*, pp. 88–90; *Chicago Defender*, Nov. 24, 1928, p. 10; Feature on Philmore "Shorty" Hall, *Reflections*, WTVD-TV, Durham, N.C., Sept. 27, 1987; Author's interview with Dizzy Gillespie, Pembroke, N.C., April 7, 1985; Brian Rust, *Jazz Records*, pp. 138, 208, 1564. The Bunch and Blackbirds sides are reissued on *Byways of Jazz* (Origin Jazz Library OJL9).

13. Albert J. McCarthy, *Big Band Jazz*, pp. 96–98; *Chicago Defender*, Feb. 4, 1928, p. 9; Dec. 31, 1927, p. 7; March 17, 1928, p. 11; July 21, 1928, p. 10. Two Morgan sides are on *Steppin On the Gas* (NW 269). Eight including "Sing On," "Down by the Riverside," and "Over In the Gloryland," are included on *The Sound of New Orleans* (Columbia C3L 30); Brian Rust, *Jazz Records*, pp. 301–302, 1095–1096.

14. *Chicago Defender*, Sept. 11, 1926, p. 6; Oct. 30, 1926, p. 6; April 16, 1927, p. 8; Sept. 10, 1927, p. 9; Feb. 11, 1928, p. 8; Stanley Dance, *The World of Swing*, pp. 193, 206–207, 214–215; Eric Townley, "Bama State Collegian, Interview with Haywood Henry," *Storyville* (June–July, 1978) pp. 181–182.

15. Gunther Schuller, *Swing Era*, pp. 773–777 gives a very positive review while Albert J. McCarthy, *Big Band Jazz*, pp. 93–94 is very negative. *Chicago Defender*, Sept. 11, 1926, p. 6; Oct. 16, 1926, p. 6; Oct. 30, 1926, p. 6; Dec. 4, 1926, p. 8; Jan. 22, 1927, p. 6; Sept. 24, 1927, p. 8; Oct. 22, 1927, p. 8; March 10, 1928, p. 8; Brian Rust, *Jazz Records*, p. 1338. All eight sides were reissued on *Territory Bands, 1925–1932* (RCA-France, FXM1 7205).

16. On *Jammin' For the Jackpot: Big Bands and Territory Bands of the 1930s*, (New World Records, NW217). J. Neal Montgomery's Collegians, Montgomery's Black Rocks, the Black Rock Country Club Orchestra, and the Collegiate Ramblers were all names for a group of Atlanta U. students. They were defensive of their "respectable" position, complaining about misunderstandings of the "Black Rocks" name which came from a fashionable country club. *Chicago Defender*, Sept. 4, 1926, p. 6; April 9, 1927, p. 8; April 13, 1929, p. 10; Albert J. McCarthy, *Big Band Jazz*, p. 93; Gunther Schuller, *Early Jazz*, pp. 311–312; Brian Rust, *Jazz Records*, p. 1089.

17. Albert J. McCarthy, *Big Band Jazz*, pp. 98–99; Brian Rust, *Jazz Records*, p. 1089; *Chicago Defender*, Nov. 2, 1929, p. 13.

18. Albert J. McCarthy, *Big Band Jazz*, pp. 94–95; *Chicago Defender* Sept. 11, 1926, p. 6; Sept. 10, 1927, p. 9; Dec. 17, 1927, p. 11; June 9, 1928, p. 11; March 16, 1929, p. 10; July 20, 1929, p. 9; March 3, 1928, p. 9; Oct. 6, 1928, p. 10; Nov. 2, 1929, p. 13; Nov. 16, 1929, p. 9.

19. Albert J. McCarthy, *Big Band Jazz*, p. 249; Gunther Schuller, *Swing Era*, pp. 201–205; George Hoefer, notes on Jimmie Lunceford, Jimmie Lunceford file, I.J.S.

20. Florette Henri, *Black Migration*, p. 69; *Chicago Defender* June 4, 1927, p. 8; March 5, 1927, p. 6; March 26, 1927, p. 8; Oct. 22, 1927, p. 8; April 9, 1927,

p. 8; May 14, 1927, p. 10; Dec. 17, 1927, p. 10; May 18, 1929, p. 11; Oct. 13, 1928, p. 9.

21. Albert J. McCarthy, *Big Band Jazz*, pp. 43–45; Gunther Schuller, *Swing Era*, p. 302; George W. Kay, "The Springfield Story," in McKinney's Cotton Pickers file I.J.S.; H. B. M. "Everybody Loves Cecil," in Art Hodes and Chadwick Hansen, *Selections From the Gutter*, p. 215; Richard Congdon, "Great Scott," *Record Changer* (Sept., 1953) p. 7–8; Thurman and Mary Grove, "Cecil Scott and His Bright Boys," *Jazz Journal* 6, 12 (Dec., 1953) pp. 29–30; *Chicago Defender*, April 10, 1926, p. 6; Oct. 8, 1927, p. 8; June 2, 1928, p. 8; April 20, 1929, p. 8.

22. Albert J. McCarthy, *Big Band Jazz*, pp. 75–79; Gunther Schuller, *Swing Era*, pp. 301–317; Claude Jones with David Ives "Claude Jones," *Jazz Journal* 15, 6 (June 1962) pp. 13–14; Claude Jones with John E. Mann, "Fragment of an Autobiography," *Jazz Monthly* 8, 1 (March, 1962) pp. 3–4; *Chicago Defender*, June 4, 1927, p. 8; Frank Driggs, "Don Redman, Jazz Composer-Arranger," in Martin Williams, ed., *Jazz Panorama*, pp. 98–100; Barry Ulanov, "Thanks, Mr. Redman, For Modern Style," *Metronome*, (June, 1941), pp. 20–21; Buddy Howard, "Old Cotton Pickers Band Could Outrock Moderns," *Downbeat* 9, 11 (June 1, 1942) p. 8. Two John Nesbitt arrangements by the Detroit band "Put It There" and "Stop Kidding" are included in *Big Band Jazz* (Smithsonian R 030 DMM-0610).

23. *Chicago Defender*, April 10, 1926, p. 6; Jan. 8, 1917, p. 6; Feb. 12, 1927, p. 6; Oct. 6, 1928, p. 10; Albert J. McCarthy, *Big Band Jazz*, pp. 123–125; Duncan P. Scheidt, "Speed Webb" in *Sounds and Fury* 1, 2 (Sept.-Oct., 1965) pp. 46–52, reprinted in Scheidt, *The Jazz State of Indiana*, pp. 153–174.

24. Stanley Dance, *World of Swing*, p. 303.

25. Ibid.; Teddy Wilson with Tom Scanlon, "The Impeccable Mr. Wilson," *Downbeat*, 26, 2 (Jan. 22, 1959) p. 20.

26. Ibid.

27. *Chicago Defender*, Jan. 8, 1927, p. 6; June 4, 1927, p. 8; Sept. 24, 1927, p. 8; Dec. 17, 1927, p. 10; Feb. 11, 1928, p. 8; July 7, 1928, p 8; Albert J. McCarthy, *Big Band Jazz*, pp. 164–165; Brian Rust, *Jazz Records*, p. 863.

28. *Chicago Defender*, Jan. 8, 1927, p. 6; Feb. 5, 1927, p. 6; June 4, 1927, p. 8; Oct. 8, 1927, p. 8; Nov. 26, 1927, p. 8; Albert J. McCarthy, *Big Band Jazz*, pp. 164–165; Brian Rust, *Jazz Records*, p. 806.

29. Melvin "Sy" Oliver with Frank Driggs, "Sy Oliver," *Sounds and Fury* 1, 1 (July-Aug., 1965) p. 51; Oliver gives a picture of the Whyte band as roughnecks in Stanley Dance, *World of Swing*, pp. 129–130. Whyte's versions of "West End Blues" and "Good Feelin Blues" are on *Jammin' For The Jackpot: Big Bands and Territory Bands of the 1930s*, (New World Records, NW217); Albert McCarthy, *Big Band Jazz*, pp. 159–162; Gunther Schuller, *Early Jazz*, p. 310.

30. Melvin "Sy" Oliver with Frank Driggs, "Sy Oliver," *Sounds and Fury* 1, 1 (July-Aug., 1965) p. 51.

31. Sylvester Rice, letter to Marshall Stearns, Sylvester Rice file, I.J.S.

32. Sylvester Rice to Marshall Stearns, Eli Rice file, I.J.S.

33. Frank Driggs, "Tommy Douglas," *Jazz Monthly* 6, 2 (April, 1960) p. 5; Stanley Dance, *The World of Count Basie*, (New York: Da Capo, 1980) p. 318; Nathan W. Pearson, Jr., *Goin' To Kansas City*, pp. 41–42, 51–52.

34. Ibid., p. 312–318, 343; Eli Rice file, I.J.S.; Sylvester Rice file I.J.S.; *Chicago Defender*, Sept. 8, 1926, p. 6; Sept. 18, 1926, p. 6; Feb. 19, 1927, p. 8; Nov. 26, 1927, p. 8; Aug. 25, 1928, p. 8; Aug. 10, 1929, p. 8; Albert J. McCarthy, *Big Band Jazz*, p. 121.

35. Grant Moore file, I.J.S.; *Chicago Defender*, April 16, 1927, p. 8; June 11, 1927, p. 8; Oct. 1, 1927, p. 8; Nov. 26, 1927, p. 8; March 17, 1928, p. 10; June 16, 1928, p. 10; Feb. 9, 1929, p. 8; Feb. 16, 1929, p. 8; June 22, 1929, p. 8; Albert J. McCarthy, *Big Band Jazz*, p. 122; Gunther Schuller, *Early Jazz*, pp. 307–310.

36. Frank Driggs, "Red Perkins and His Dixie Ramblers," pp. 15–16; *Chicago Defender*, Oct. 13, 1928, p. 8; Dec. 8, 1928, p. 10; Jan. 26, 1929, p. 10; Nov. 4, 1929, p. 9; Frank Driggs, "Elmer Crumbley, His Story," *Coda* 1, 10 (Feb., 1959) p. 9; Albert J. McCarthy, *Big Band Jazz*, pp. 126–131.

37. Brian Rust, *Jazz Records*, p. 318; Vocalion 1050, Vocalion 15641, both reissued on *West Coast Jazz v. I*, (Arcadia 2001); Lawrence Gushee, "New Orleans Area Musicians On the West Coast," *Black Music Research Journal* 9, 1 (1989), pp. 4, 9; Gunther Schuller, *Swing Era*, pp. 779–780; Albert J. McCarthy, *Big Band Jazz*, p. 173.

38. Jack Mitchell, "Colored Ideas," *Storyville*, 61 (Oct.–Nov., 1975) pp. 19–23; *Chicago Defender*, March 10, 1928, p. 9; May 12, 1928, p. 11; April 7, 1928, p. 10; May 5, 1928, p. 10; August 18, 1928; p. 11; Albert J. McCarthy, *Big Band Jazz*, p. 173. It is interesting that some of the press blamed Clay rather than attacking the racism and exclusion of the Australian government and press, which threw around epithets like "coon" and "nigger." In 1975, Jack Mitchell argued that the Australian government's reaction in expelling the six musicians involved and convincing five more to leave was basically the result of pressure from the Australian Musician's Union, which was trying, successfully, to protect the jobs of its members from black American competition.

39. Albert J. McCarthy, *Big Band Jazz*, p. 174; Dick Raichelson, notes to *West Coast Jazz v. I*, (Arcadia 2001); John Bentley and Ralph W. Miller, "West Coast Jazz in the Twenties," *Jazz Monthly* 7, 3 (May, 1961) pp. 4–5; Brian Rust, *Jazz Records*, p. 1108.

40. Peter Vacher, "Andrew Blakeney—A Lifetime in Music," *Storyville* 58 (April–May, 1975) p. 126.

41. Albert J. McCarthy, *Big Band Jazz*, pp. 170–172; Lionel Hampton with James Haskins, *Hamp*, pp. 28–39; Berta Wood, "Charlie Lawrence," *Jazz Journal* 9, 10 (Oct., 1956) pp. 6–7; Berta Wood, "George Orendorf, Quality Serenader," *Jazz Journal* part 1, 10, 1 (Jan., 1957) pp. 4–6; part 2, 10, 2 (Feb., 1957) pp. 4–5; Berta Wood, "Paul Leroy Howard," *Jazz Journal* 10, 11 (Nov., 1957) pp. 6–8; Gunther Schuller, *Swing Era*, p. 393; Stanley Dance, *World of Count*

Basie, pp. 165–167; *Californian Jazz 1929–1930* (RCA-France FXMI7106) includes seven Paul Howard sides from 1929 and six from 1930.

42. Frank Driggs, "Kansas City and the Southwest," in Nat Hentoff and Al Mc-Carthy, *Jazz*, pp. 191–230; Paul Oliver, *Story of the Blues*, pp. 36–41; Gunther Schuller, *Early Jazz*, pp. 279–317; Gunther Schuller, *Swing Era*, pp. 781–786, 792–805; Nathan W. Pearson, Jr., "Political and Musical Forces . . . Kansas City," pp. 181–183, 188–189; Nathan W. Pearson, Jr., *Goin' To Kansas City*, pp. 33–40.

43. Ed Lewis with Frank Driggs, "Kansas City Brass," part 2, *Jazz Review* 2, 9 (Oct., 1959) p. 23.

44. Budd Johnson file, I.J.S.; Keg Johnson file, I.J.S.; Frank Driggs, "Booker Pittman," *Coda* 6, 3 (Oct., 1963) p. 8; George Corley with Bertrand DeMeusy, "Two Musical Careers," *Jazz Monthly* 12, 12 (Feb., 1967) pp. 2–5; Bertrand DeMeusy, "Lloyd Glenn—Texas Pianist," *Jazz Journal* 18, 10 (Oct., 1965) pp. 12–13; Valerie Wilmer, "The Lee Young Story," *Jazz Journal* 14, 1 (Jan., 1961) p. 3, Johnny Simmen, "The Lem Johnson Story," *Jazz Journal* 20, 12 (Dec., 1967) p. 16; Frank Driggs, "LaForest Dent," *Jazz Journal* 12, 5 (May, 1959) pp. 2–3.

45. Valerie Wilmer, "The Lee Young Story," *Jazz Journal* 14, 1 (Jan., 1961) p. 3.

46. Johnny Simmen, "The Lem Johnson Story," *Jazz Journal* 20, 12 (Dec., 1967) p. 16; Ed Lewis with Frank Driggs, "Kansas City Brass," part 1, *Jazz Review* 2, 4 (May, 1959) pp. 16–17; Frank Driggs, "LaForest Dent," *Jazz Journal* 12, 5 (May, 1959) pp. 2–3.

47. Don Gazzaway, "Before Bird—Buster," *Jazz Monthly* 7, 11 (Jan., 1962) pp. 7–8.

48. Frank Driggs, "Booker Pittman," p. 8; Budd Johnson file, I.J.S.; Keg Johnson file, I.J.S.; Frank Driggs, "LaForest Dent," *Jazz Journal* 12, 5 (May, 1959) pp. 2–3; Frank Driggs, "Walter Page, About My Life In Music," *Jazz Review* 1, 1 (Nov., 1958) p. 13–14; Nathan W. Pearson, Jr., *Goin' To Kansas City* pp. 19–21.

49. Frank Driggs, "Kansas City and the Southwest," in Nat Hentoff and Albert McCarthy, *Jazz*, p. 199; Gunther Schuller, *Early Jazz*, pp. 288–291; Albert J. McCarthy, *Big Band Jazz*, pp. 139–140; Nathan W. Pearson, Jr., *Goin' To Kansas City*, pp. 46–50. Brian Rust, *Jazz Records*, p. 1507. "Starvation Blues" is on both *Big Band Jazz* Smithsonian (R 030 DMM-0610) and *Sweet and Low Blues* New World (NW 256).

50. Frank Driggs, "Kansas City and the Southwest," in Nat Hentoff and Albert McCarthy, *Jazz*, pp. 191, 203–204, 210; Gunther Schuller, *Early Jazz*, pp. 298–299; Albert J. McCarthy, *Big Band Jazz*, pp. 139–140; Budd Johnson file, I.J.S.; Brian Rust, *Jazz Records*, pp. 940–941; Nathan W. Pearson, Jr., *Goin' To Kansas City*, pp. 148–153. "Ruff Scufflin" is on *Sweet and Low Blues* New World (NW 256).

51. Frank Driggs, "Kansas City and the Southwest," in Nat Hentoff and Albert McCarthy, *Jazz* p. 199; Gunther Schuller, *Early Jazz*, pp. 288–291; Albert J.

NOTES TO CHAPTER 6

McCarthy, *Big Band Jazz*, pp. 139–140; Walter Page file, I.J.S.; Oran Page file, I.J.S.; Frank Driggs, "Walter Page," *Jazz Review* 1, 1 (Nov., 1958) pp. 13–14; Jimmy Rushing with Frank Driggs, "Jimmy Rushing's Story," *Evergreen Review* (April, 1966) pp. 65–67; Don Gazzaway, "Before Bird—Buster," *Jazz Monthly* 7, 11 (Jan., 1962) pp. 7–8; Count Basie with Albert Murray, *Good Morning Blues*, pp. 3–23; Nathan W. Pearson, Jr., *Goin' To Kansas City*, pp. 64–68; Brian Rust, *Jazz Records*, p. 1204. "Blue Devil Blues" and "Squabblin'" are on *Sweet and Low Blues* New World (NW 256).

52. Frank Driggs, "Kansas City and the Southwest," in Nat Hentoff and Albert McCarthy, *Jazz*, pp. 198, 202–204; Gunther Schuller, *Early Jazz*, pp. 284–288; Albert J. McCarthy, *Big Band Jazz*, pp. 135–137; Ed Lewis with Frank Driggs, "Kansas City Brass," part 1, *Jazz Review* 2, 4 (May, 1959) p. 18; Paul Banks with Frank Driggs, "Paul Banks Tells His Story," *Jazz Journal* 11, 8 (Aug., 1958) pp. 4–5; *Chicago Defender*, June 11, 1927, p. 8; Oct. 22, 1927, p. 8; May 5, 1928, p. 10; Oct. 6, 1928, p. 10; July 13, 1929, p. 8; Nathan W. Pearson, Jr., *Goin' To Kansas City*, pp. 121–126; Brian Rust, *Jazz Records*, pp. 1109–1111. Moten recordings are available in various reissues but most are from the 1932 sessions, which will be discussed in chapter seven, not examples of the music referred to here.

53. *Chicago Defender*, July 31, 1926, p.6; April 23, 1927, p. 8; April 30, 1927, p. 8; May 21, 1927, p. 10; Oct. 29, 1927, p. 11; Jan. 7, 1928, p. 8; Jan. 28, 1928, p. 8; June 23, 1928, p. 10; Jan. 19, 1929, p. 10; June 29, 1929, p. 8; Frank Driggs, "Buddy Tate's Story," *Jazz Review* 1, 2 (Dec., 1958) p. 18; Frank Driggs, "Kansas City and the Southwest," in Nat Hentoff and Al McCarthy, *Jazz*, pp. 199–202; Gunther Schuller, *Early Jazz*, pp. 299–303; Albert J. McCarthy, *Big Band Jazz*, pp. 99–102; Nathan Pearson, Jr., *Goin' To Kansas City*, pp. 43–45; Brian Rust, *Jazz Records*, pp. 1563–1564. "Black and Blue Rhapsody" (1928) "After You've Gone," (1930) and "I've Found a New Baby," are on *Sweet and Low Blues* New World (NW 256).

54. *Chicago Defender*, April 7, 1928, p. 10; May 5, 1928, p. 10; Jan. 19, 1929, p. 10; Jan. 26, 1929, p. 10; Feb. 23, 1929, p. 8; June 8, 1929, p. 10; Frank Driggs, "Kansas City and the Southwest," in Nat Hentoff and Al McCarthy, *Jazz*, p. 214; Gunther Schuller, *Early Jazz*, pp. 291–293; Albert J. McCarthy, *Big Band Jazz*, pp. 103–104; Troy Floyd file, I.J.S.; Don Albert file, I.J.S.; Nathan W. Pearson, Jr., *Goin' to Kansas City*, pp.45–46; Brian Rust, *Jazz Records*, pp. 209, 533, 1156, 1338. "Dreamland Blues" parts I and II, are on *Sweet and Low Blues* New World (NW 256).

55. *Chicago Defender*, April 30, 1927, p. 8; June 2, 1928, p. 8; Aug. 4, 1928, p. 8; March 2, 1929, p. 9; Frank Driggs, "Kansas City and the Southwest," in Nat Hentoff and Al McCarthy, *Jazz*, pp. 199–200; Gunther Schuller, *Early Jazz*, pp. 281, 286, 288; Albert J. McCarthy, *Big Band Jazz*, pp. 102–103; Keg Johnson file, I.J.S.; Budd Johnson file, I.J.S.; Frank Driggs, "Booker Pittman," *Coda* 6, 3 p. 8; Nathan W. Pearson, Jr., *Goin' To Kansas City*, pp. 54–59.

56. Max Jones and John Chilton, *Louis*, pp. 58, 210; Johnny St. Cyr, "Jazz As I Remember It," part 3, *Jazz Journal* 19, 11 (Nov., 1966), p. 9; James Lincoln Collier, *Louis Armstrong*, p. 81; "Pops" Foster with Tom Stoddard, *The Autobiography of a New Orleans Jazzman*, p. 115; Warren "Baby" Dodds with Larry Gara, "The Baby Dodds Story," *Jazz Journal* 8, 6 (June, 1955) part 2, pp. 4–5.

57. Jerome Don Pasquall, Frank Driggs, and Thornton Hagert, "Jerome Don Pasquell," part 1 p. 24; Harry Dial, "Drums on the Mississippi," in Art Hodes and Chadwick Hansen, *Selections from the Gutter*, pp. 211–212; Louis Metcalf with Derrick Stewart-Baker, "Louis Metcalf," part 1, *Jazz Journal* 19, 11 (Nov., 1966) p. 15; John Chilton, *Who's Who of Jazz*, pp. 88, 105, 244, 300, 375–376; Leonard Kunstadt, "Eugene Sedric—Gentleman Musician," *Record Research*, 53 (Sept., 1963) pp. 3–5; Jack Bradley, "Honey Bear, Gene Sedric 1907–1963," *Coda* 5, 10 (May, 1963) pp. 21; Albert J. McCarthy, *Big Band Jazz*, pp. 79–80; Brian Rust, *Jazz Records*, pp. 349, 1245.

58. Albert J. McCarthy, *Big Band Jazz*, pp. 113–120; Douglas Hague, "Ed Allen," *Jazz Journal* 11, 1 (Jan. 1958) pp. 11 14; Bartlett D. Simms, "Jazz In St. Louis," *Record Changer* (Nov., 1945) pp. 4 5, 30; Marshall Stearns, "Dark Lad Creath Introduced the Stomach Vibrato," *Downbeat* 4, 10 (Oct., 1937) p. 12; Ed Crowder and A.F. Neimoeller, "Dewey Jackson, St. Lewis Jazzman," pp. 208–211, and Harry Dial, "Drums on the Mississippi," pp. 211–212 in Art Hodes and Chadwick Hansen, *Selections From The Gutter*; Bertrand De-Meusy, "Floyd Campbell's Story," *Storyville* 74 (Dec. 1977–Jan. 1978) pp. 63–66; Frank Driggs, "Kansas City and the Southwest," in Nat Hentoff and Al McCarthy, *Jazz*, pp. 217–220; David Chevan, "Riverboat Music From St. Louis," *Black Music Research Journal* 9, 2 (Fall, 1989), pp. 163–177.

59. *Chicago Defender*, Sept. 10, 1927, p. 9; Frank Driggs, "Red Perkins and His Dixie Ramblers," *Jazz Journal* 17, 11 (Nov., 1964) pp. 15–16; Ed Lewis with Frank Driggs, "Kansas City Brass," *Jazz Review*, 2, 4 (May, 1959) part 1, p. 18.

Chapter 7

1. Walter C. Allen, documents the *Great Day* episode in detail in *Hendersonia*, pp. 228–238, 242–243. When casting began for Vincent Youmans's show in April, Duke Ellington was listed as the band leader according to the *Chicago Defender*, April 27, 1929, p. 7 (*Hendersonia*, p. 228). The *Pittsburg Courier* reported May 4, 1929, "Because of some misunderstanding between Vincent Youmans and Irving Mills, the latter, manager of Duke Ellington, Duke and his orchestra will not open" (*Hendersonia*. p. 228). In late May and early June, some white musicians were added and some of Henderson's men, (including apparently Kaiser Marshall and Louis Armstrong) were let go, apparently without his protesting (Percy Outram in *New York Age*, June 8, 1929, p. 7; Walter C. Allen, *Hendersonia*, pp. 229–230). Out-of-town tryouts continued in Philadelphia, Atlantic City, and Long Branch, New Jersey when

Fletcher and the last of his men were fired and replaced by whites (Walter C. Allen, *Hendersonia*, pp. 231–32, 242). Fletcher Henderson then scuffled some tour dates to survive the summer but had to rebuild the band significantly before finally returning to Roseland on Oct. 30, 1929 with a band of Russell Smith, Bobby Stark, Rex Stewart on trumpet and cornet; Claude Jones, Jimmy Harrison on trombone; Arville Harris, Harvey Boone, Coleman Hawkins on reeds; Fletcher Henderson, as pianist arranger; Clarence Holiday on banjo; Bob Ysaguirre on tuba; Walter Johnson on drums (*Hendersonia*, p. 235, 242–243). For Duke Ellington and *Show Girl*, see Roger D. Kinkle, *Encyclopedia of Popular Music and Jazz*, p. 199; James L. Collier, *Duke Ellington*, pp. 97–98.

2. Brian Rust, *Jazz Records*, pp. 472–483, 710–724.

3. Mark Tucker, *Ellington: The Early Years*, pp. 1–110; Barry Ulanov, *Duke Ellington* (New York: Creative Age Press, 1946) pp. 1–63; James L. Collier, *Ellington*, pp. 3–53; Samuel Charters and Leonard Kunstadt, *Jazz: New York*, pp. 201–210; Stanley Dance, *The World of Duke Ellington*, (New York: Scribner's 1970) pp. 7, 55–56, 62–63; Stanley Dance, *World of Swing*, pp. 47–53.

4. Mark Tucker, *Ellington: The Early Years*, pp. 98–210; Walter C. Allen, *Hendersonia*, pp. 84–118.

5. Brian Rust, *Jazz Records,* pp. 472, 712–720, 1564; Mark Tucker, *Ellington: The Early Years*, pp. 98–118, 140–170; Gunther Schuller, *Early Jazz*, pp. 318–325; Gunther Schuller, "The Ellington Style: Its Origins and Early Development" in Nat Hentoff and Albert McCarthy, *Jazz*, pp. 233–242. Mark Tucker reprints Green's review on pp. 99–100.

6. Mark Tucker, *Ellington: The Early Years*, pp. 183–210; Barry Ulanov, *Duke Ellington*, pp. 45–51; Albert J. McCarthy, "Bubber Miley," Bubber Miley file, I.J.S.; Roger Pryor Dodge, "Bubber," *HRS Society Rag*, pp. 10–14; John Chilton, *Who's Who of Jazz*, pp. 65, 168, 177, 246, 272; Gunther Schuller, *Early Jazz*, pp. 326–339; James L. Collier, *Duke Ellington*, pp. 46–48, 60–63, 82–84; Stanley Dance, *World of Duke Ellington*, p. 70.

7. Anne Judd, "Barney Goin' Easy," *Jazz Journal* 20, 9 (Sept., 1967) pp. 4–7; George Hoefer, "New Orleans Clarinets: 6: Barney Bigard," *Jazz Information* 2, 8 (Nov., 1940) pp. 6–13; *Chicago Defender*, Oct. 15, 1927, p. 9; Rudy Jackson, "My Story," *Jazz Music* 3, 6 (1947) pp. 3–4; Charles Chilton, "Jackson and the Oliver Band," *Jazz Music* 3, 6 (1947) pp. 5–9; Derrick Stewart-Baker, "Louis Metcalf," *Jazz Journal* 19, 12 (Dec., 1966) part 2, p. 20–21; Mark Tucker, *Ellington: The Early Years*, pp. 202–203; James L. Collier, *Duke Ellington*, 60–62, 80–82.

8. Mark Tucker, *Ellington: The Early Years*, pp. 195–198; James L. Collier, *Duke Ellington*, pp. 64-72; Barry Ulanov, *Duke Ellington*, pp. 56–58, 62–65.

9. James L. Collier, *Duke Ellington*, pp. 64–105; Barry Ulanov, *Duke Ellington*, pp. 56–58, 62–65; Samuel Charters and Leonard Kunstadt, *Jazz: New York*, pp. 208–210, 216–221; Stanley Dance, *World of Duke Ellington*, p. 67; Cab Calloway and Bryant Rollins, *Of Minnie the Moocher*, pp. 106–117.

10. For an example of this see Irving Mills's release in the *Chicago Defender*,

Aug. 27, 1927, p. 8, which is both good publicity for Duke Ellington and counter programming against a Fletcher Henderson appearance in Chicago.

11. Barry Ulanov, *Duke Ellington*, pp. 57–58, 62–65, 82–83, 90–91; James L. Collier, *Duke Ellington*, pp. 67–105, 124–133, 152–159; Samuel Charters and Leonard Kunstadt, *Jazz: New York*, p. 220; Stanley Dance, *World of Duke Ellington*, pp. 67–68; *Chicago Defender*, Nov. 16, 1929, p. 11; April 27, 1929, p. 8; June 15, 1929, p. 10; Dec. 27, 1930, p. 7; Jan. 24, 1931, p. 9; March 7, 1931, pp. 8, 9; Aug. 27, 1932, p. 8; April 22, 1933, p. 8; July 24, 1933, p. 9; Oct. 7, 1933, p. 8.

12. Gunther Schuller, *Early Jazz*, pp. 326–357; Mark Tucker, *Ellington: The Early Years*, pp. 236–260; James L. Collier, *Duke Ellington*, pp. 106–123, 134–151; Albert J. McCarthy, *Big Band Jazz*, pp. 328–338; Charles Emge, "Irving Mills Tells His Story," *Downbeat* 19, 22 (Nov. 5, 1952) p. 6; *Chicago Defender*, Sept. 30, 1933, p. 9; Oct. 7, 1933, p. 8.

13. Leo Walker, *The Wonderful Era of the Great Dance Bands*, (Berkley: Howell-North, 1964) pp. 170–182, 190–196, 235–257; Irving Kolodin, "The Dance Band Business: A Study in Black and White," *Harper's Magazine* 183 (1941) pp. 72–82; Artie Shaw with Bob Maxwell, "Music is a Business," *Saturday Evening Post* (Dec. 2, 1938) pp. 66–68.

14. Coy Herndon column, *Chicago Defender*, Jan. 27, 1927, p. 7; Tim Owlsey column, *Chicago Defender* June 27, 1927, p. 8; S.H Dudley column, *Chicago Defender*, July 9, 1927, p. 6; St. Clair Drake and Horace Cayton, *Black Metropolis*, p. 84.

15. Dave Peyton column, *Chicago Defender* May 5, 1928, p. 10; June 30, 1928, p. 10; July 28, 1928, p. 8; Sept. 8, 1928, p. 8; Oct. 6, 1928, p. 10; Tom Hennessey, "Chicago's Black Establishment," *Journal of Jazz Studies* 2, 1 (Dec., 1974) pp. 28–31.

16. *Chicago Defender*, Jan. 11, 1930, p. 10; Feb. 1, 1930, p. 10; Feb. 15, 1930, p. 10; March 8, 1930, p. 8; Oct. 18, 1930, p. 6; Dec. 27, 1930, p. 6; Jan. 3, 1931, p. 6; Jan. 17, 1931, p. 6; July 4, 1931, p. 6; Aug. 15, 1931, p. 8; Dempsey J. Travis, *An Autobiography of Black Jazz*, pp. 145–155; Tom Hennessey, "Chicago's Black Establishment," *Journal of Jazz Studies* 2,1 (Dec., 1974) pp. 30–31.

17. Chart titled, "Bands in Harlem Theaters," compiled by Walter C. Allen and Jerry Valburn, in Stanley Dance, *World of Swing*, pp. 404–416.

18. *Chicago Defender*, Nov. 19, 1927, p. 3; Feb. 25, 1928, p. 8; Dec. 1, 1928, p. 8; Nov. 12, 1927, pp. 5, 12; March 17, 1928, p. 10; April 14, 1928, p. 10; May 12, 1928, p. 10; Sept, 22, 1928, p. 2; Oct. 12, 1929, p. 10; Jan. 11, 1930, p. 8; May 24, 1930, p. 12; July 26, 1930, p. 6; Oct. 4, 1930, p. 7; Dec. 6, 1930, p. 9; Jan. 10, 1931, p. 6; Feb. 28, 1931, pp. 8, 9; March 28, 1931, p. 8; May 2, 1931; p. 8; Sept. 19, 1931, p. 6; Dempsey J. Travis, *Autobiography of Black Jazz*, pp. 93–98; Tom Hennessey, "Chicago's Black Establishment," *Journal of Jazz Studies* 2,1 (Dec., 1971) pp. 36–37.

19. John Norris, "Harold Holmes, His Story," *Coda* (4, 4) p. 24.

20. *Chicago Defender*, Oct. 6, 1928, p. 10; July 29, 1929, p. 9; March 29, 1930, p. 11; April 5, 1930, p. 10; Cab Calloway and Bryant Rollins, *Of Minnie the Moocher*, pp. 122–130; Roger Pryor Dodge, "Bubber" *HRS Society Rag* (Oct., 1940) p. 14; Dempsey J. Travis, *Autobiography of Black Jazz*, pp. 287–292.

21. Dempsey J. Travis, *Autobiography of Black Jazz*, p. 292; Walter C. Allen, *Hendersonia*, pp. 221–223, 242; *Chicago Defender*, April 5, 1930, p. 10; Oct. 18, 1930, p. 6.

22. John Chilton, *Who's Who in Jazz*, p. 18; Albert J. McCarthy, *Big Band Jazz*, pp. 31–32; Albert J. McCarthy, "The Life and Death of Walter Barnes," *Jazz Monthly* 179 (Jan., 1970) pp. 7–10. Admittedly white bands also ran risks, as the Coconut Grove fire proved. Still the relative lack of publicity for the Barnes fire versus the Coconut Grove blaze is another example of the continued invisibility of black Americans particularly in the territories.

23. *Chicago Defender*, March 2, 1931, p. 9.

24. Albert J. McCarthy, *Big Band Jazz*, pp. 52, 94–95; *Chicago Defender*, March 16, 1929, p. 10; July 20, 1929, p. 9; March 3, 1928, p. 9; Oct. 6, 1928, p. 10; Nov. 2, 1929, p. 13; Nov. 16, 1929, p. 9; Aug. 16, 1930, p. 11; Stanley Dance, *World of Count Basie*, p. 54.

25. Ronald Priestly, *Jazz on Record*, pp. 43–49; Roland Gelatt, *The Fabulous Phonograph*, pp. 245–277.

26. *Chicago Defender*, Nov. 2, 1929, p. 13; Jan. 11, 1930, p. 8; Aug. 16, 1930, p. 11; Philip K. Eberly, *Music in the Air*, pp. 18–22, 42–50; Walter C. Allen, *Hendersonia*, p. 236.

27. *Chicago Defender*, March 28, 1931, p. 9.

28. *Chicago Defender*, Dec. 20, 1930, p. 6; Nov. 26, 1932, p. 6; Jan. 7, 1933, p. 6.

29. *Chicago Defender*, Jan. 24, 1931, p. 9; March 14, 1931, p. 8; April 18, 1931, p. 9; May 2, 1931, p. 8.

30. *Chicago Defender*, Jan. 10, 1931, p. 6.

31. *Chicago Defender*, Jan. 24, 1931, p. 9, May 16, 1931, p. 8; July 18, 1931, p. 7; Feb. 18, 1933, p. 7; July 16, 1932, p. 6; Rex Stewart, "Coleman Hawkins," *Downbeat* (May 19, 1966) pp. 23–25; Milt Hinton and David G. Berger, *Brass Line*, pp. 115–119; Calloway and Rollins, *Of Minnie the Moocher*, pp. 139–141.

32. *Chicago Defender*, Feb. 18, 1933, p. 7.

33. Anne Judd, "Barney Goin' Easy," *Jazz Journal* 20, 9 (Sept., 1967) p. 5; Roger Pryor Dodge, "Bubber," *HRS Society Rag* (Oct., 1940) p. 14.

34. *Chicago Defender*, May 12, 1928, p. 10; James L. Collier, *Duke Ellington*, pp. 132–133.

35. James L. Collier, *Making of Jazz*, pp. 127–140; *Chicago Defender*, May 16, 1931, p. 9.

36. *Chicago Defender*, Sept. 4, 1926, p. 6; Sept. 18, 1926, p. 6; April 9, 1927, p. 8.

37. *Chicago Defender*, April 11, 1931, p. 9.

38. Preston Love, "Chords and Dischords," *Sounds and Fury* 1, 1 (July–Aug., 1965) p. 59.

39. Ibid.

40. Lewis Porter, *Lester Young*, (Boston: Twayne, 1985) pp. 1–16; Allen, *Hendersonia*, pp. 292–296, 298, 302.

41. Gunther Schuller, *Swing Era*, pp. 6–8, 192–207; Morroe Berger, Edward Berger, and James Patrick, *Benny Carter*, pp. 172–186.

42. Gunther Schuller, *Early Jazz*, pp. 271–279; Frank Tirro, *Jazz: A History* pp. 237–238; James L. Collier, *Making of Jazz*, pp. 188–192.

43. John Chilton, *Who's Who in Jazz*, pp. 65, 66, 388.

44. John Chilton, *Who's Who in Jazz*, pp. 66, 158, 376, 347, 394, 398.

45. Gunther Schuller, *Early Jazz*, p. 277. James L. Collier, *Making of Jazz*, pp. 188–192, sees similar changes in Fletcher Henderson's arrangements of "Radio Rhythm" and "Low Down on the Bayou" from the same period.

46. Brunswick 6074, Brunswick 6211, Brunswick 01463; Brian Rust, *Jazz Records*, pp. 253, 1072, 1276; George Hoefer, notes to *Sound of Harlem*, pp. 19–20, 35.

47. Gunther Schuller, *Swing Era*, pp. 3–23.

48. Count Basie with Albert Murray, *Good Morning Blues*, pp. 141–143; Gunther Schuller, *Early Jazz*, pp. 304–306, 312–317. "Toby" arr. by Eddie Barefield and "Moten Swing" arr. by Eddie Durhan are on *Big Band Jazz*, Smithsonian (R 030 DMM-0610) and Bennie Moten, *Basie Beginnings* (BMG 9768-2-RB).

Chapter 8

1. Walter C. Allen, *Hendersonia*, pp. 228–238, 242–243; Max Jones and John Chilton, *Louis*, pp. 101–161; James L. Collier, *Armstrong*, pp. 199–300; Albert J. McCarthy, *Big Band Jazz*, pp. 271–272; Gunther Schuller, *Swing Era*, pp. 158–193; *Chicago Defender*, Aug. 31, 1929, p. 8; Sept. 14, 1929, p. 5; Sept. 21, 1929, p. 7; Oct. 26, 1929, p. 11; April 26, 1930, p. 8; Dec. 27, 1930, p. 7; Jan. 21, 1933, p. 6; March 4, 1933, p. 9; May 13, 1933, p. 8; Oct. 21, 1933, p. 8.

2. Steve Voce, "The Marquis of Harlem," *Jazz Journal* 11, 6 (June, 1958) p. 9.

3. Cab Calloway and Bryant Rollins, *Of Minnie the Moocher*, pp. 65–185; Dempsey Travis, *Autobiography of Black Jazz*, pp. 219–236; Albert J. McCarthy, *Big Band Jazz*, pp. 210–213; Gunther Schuller, *Swing Era*, pp. 326–345; *Chicago Defender*, July 5, 1930, p. 6; Jan. 31, 1931, p. 9; March 7, 1931, p. 8; Oct. 8, 1932, p. 8; Jan. 7, 1933, p. 6; May 27, 1933, p. 9; Aug. 12, 1933, p. 8; Sept. 30, 1933, p. 9; Oct. 7, 1933, p. 8; Jan. 13, 1934, p. 8; June 2, 1934, p. 9; June 23, 1934, p. 8; clippings, Eddie Barefield file, I.J.S.

4. Frank Driggs, "Good-bye Fess," *Storyville* 67 (Oct.-Nov., 1976) pp. 14–19; Stanley R. Williams with Harrison Smith, "Fess Williams Story," pp. 3–5; Albert J. McCarthy, *Big Band Jazz*, pp. 51–53; *Chicago Defender*, Aug. 31, 1929, p. 8; Oct. 29, 1929, p. 9; March 17, 1933, p. 8; June 2, 1934, p. 9.

5. Albert J. McCarthy, *Big Band Jazz*, pp. 80–88; "Pops" Foster with Tom Stoddard, *The Autobiography of a New Orleans Jazzman*, pp. 135–144, Gunther Schuller, *Swing Era*, pp. 186–189; David Innes, "Luis Russell, 1902–1963," *Jazz Journal* 20, 6 (June, 1967) pp. 4–5; Harold Grut, "Luis Russell," *Jazz Journal* 17, 3 (March, 1964) pp. 19, 22; Stanley Dance, *World of Swing*, pp. 253–254; *Chicago Defender*, April 7, 1933, p. 8; Dec. 30, 1933, p. 8; "Ol' Man River" (Aug. 8, 1934) is on *Big Band Jazz* Smithsonian (R 030 DMM-0610).

6. Albert J. McCarthy, *Big Band Jazz*, pp. 286–289; Gunther Schuller, *Swing Era*, pp. 317–322; Stanley Dance, *World of Swing*, pp. 31–45; 232–238; Charles Fox, "Claude Hopkins Orchestra," *Jazz Forum* 3 (Jan., 1947) pp. 3–5; Herman Rosenberg and Eugene Williams, "New Orleans Clarinets; 2: Edmond Hall," *Jazz Information* 2, 2 (Aug. 9, 1940) pp. 9–12; George Hoefer, notes to *Sound of Harlem*, p. 19; *Chicago Defender*, May 12, 1931, p. 8; Aug. 20, 1932, p. 8; March 4, 1933, p. 8; June 24, 1933, p. 8; Dec. 9, 1933, p. 9; May 12, 1934, p. 8; June 20, 1934, p. 7.

7. Albert J. McCarthy, *Big Band Jazz*, pp. 255–256; Gunther Schuller, *Swing Era*, pp. 385–389; George Hoefer, notes to *Sound of Harlem*, pp. 19–20; clippings, Edgar Hayes file, I.J.S.; Bingie Madison with Bertrand DeMeusy, "Biography of a Career," *Jazz Monthly* 10, 7 (Sept., 1964) p. 9; *Chicago Defender*, Aug. 27, 1932, p. 8; Sept. 10, 1932, p. 7; Jan. 7, 1933, p. 6; April 14, 1933, p. 9; May 13, 1933, p. 8; July 15, 1933, p. 8; Aug. 5, 1933, p. 9; Nov. 4, 1933, p. 8; Nov. 18, 1933, p. 9; Jan. 27, 1934, p. 9; June 2, 1934, p. 9.

8. Albert J. McCarthy, *Big Band Jazz*, pp. 265–268; Gunther Schuller, *Swing Era*, pp. 292–301; Stanley Dance, *World of Swing*, pp. 84–89, 68–74, 384–390; Stanley Dance, liner notes to *Chick Webb, a Legend* (Decca DL 79222); George Hoefer, booklet for *Harlem*, p. 20; *Chicago Defender* March 24, 1933 p. 8. "Stomping At The Savoy" (May 18, 1934) and "Don't Be That Way" both arranged by Edgar Sampson, whose scores (like Fletcher Henderson's) were very important to Benny Goodman, are on *Big Band Jazz* Smithsonian (R 030 DMM-0610).

9. Albert J. McCarthy, *Big Band Jazz*, pp. 249–255; Gunther Schuller, *Swing Era*, pp. 201–222; Dempsey J. Travis, *Autobiography of Black Jazz*, pp. 435–449; George Hoefer, notes, Jimmie Lunceford file, I.J.S.; *Chicago Defender*, Jan. 24, 1931, p. 9; March 24, 1933, p. 8; Oct. 21 1933, p. 8; Nov. 18, 1933, p. 9; Feb. 3, 1934, p. 8; June 23, 1934, p. 8; Aug. 25, 1934, p. 7; Oct. 13, 1934, p. 6; Ralph Gleason, liner notes to *Jimmie Lunceford, Rhythm Is Our Business* Decca DL 79237; Ralph Gleason, liner notes to *Jimmie Lunceford, For Dancers Only* Decca DL 79239. "Mood Indigo," arranged by Willie Smith, and "Stratosphere," arranged by Jimmie Lunceford, (both Sept. 4, 1934), and "Stomp It Off" (Oct. 29, 1934) and "Organ Grinder's Swing" (Aug. 31, 1936), both arranged by Sy Oliver, are on *Big Band Jazz* Smithsonian (R 030 DMM-0610).

10. Walter C. Allen, *Hendersonia*, pp. 235–289; Albert J. McCarthy, *Big Band*

Jazz, pp. 66–70, 72–73; Gunther Schuller, *Early Jazz*, pp. 275–279; John Hammond, *On Record*, (New York: Ridge Press, 1977) pp. 70, 75–76, 86–89, 142; Gunther Schuller, *Swing Era*, pp. 323–326; *Chicago Defender*, Jan. 3, 1931, p. 6; March 17, 1933, p. 8; April 7, 1933, p. 8; Sept. 9, 1933, p. 9; May 5, 1934, p. 8.

11. Albert J. McCarthy, *Big Band Jazz*, pp. 155–156, 166–167; Russ Shor, "Charlie Gaines," *Storyville* (Dec. 1976–1977) pp. 45–46; Stanley Dance, *World of Swing*, pp. 79–83, 310–311.

12. Tom Hennessey, "Chicago's Black Establishment," *Journal of Jazz Studies* 2, 1 (Dec., 1974) pp. 36–38; St. Clair Drake and Horace R. Cayton, *Black Metropolis*, pp. 82–87, 465–467; Dempsey J. Travis, *Autobiography of Black Jazz*, pp. 77–110, 145–156; Fred Moore, "King Oliver's Last Tour" in Art Hodes and Chadwick Hansen, eds. *Selection from the Gutter*, pp. 86–88; Alan Lomax, *Mister Jelly Lord*, p. 198–255; John Chilton, *Who's Who in Jazz*, pp. 82, 116, 287–288, 366, 371; *Chicago Defender*, Aug. 2, 1930, p. 7; Dec. 6, 1930, p. 8; Feb. 28, 1931, p. 8; Feb. 7, 1931, p. 8.

13. Albert J. McCarthy, *Big Band Jazz*, pp. 30–31; *Chicago Defender*, Jan. 31, 1931, p. 8; May 9, 1931, p. 9; Sept. 9, 1931, p. 6.

14. *Chicago Defender*, Aug. 29, 1931, p. 6; Clark Halker, "A History of Local 208," *Black Music Research Journal*, 8, 2 (Fall, 1988) pp. 207, 211–215; Robert D. Leiter, *The Musicians and Petrillo*, (New York: Bookman, 1953) pp. 45–70.

15. *Chicago Defender*, Sept. 21, 1929, p. 11; Oct. 12, 1929, p. 10; April 26, 1930, p. 5; May 24, 1930, p. 12; July 5, 1930, p. 8; Aug. 9, 1930, p. 8; Dec. 27, 1930, p. 6; Feb. 28, 1931, p. 8; Aug. 27, 1932, p. 7; June 30, 1934, p. 6; Dempsey J. Travis, *Autobiography of Black Jazz*, pp. 107, 110, 114–116, 371, 390–391; Hinton and Berger, *Bass Line*, pp. 49–51, 44–46; Gunther Schuller, *Swing Era*, pp. 170–181.

16. Dempsey J. Travis, *Autobiography of Black Jazz*, pp. 39–49, 287–292; Earl Hines, "How Gangsters Ran the Band Business," *Ebony* (Sept., 1949) pp. 40–47; Barry Ulanov, "Fatha," *Metronome* (Feb., 1945) pp. 18–19, 33; Albert J. McCarthy, *Big Band Jazz*, pp. 237–240; Gunther Schuller, *Swing Era*, pp. 263–286; *Chicago Defender* Jan. 7, 1933, p. 6; Feb. 18, 1933, p. 8; May 20, 1933, p. 8; Sept. 2, 1933, p. 9; Jan. 13, 1934, p. 9. "Madhouse" (March 26, 1934), "Fat Babes" (Sept. 12, 1934), and "Rock and Rye" (Sept. 13, 1934), all arranged by Jimmy Mudy, show how national sounding the Hines band was by the beginning of the Swing Era on *Big Band Jazz* Smithsonian (R 030 DMM-0610).

17. Albert J. McCarthy, *Big Band Jazz*, pp. 75–79; Gunther Schuller, *Swing Era*, pp. 301–317; Barry Ulanov, "Thanks, Mr. Redman, For Modern Style," *Metronome*, (June, 1941) pp. 20–21; Buddy Howard, "Old Cotton Pickers Band Could Outrock Moderns," *Downbeat* 9, 11 (June 1, 1942) p. 8; "Meet Todd Rhodes," Todd Rhodes file, I.J.S.; *Chicago Defender*, Aug. 2, 1930, p. 7; Dec. 23, 1933, p. 9.

18. Melvin "Sy" Oliver with Frank Driggs, "Sy Oliver," *Sounds and Fury* 1, 1 (July–Aug., 1965) p. 51; Stanley Dance, *World of Swing*, pp. 129–130, 301; Dempsey J. Travis, *Autobiography of Black Jazz*, pp. 435–438; Albert J. McCarthy, *Big Band Jazz*, pp. 123–126, 159–165; Gunther Schuller, *Swing Era*, p. 781; Duncan P. Sheidt, *Jazz State of Indiana*, pp. 153–174.

19. Albert J. McCarthy, *Big Band Jazz*, pp. 89–90, 94–95; Paul Oliver, *The Story of the Blues*, pp. 116–134; *Chicago Defender*, Sept. 28, 1929, p. 11; Jan. 11, 1930, p. 8; Feb. 22, 1930, p. 9; March 29, 1930, p. 9; April 19, 1930, p. 10; May 24, 1930, p. 12; June 7, 1930, p. 11; Aug. 6, 1930, p. 10; March 17, 1933, p. 8.

20. Albert J. McCarthy, *Big Band Jazz*, pp. 90–92; Gunther Schuller, *Swing Era*, pp. 776–778.

21. Albert J. McCarthy, *Big Band Jazz*, pp. 88–90, 233–234; Gunther Schuller, *Swing Era*, pp. 405–409; Stanley Dance, *World of Swing*, pp. 192–197, 203–211; *Chicago Defender*, March 17, 1933, p. 8; Aug. 26, 1933, p. 7; Dec. 9, 1933, p. 9.

22. Sylvester Rice to Marshall Stearns, Eli Rice file, I.J.S.

23. Sylvester Rice file, I.J.S.; Eli Rice file, I.J.S.; Albert J. McCarthy, *Big Band Jazz*, p. 121; Gunther Schuller, *Swing Era*, p. 781; Stanley Dance, *World of Count Basie*, p. 318; Lewis Porter, *Lester Young*, pp. 6–8.

24. *Chicago Defender*, March 29, 1930, p. 10; Aug. 2, 1930, p. 7; Jan. 31, 1931, p. 9; March 11, 1933, p. 8; Feb. 24, 1934 p. 9; Albert J. McCarthy, *Big Band Jazz*, pp. 121–123, 126–133, Gunther Schuller, *Swing Era*, pp. 787–790; Gunther Schuller, *Early Jazz*, pp. 306–307; Grant Moore file, I.J.S.; Preston Love, "Chords and Dischords," *Sounds and Fury* 1, 1 (July–Aug. 1965) pp. 23, 25; Frank Driggs, "Red Perkins" *Jazz Journal* 17, 11 (Nov., 1964) p. 16, part 2, *Jazz Journal* 17, 12 (Dec., 1964) pp. 16–18; Albert J. McCarthy, "The Nat Towles Story," *Jazz Monthly* 168 (Feb., 1969) pp. 2–7; Lloyd Hunter's "Sensational Mood" and Grant Moore's "Original Dixieland One-Step" are both on *Jammin' For the Jackpot* (NW 217).

25. Floyd Levin, "The Spikes Brothers," *Jazz Journal* 4, 12 (Dec., 1951) pp. 14–15; John Bentley and Ralph W. Miller, "West Coast Jazz in the Twenties," *Jazz Monthly* 5, 3 (May, 1959) pp. 4–5; Albert J. McCarthy, *Big Band Jazz* pp. 168, 172–174; *Chicago Defender*, Sept. 28, 1929, p. 10; Oct. 19, 1929, p. 10.

26. Lionel Hampton with James Haskins, *Hamp*, pp. 33–53; Milt Hinton and David Berger, *Bass Line*, pp. 46–47; Albert J. McCarthy, *Big Band Jazz*, 176–177; Gunther Schuller, *Swing Era*, pp. 166–171, 181, 393; *Chicago Defender*, July 19, 1930, p. 9; Oct. 11, 1930, p. 7; Oct. 25, 1930, p. 5; Nov. 8, 1930, p. 7; Nov. 29, 1930, p. 7; Jan. 7, 1933, p. 6; Jan. 27, 1933, p. 7, July 7, 1934, p. 6.

27. Compare charts in Gunther Schuller, *Early Jazz*, p. 281 and *Swing Era*, p. 781; Nathan W. Pearson, Jr., "Political and Musical Forces . . . Kansas City," *Black Music Research Journal* 9, 2 (Fall, 1989) pp. 181–183; Nathan W. Pearson, Jr. *Goin' To Kansas City*, pp. 68–69, 77–113; Leroy Ostransky, *Jazz City*,

pp. 136–146; Ross Russell, *Jazz Style in Kansas City*, pp. 77–87, 118; Albert J. McCarthy, *Big Band Jazz*, pp. 100–106, 138, 144–145; Frank Driggs, "Kansas City and the Southwest," in Nat Hentoff and Al McCarthy, *Jazz*, pp. 199–202, 204–209.

28. Keg Johnson file, I.J.S.; Budd Johnson file I.J.S.; Frank Driggs, "Kansas City and the Southwest', in Nat Hentoff and Al McCarthy, *Jazz*, pp. 191–225; Albert J. McCarthy, *Big Band Jazz*, pp. 100–103, 105–106, 136–138, 139–140.

29. Frank Driggs, "Kansas City and the Southwest," in Nat Hentoff and Al McCarthy, *Jazz* p. 203, 212–214; Albert J. McCarthy, *Big Band Jazz*, pp. 141–144, 145–150; Nathan W. Pearson, Jr. *Goin' To Kansas City*, pp. 154–160.

30. Frank Driggs, "Clarence Love," *Jazz Monthly* 5, 10 (Dec., 1959) pp. 7–8.

31. Frank Driggs, "Tommy Douglas," *Jazz Monthly* 6, 2 (April, 1960) pp. 7–8.

32. Frank Driggs, "Andy Kirk's Story," in Martin Williams, *Jazz Panorama*, pp. 119–128; Frank Driggs, "Don Albert," *Jazz Monthly* 5, 5 (July, 1959) pp. 4–6; Leonard Feather column on Don Albert in *Melody Maker* (Sept. 4, 1934) in Don Albert file, I.J.S.; Albert J. McCarthy, *Big Band Jazz*, pp. 135–138, 141–144, 145–150; Frank Driggs, "Kansas City and the Southwest," in Nat Hentoff and Al McCarthy, *Jazz*, pp. 203, 212–214.

33. Albert J. McCarthy, *Big Band Jazz*, pp. 99-102; Frank Driggs, "Kansas City and the Southwest," pp. 209–210; Gunther Schuller, *Early Jazz*, pp. 299–303. Five Trent sides were reissued on two different collections called *Territory Bands* (Historical HLP24) and (Classic Jazz Masters CJM10). "Black and Blue Rhapsody" (1928), "After You've Gone" (1930), and "I've Found A New Baby" are on *Sweet and Low Blues* New World (NW 256).

34. Frank Driggs, "Kansas City and the Southwest," in Nat Hentoff and Al McCarthy, *Jazz*, pp. 202–207; Albert J. McCarthy, *Big Band Jazz*, pp. 104–106, 135–136; Gunther Schuller, *Early Jazz*, pp. 293–298, 303–306, 312–317; Count Basie with Albert Murray, *Good Morning Blues*, pp. 22-23, 107–155; Walter Page file, I.J.S.; Oran Page file, I.J.S.; Frank Driggs, "Walter Page," *Jazz Review* 1 1 (Nov., 1958) pp. 13–14; Jimmy Rushing with Frank Driggs, "Jimmy Rushing's Story," *Evergreen Review* (April, 1966) pp. 65–67; Don Gazzaway, "Before Bird Buster," *Jazz Monthly* 7, 11 (Jan. 1962) pp. 7–8; *Chicago Defender*, Jan. 17, 1931, p. 7; Nathan W. Pearson, Jr., *Goin' To Kansas City*, pp. 68–69, 126–134.

35. Frank Driggs, "Andy Kirk's Story," in Martin Williams, *Jazz Panorama*, pp. 119–128; Albert J. McCarthy, *Big Band Jazz*, pp. 242–246; Gunther Schuller, *Swing Era*, pp. 350–367; Nathan W. Pearson, Jr. *Goin' To Kansas City*, pp. 59–63; Sally Placksin, *American Women in Jazz*, (New York: Wildview Books, 1982) pp. 44–45. "Dallas Blues" (Oct. 9, 1930) is on *Jammin' For The Jackpot*, (NW 217).

36. Frank Driggs, "Don Albert," *Jazz Monthly* 5, 5 (July, 1959) pp. 4–6; Albert J. McCarthy, *Big Band Jazz*, pp. 107–109; Gunther Schuller, *Swing Era*, pp. 798–799; Sam Charters, *Jazz: New Orleans*, pp. 111, 74, 84; Nathan W. Pearson, Jr., *Goin' To Kansas City*, p. 41.

37. Albert J. McCarthy, *Big Band Jazz*, p. 109; Gunther Schuller, *Swing Era*, pp. 799–802. "Blues of Avalon" (Sept. 13, 1937) is on *Jammin' For The Jackpot* (NW 217).

38. David Chevon, "Riverboat Music From St. Louis," *Black Music Research Journal* 9, 2 (Fall, 1989) pp. 170–177; Albert J. McCarthy, *Big Band Jazz*, pp. 113–120, Gunther Schuller, *Swing Era*, pp. 782–786; Jerome Don Pasquall, Frank Driggs and Thornton Hagert, "Jerome Don Pasquall," *Jazz Journal* 17, 4 (April, 1964) pp. 23–24; Douglas Hague, "Ed Allen," *Jazz Journal* 11, 1 (Jan., 1958) pp. 11–14; Bartlett D. Simms, "Jazz In St. Louis," *Record Changers* (Nov., 1945) pp. 4–5, 30; Ed Crowder and A.F. Niemoeller, "Dewey Jackson, St. Louis Jazzman," in Art Hodes and Chadwick Hansen, *Selections From the Gutter* pp. 210–211; Harry Dial, "Drums on the Mississippi," in Art Hodes and Chadwick Hansen, *Selections From the Gutter*, p. 212; Jack Bradley, "Honey Bear, Gene Sedric," *Coda* 5, 10 (May, 1963) p. 21.

Bibliography

Allen, Walter C. *Hendersonia: The Music of Fletcher Henderson and his Musicians.* Highland Park, N.J.: Walter C. Allen, 1973.

Allen, Walter C., and Brian Rust. *King Joe Oliver.* London: Jazz Book Club, 1957.

Anderson, Jervis. *Harlem. The Great Black Way.* London: Orbis, 1982.

Armstrong, Louis. *Satchmo: My Life in New Orleans.* New York: Prentice Hall, 1954.

Badger, R. Reid, "James Reese Europe and the Prehistory of Jazz," *American Music* (Spring, 1989): 48–67.

Banks, Paul, with Frank Driggs. "Paul Banks Tells His Story." *Jazz Journal* 11, 8 (Aug. 1958): 4–5.

Barnouw, Erik. *A Tower In Babel.* New York: Oxford University Press, 1966.

Basie, Count, as told to Albert Murray. *Good Morning Blues, The Autobiography of Count Basie.* New York: Random House, 1985.

Bentley, John, and Ralph W. Miller. "Andrae Nordskog: Record Man." *Jazz Monthly* 5, 3 (May 1959): 8–9.

———. "West Coast Jazz in the Twenties." *Jazz Monthly* 7, 3 (May 1961): 4–7.

Berger, Morroe, Edward Berger, and James Patrick. *Benny Carter: A Life in American Music.* Metuchen, N.J.: Scarecrow Press, 1982.

Bernhardt, Clyde. *I Remember: Eighty Years in Black Entertainment, Big Bands, and Blues.* Philadelphia: University of Pennsylvania Press, 1986.

Blake, Eubie. Interview with the author. Brooklyn, N.Y., Nov. 15, 1971.

Blesh, Rudi, and Harriet Janis. *They All Played Ragtime.* New York: Oak Publications, 1971.

Bradford, Perry. *Born with the Blues.* New York: Oak Publications, 1965.

Bradley, Jack. "Honey Bear, Gene Sedric 1907–1963." *Coda* 5, 10 (May 1963): 21.

Brunn, H.O. *The Story of the Original Dixieland Jazz Band.* Baton Rouge: Louisiana State University Press, 1960.

Buerkle, Jack V., and Danny Barker. *Bourbon Street Black.* New York: Oxford University Press, 1973.

Bushell, Garvin, with Nat Hentoff. "Garvin Bushell and New York Jazz in the 1920s." Part 2, *Jazz Review* 2, 2 (Feb. 1959): 9–10.

BIBLIOGRAPHY

Bushell, Garvin, with Mark Tucker. *Jazz from the Beginning*. Ann Arbor: University of Michigan Press, 1988.

Calloway, Cab, and Bryant Rollins. *Of Minnie the Moocher and Me*. New York: Thomas Y. Crowell, 1976.

Carner, Gary. *Jazz Performers: An Annotated Bibliography of Biographical Materials*. New York: Greenwood Press, 1990.

Castle, Vernon, and Irene Castle. *Modern Dancing*. New York: World Syndicate Co., 1914.

Charters, Samuel. *Country Blues*. New York: Rinehart, 1959.

――――. *Jazz: New Orleans, 1885–1957*. Rev. ed. New York: Oak Publications, 1963.

Charters, Samuel, and Leonard Kunstadt. *Jazz: A History of the New York Scene*. New York: Doubleday, 1962.

Chevan, David. "Riverboat Music from St. Louis and the Streckfus Steamboat Line." *Black Music Research Journal* 9, 2 (Fall, 1989): 153–180.

Chicago Commission on Race Relations. *The Negro in Chicago: A Study of Race Relations and a Race Riot*. Chicago: University of Chicago Press, 1922.

Chicago Defender. (Weekly) entertainment pages from March 1910 to April 1936.

Chilton, John. *A Jazz Nursery: The Story of the Jenkins' Orphanage Jazz Bands*. Chicago: Chicago Public Library, 1980.

――――. *Who's Who of Jazz*. Philadelphia: Chilton Book Co., 1972.

Chudacoff, Howard P., and Judith E. Smith. *The Evolution of American Urban Society*. 3d ed. Englewood Cliffs, N.J.: Prentice Hall, 1988.

Clayton, Buck, with Nancy Miller Elliott. *Buck Clayton's Jazz World*. New York: Oxford University Press, 1987.

Collier, James L. *Duke Ellington*. New York: Oxford University Press, 1987.

――――. *Louis Armstrong: An American Genius*. New York: Oxford University Press, 1983.

――――. *The Making of Jazz*. Boston: Houghton Mifflin, 1978.

Congdon, Richard. "Great Scott." *Record Changer* (Sept. 1953): 6–7.

Cruse, Harold. *The Crisis of the Negro Intellectual*. New York: Morrow, 1967.

Dance, Stanley. *The World of Count Basie*. New York: Da Capo, 1980.

――――. *The World of Duke Ellington*. New York: Scribner's, 1970.

――――. *The World of Swing*. New York: Da Capo, 1979.

Darensbourg, Joe, with Peter Vacher. *Jazz Odyssey: The Autobiography of Joe Darensbourg*. Baton Rouge: Louisiana State University Press, 1988.

Divine, Robert A., et. al. *America Past and Present*, 3rd ed. New York: Harper Collins, 1991.

Dixon, Robert M.W., and John Goodrich. *Recording The Blues*. London: Studio Vista, 1970.

Dodds, Warren "Baby," with Larry Gara. "The Baby Dodds Story." Parts 2–4, 6. *Jazz Journal* 8, 6–8, 8, 8, 10 (June–August, October 1955): 4–5, 8–10, 4–5, 26–27.

Dodge, Roger Pryor. "Bubber." *HRS Society Rag* (Oct. 1940): 10–14.

Bibliography

Drake, St. Clair, and Horace R. Cayton. *Black Metropolis: A Study of Negro Life in a Northern City.* Rev. ed. New York: Harcourt Brace, 1970.

Driggs Frank, "Don Albert." *Jazz Monthly* 5, 5 (July, 1959): 4–6.

———. "LaForest Dent." *Jazz Journal* 12, 5 (May, 1959): 2–3.

———. "Red Perkins and His Dixie Ramblers." Parts 1–2 *Jazz Journal* 17, 11–17, 12 (Nov.–Dec. 1964); 14–16, 16–18.

———. "Walter Page, About My Life in Music." *Jazz Review* 1, 1 (Nov. 1958): 12–15.

———. "Tommy Douglas." *Jazz Monthly* 6, 2 (April 1960): 4–8.

DuBois, W. E. B. *The Philadelphia Negro.* New York: Schocken, 1967.

Eberly, Philip K. *Music in the Air: America's Changing Tastes in Popular Music, 1930–1980.* New York: Hastings House, 1982.

Ellington, Edward K. "Duke." "Jazz As I Have Seen It." Part 4, *Swing* (June, 1940): 11, 22.

Erenberg, Lewis A. *Steppin' Out: New York Nightlife and the Transformation of American Culture, 1890–1930.* Westport, Conn: Greenwood Press, 1981.

Europe, James Reese, "A Negro Explains Jazz." *Literary Digest* (April 26, 1919): 28.

Fass, Paula S. *The Damned and the Beautiful: American Youth in the 1920s.* New York: Oxford University Press, 1977.

Fernett, Gene. *Swing Out: Great Negro Dance Bands.* Midland, Mich.: Pendell Publishing, 1970.

Floyd, Samuel A., Jr., ed. *Black Music in the Harlem Renaissance.* New York: Greenwood Press, 1990.

Foster, George "Pops," with Tom Stoddard. *Pops Foster: The Autobiography of a New Orleans Jazzman.* Berkeley: University of California Press, 1971.

Fox, Ted. *Showtime at the Apollo.* New York: Holt, Reinhart and Winston, 1983.

Franklin, John Hope. *From Slavery to Freedom.* 6th ed. New York: Alfred A. Knopf, 1988.

Gazzaway, Don. "Before Bird—Buster." *Jazz Monthly* 7, 11 (Jan. 1962): 4–8.

Gelatt, Roland. *The Fabulous Phonograph* Philadelphia: Lippincott, 1955.

Gillespie, Dizzy. Interview with the author. Pembroke, N.C., April 7, 1985.

Gleason, Ralph J. *Celebrating the Duke and Other Heroes.* New York: Delta, 1977.

Goldfield, David R., and Blaine A. Brownell. *Urban America: From Downtown to No Town.* 2d ed. Boston: Houghton Mifflin, 1990.

Grove, Thurman, and Mary Grove. "Cecil Scott and His Bright Boys." Parts 1–2. *Jazz Journal* 6, 12; 7, 1 (Dec. 1953, Jan. 1954): 29–30, 3–4.

Gulliver, Ralph. "The Band from Columbus: Sammy Stewart and His Orchestra." *Storyville* 48 (Aug.–Sept. 1973): 213–217.

Gushee, Lawrence. "How the Creole Band Came To Be." *Black Music Research Journal* 8, 1 (1988): 83–100.

———. "New Orleans-Area Musicians on the West Coast, 1908–1925." *Black Music Research Journal* 9, 1 (1989): 1–19.

Hadlock, Richard. *Jazz Masters of the Twenties.* New York: Macmillan, 1965.

BIBLIOGRAPHY

Hague, Douglas. "Ed Allen." *Jazz Journal* 11, 1 (Jan. 1958) 11–14.

Halker, Clark. "A History of Local 208 and the Struggle for Racial Equality in the American Federation of Musicians." *Black Music Research Journal* 8, 2 (Fall 1988): 207–211.

Hammond, John. *On Record*. New York: Ridge Press, 1977.

Hampton, Lionel, with James Haskins. *Hamp*. New York: Warner Books, 1989.

Handy, W.C. *Father of the Blues*. New York: MacMillan, 1941.

Hansen, Chadwick C. "Social Influences on Jazz Style: Chicago, 1920–30." *American Quarterly* 12, 4 (Winter 1960): 493–497.

Harper, Emerson "Geechie," with Bertrand DeMeusy. "Leroy Smith and His Band." *Jazz Monthly* 170 (n.d.): 5–7.

Harris, Michael W. *The Rise of Gospel Blues: The Music of Thomas Andrew Dorsey in the Urban Church*. New York: Oxford University Press, 1992.

Haskins, Jim. *The Cotton Club*. New York: Random House, 1977.

Hegamin, Lucille, and Leonard Kunstadt. "The Lucille Hegamin Story." *Record Research* 39 (Nov. 1961): 3–7.

Hennessey, Thomas J. "Chicago's Black Establishment." *Journal of Jazz Studies* 2, 1 (Dec. 1974): 15–45.

Henri, Florette. *Black Migration: Movement North, 1900–1920*. New York: Doubleday, 1975.

Hentoff, Nat. *Jazz Is*. New York: Avon, 1978.

Hentoff, Nat, and Albert J. McCarthy. eds. *Jazz*. New York: Reinhart, 1959.

Hines, Earl. "How Gangsters Ran the Band Business." *Ebony* 4, 11 (Sept. 1949): 40–47.

Hinton, Milt, and David G. Berger. *Bass Line: The Stories and Photographs of Milt Hinton*. Philadelphia: Temple University Press, 1988.

Hodeir, Andre. *Jazz: Its Evolution and Essence*. New York: Grove Press, 1956.

Hodes, Art, and Chadwick Hansen. eds. *Selections from the Gutter*. Berkeley: University of California Press, 1977.

Hoefer, George. Booklet of notes for *The Sound of Harlem*. Columbia C3L 33.

———. "Jimmy Harrison, Forgotten Giant." Parts 1–2. *Jazz* 2, 5–6 (June, July–Aug. 1963): 10–12, 12–13.

Holmes, Harold, with John Norris. "Harold Holmes, His Story." *Coda* 4, 4 (Nov. 1961): 23–24.

Houghton, Bernard. "Joe Smith: A Biography and Appreciation." *Jazz Journal* 18, 12 (Dec. 1965): 18–19, 44.

Howard, Buddy. "Old Cotton Pickers Band Could Outrock Moderns." *Downbeat* 9, 11 (June 1, 1942): 8.

Howard, Paul L. and Berta Wood. "Paul Leroy Howard." Part 1, *Jazz Journal* 10, 11 (Nov. 1957): 6–8.

Huggins, Nathan I. *Harlem Renaissance*. New York: Oxford University Press, 1971.

Institute of Jazz Studies, (I.J.S.) Rutgers University-Newark, N.J. clippings files on various musicians.

Bibliography

Johnson, James Weldon. *Black Manhattan*. New ed. New York: Atheneum, 1969.

Jones, Claude, with David Ives. "Claude Jones." *Jazz Journal* 15, 6 (June, 1962): 13–14.

Jones, Claude, with John E. Mann. "Claude Jones, Fragment of an Autobiography." *Jazz Monthly* 8, 1 (March, 1962): 3–4.

Jones, Leroi. *Blues People*. New York: William Morrow, 1963.

Jones, Max, and John Chilton. *Louis: The Louis Armstrong Story*. Boston: Little, Brown and Co., 1971.

Judd, Anne. "Barney Goin' Easy." *Jazz Journal* 20, 9 (Sept. 1967): 4–7.

Kay, George W. "The Springfield Story," in McKinney Cotton Pickers file, IJS.

Keck, George R., and Sherrill V. Martin. *Feel the Spirit: Studies in Nineteenth-Century Afro-American Music*. New York: Greenwood Press, 1988.

Kenney, III, William H. "Jimmie Noone: Chicago's Classic Jazz Clarinetist." *American Music*, 4, 2 (Summer, 1986): 145–158.

Kinkle, Roger D. *The Complete Encyclopedia of Popular Music and Jazz, 1900–1950*. New Rochelle: Arlington House, 1974.

Kirk, Andy, with Amy Lee. *Twenty Years on Wheels*. Ann Arbor: University of Michigan Press, 1989.

Knight, Athelia. "In Retrospect, Sherman H. Dudley: He Paved the Way for T.O.B.A." *The Black Perspective in Music*, 15, 2 (Spring, 1987): 153–181.

Kunstadt, Leonard. "Eugene Sedric—Gentleman Musician." *Record Research* 53 (Sept. 1963): 3–5.

Lambin, Maria W. and Leroy S. Bowman. "Evidences of Social Relations as Seen in Types of New York City Dance Halls." *Journal of Social Forces* 3 (1924–1925): 285–291.

Lax, John. "Chicago's Black Jazz Musicians in the Twenties: Portrait of an Era." *Journal of Jazz Studies* 1, 2 (June 1974): 197–127.

Leiter, Robert D. *The Musicians and Petrillo*. New York: Bookman Associates, 1953.

Leonard, Neil. *Jazz and the White Americans*. Chicago: University of Chicago Press, 1962.

Levin, Floyd. "The Spikes Brothers—A Los Angeles Saga." *Jazz Journal* 4, 12 (Dec. 1951): 12–15.

Lewis, David Levering. *When Harlem Was in Vogue*. New York: Knopf, 1981.

Lewis, Ed, with Frank Driggs. "Kansas City Brass, The Story of Ed Lewis." Parts 1–2. *Jazz Review* 2, 4; 2, 9 (May, Oct. 1959): 16–18, 23–26.

Lomax, Alan. *Mr. Jelly Lord*. New York: Grove Press, 1950.

Love, Preston. "Chords and Dischords." *Sounds and Fury* 1, 1 (July–Aug. 1965): 22–28, 59–60, 63–64.

Lynd, Robert, and Helen Lynd. *Middletown: A Study in Modern American Culture*. New York: Harcourt, 1929.

McCarthy, Albert J. *Big Band Jazz*. New York: G.P. Putnam's Sons, 1974.

———. "The Nat Towles Story." *Jazz Monthly* 168 (Feb. 1969): 2–7.

BIBLIOGRAPHY

McLean, Albert F. *American Vaudeville as Ritual*. Lexington: University of Kentucky Press, 1965.

Madison, Bingie, with Bertrand DeMeusy. "Biography of a Career." *Jazz Monthly* 10, 7 (Sept. 1963): 7–10.

Meeker, David. *Jazz in the Movies*. New Rochelle: Arlington House, 1977.

Metcalf, Louis, with Derrick Stewart-Baker. "Louis Metcalf." Part 1, *Jazz Journal* 19, 11 (Nov. 1966): 15–16.

Morris, Ronald L. *Wait Until Dark: Jazz and the Underworld 1880–1940*. Bowling Green, Ohio: Bowling Green University Press, 1980.

Murray, Albert. *Stomping the Blues*. New York: McGraw-Hill, 1976.

Nash, Gary B., et. al. *The American People: Creating a Nation and a Society*. New York: Harper and Row, 1990.

Ogren, Kathy J. *The Jazz Revolution: Twenties America and the Meaning of Jazz*. New York: Oxford University Press, 1989.

Oliver, Melvin "Sy," with Frank Driggs. "Sy Oliver." *Sounds and Fury* 1, 1 (July–Aug. 1965): 49–51.

Oliver, Paul. *The Meaning of the Blues*. New York: Collier, 1960.

———. *Savannah Syncopators: African Retentions in the Blues*. New York: Stein and Day, 1970.

———. *The Story of the Blues*. Philadelphia: Chilton Book Co., 1969.

Osofsky, Gilbert. *Harlem: The Making of a Ghetto*. New York: Harper and Row, 1968.

Ostransky, Leroy. *Jazz City: The Impact of Our Cities on the Development of Jazz*. Englewood Cliffs, N.J.: Prentice Hall, 1978.

Ottley, Roi. *New World A-Coming*. New York: Literary Classics, 1943.

Pasquall, Jerome Don, with Frank Driggs and Thornton Hagert. "Jerome Don Pasquall." Parts 1–2. *Jazz Journal* 17, 4; 17, 5 (April, May 1964): 22–24, 21–23.

Pearson, Nathan W. Jr. *Goin' To Kansas City*. Champaign: University of Illinois Press, 1987.

———. "Political and Musical Forces That Influenced the Development of Kansas City Jazz." *Black Music Research Journal* 9, 2 (Fall, 1989): 181–192.

Peiss, Kathy. *Cheap Amusements: Working Women and Leisure in Turn-of-the-Century New York*. Philadelphia: Temple University Press, 1986.

Pittman, Booker, with Frank Driggs. "Booker Pittman." *Coda*, 6, 3 (Oct. 1963): 8–9.

Placksin, Sally. *American Women in Jazz*. New York: Wideview Books, 1982.

Porter, Lewis. *Lester Young*. Boston: Twayne, 1985.

Priestly, Brian. *Jazz on Record: A History*. New York: Billboard Books, 1991.

Raichelson, Dick. Notes to *West Coast Jazz—v. 1*. Arcadia 2001.

———. Notes to *Chicago in the Twenties, v. 1, 1926–1928*. Arcadia 2011.

Ramsey, Jr., Fredric, and Charles E. Smith. eds. *Jazzmen*. New York: Harcourt, Brace, 1939.

Bibliography

Rhodes, Todd, with Thurman Grove and Mary Grove. "Todd Rhodes—Then and Now." *Jazz Journal* 6, 2 (Feb. 1953): 18–20.

Riis, Tom. *Just Before Jazz: Black Musical Theater in New York, 1890–1915.* Washington: Smithsonian Institution Press, 1989.

Robb, F. H., ed. *The Intercollegian.* Chicago, 1927.

Rushing, Jimmy, with Frank Driggs. "Jimmy Rushing's Story." *Evergreen Review* (April 1966): 64–70.

Russell, Ross. *Jazz Style in Kansas City and the Southwest.* Berkeley: University of California Press, 1971.

Russell, Tony. *Blacks, Whites, and Blues.* New York: Stein and Day, 1970.

Rust, Brian. *Jazz Records, 1897–1942.* New Rochelle, N.Y.: Arlington House, 1978.

St. Cyr, Johnny. "Jazz As I Remember It." Parts 3–4. *Jazz Journal* 19, 11; 20, 1 (Nov. 1966, Jan. 1967) 6–7, 9, 14–16.

Schafer, William J. *Brass Bands and New Orleans Jazz.* Baton Rouge: Louisiana State University Press, 1977.

Schafer, William Jr., and Johannes Riedel. *The Art of Ragtime.* Baton Rouge: Louisiana State University Press, 1973.

Scheidt, Duncan. *The Jazz State of Indiana.* Pittsboro, Ind.: Duncan Scheidt, 1977.

———. "Speed Webb." *Sounds and Fury* 1, 2 (Sept.–Oct. 1965): 46–52.

Schoener, Allon. ed *Harlem on My Mind.* New York: Random House, 1968.

Schuller, Gunther. *Early Jazz.* New York: Oxford University Press, 1968.

———. *The Swing Era.* New York: Oxford University Press, 1989.

Shapiro, Nat, and Nat Hentoff. *Hear Me Talkin' To Ya.* New York: Rinehart and Co., 1955.

Shor, Russ. "Charlie Gaines." *Storyville* (Dec. 1976–Jan. 77): 45–50.

Simmen, Johnny. "The Lem Johnson Story." *Jazz Journal* 20,12 (Dec. 1967): 16.

Simmns, Bartlett J. "Jazz In St. Louis." *Record Changer* (Nov. 1945): 4, 5, 30.

Sklar, Robert. *Movie-Made America.* New York. Random House, 1975

Smith, Buster, with Don Gazzaway. "Conversations with Buster Smith," Part 1 *Jazz Review* 2, 12 (Dec. 1959): 18 22.

Smith, Charles Edward. Booklet to *History of Classic Jazz.* Riverside RD-005.

Smith, Russell, with Anne Judd. "A Portrait of Russell Smith," *Jazz Journal* 20, 4 (April, 1967): 5–7.

Smith, Willie "the Lion." Interview with the author. New Brunswick, N.J., Nov. 8, 1971.

Southern, Eileen. *The Music of Black Americans.* New York: Norton, 1971.

Spear, Allan H. *Black Chicago: The Making of a Negro Ghetto, 1890–1920.* Chicago: University of Chicago Press, 1967.

Spencer, Onah L., and Amy Lee. "The Purest Trumpet Tone of All." *Downbeat* Aug. 1, 1943; 13.

Stearns, Marshall and Jean Stearns. *Jazz Dance.* New York: Macmillan, 1968.

Steiner, John. Booklet to *The Sound of Chicago* Columbia C3L 32.

Stewart, Rex. "Coleman Hawkins." *Downbeat* May 19, 1966: 23–25.

BIBLIOGRAPHY

Tirro, Frank. *Jazz: A History*. New York: Norton, 1977.

Travis, Dempsey J. *An Autobiography of Black Jazz*. Chicago: Urban Research Institute, 1983.

Tucker, Mark. *Ellington: The Early Years*. Urbana: University of Illinois Press, 1991.

Ulanov, Barry. *Duke Ellington*. New York: Creative Age Press, 1946.

Wang, Richard. "Researching the New Orleans-Chicago Jazz Connection." *Black Music Research Journal* 8, 1 (1988): 101–112.

Welburn, Ron. "James Reese Europe and the Infancy of Jazz Criticism." *Black Music Research Journal* 7 (1987): 35–44.

Wells, Dickie with Stanley Dance. *The Night People*. Boston: Crescendo Publishing, 1971.

Williams, Martin. *Jazz Panorama*. New York: Collier, 1964.

Williams, Stanley R. "Fess," with Harrison Smith. "The Fess Williams Story." *Record Research*, n. 15 (Oct.–Nov. 1958): 1–5.

Wilmer, Valerie. "The Lee Young Story." *Jazz Journal* 14, 1 (Jan. 1961): 3–5.

Wilson, Teddy, with Tom Scanlon. "The Impeccable Mr. Wilson." *Downbeat* 26, 2 (Jan. 22, 1959): 18–21.

Writer's Project, (WPA), oral history files on "The Negro in Illinois" presently housed in the Carter G. Woodson branch of the Chicago Public Library.

Index

Adams, Ted, 113, 134
Adolphus Hotel, 118–119
Aeolion record label, 43
African musical roots, 16
"After You've Gone," 188, 197
Aiken, Buddy, 46, 54
Aiken, Gus, 46, 54, 100
"Ain't Misbehavin'," 100, 140, 142
Alabama State College, 150
(The) Alabamians, 75, 141
Albany, New York, 96
Albert, Don, 119, 135, 152, 154
Alcorn, Alvin, 154
Alger Bass Band, 183
Allen, Ed, 62, 120
Allen, Henry "Red," 143
Allen, Jasper "Jap," 116, 151
Allen, Moses, 109
Allen, Walter C., 177, 189–190
"Alligator Hop," 39
Alston, James, 106
Amarillo, Texas, 116
American Conservatory of Music, 23
American Federation of Musicians, 148;
    Local 208, 23, 67–69, 148; Local 10,
    69, 147–148
"Amos N' Andy," 126, 131
Anderson, Cat, 150
Apex Club, 74
Arcadia Ballroom, 71, 147
Arment, Alex, 23
Armstrong, Alpha Smith, 141
Armstrong, Lil Hardin, 39, 52, 77–78, 91,
    176
Armstrong, Louis, 30, 34–35, 39, 51,

61–62, 67–68, 70, 73–83, 88–89,
    91–92, 94–95, 100, 112, 119, 128,
    130–131, 135, 140–143, 147, 148,
    150–151, 154, 174–176, 180–181, 189;
    Hot Five, 60, 67, 75–80, 83, 87, 128,
    176; Hot Seven, 75, 78; Savoy Ballroom
    Five, 78
Atkins, Boyd, 119
Atlanta, Georgia, 19, 30, 51, 83, 103, 108,
    134
"Atlanta Lowdown," 108
Atlanta University, 83, 108
Atlantic City, New Jersey, 50, 99, 104, 122,
    143, 189
"Auburn Avenue Stomp," 108
Austin, Cuba, 149
Austin High Gang, 40, 81
Austin, Lovie, 70
Austin, Texas, 116

Bailey, Bert, 62
Bailey, Buster, 36, 52, 90–91
Bailey, "Professor" Ed, 40
Baker, Shorty, 154
"Ballin' the Jack," 74
Ballrooms. See Dance halls (and check
    specific locations)
Baltimore, Maryland, 16–17, 50, 97,
    104–105, 144
'Bama State Collegians, 150
Banks, Paul, 63–64, 116, 152
Barbarin, Paul, 143
Barefield, Eddie, 113–114, 136, 142, 148,
    150, 153, 193
Barnes, Walter, 73, 81, 129–130, 147, 192;

Royal Creolians, 147
Basie, William "Count," 19, 50, 117–118, 135, 137, 152–153; and his Orchestra, 117–118, 137, 153
Bechet, Sidney, 46
Beiderbecke, Bix, 48, 92, 111–113, 115, 133
Bell, Jimmy, 70, 73
Belton, C. S., 109, 121, 130, 149
Benford brothers, 54
Bernie, Ben, 133
Bess, Druie, 117
Bethune-Cookman College, 109
Bigard, Barney, 76, 125–126
Big band arranged style, 41, 46–48, 60–63, 71–75, 81–83, 87–95, 99–102, 108–112, 115, 117–121, 133–156
Binga Bank, 128, 147
Birmingham, Alabama, 17, 30, 51, 53, 106–107, 150
"Birmingham Breakdown," 111
"Black and Blue Rhapsody," 188, 197
"Black and Tan Fantasy," 126
Black and Tan Fantasy (film), 126
Black and Tan Orchestra, 59
Blackbirds of Paradise, 106–107, 184
Black, Clarence, 73, 76
"Black Maria," 72
Black Patti Troubadours, 19, 50
Black Rock Collegians, 134, 184. See also Montgomery, J. Neal
Black Swan Record Company, 47, 83
Blake, Eubie, 20, 26–27, 43–44, 50, 84, 130
Blakeny, Andrew, 115
"Blue Devil Blues," 118, 188
Blue Devils, 116, 118, 151, 153
Blue Moon Chasers, 116
Blue Rhythm Band, 125, 127, 137, 144, 148. See also Mills Blue Rhythm Band
Blues, 16, 20–21, 24, 40–47, 50–54, 63–65, 72, 105–107, 117–118, 150
"Blues for Avalon," 198
Boarman, George, 22, 24
Bocage, Peter, 35, 61
Boone, Harvey, 190
Boots and His Buddies, 154
"Boot to Boot," 117
Boston, Massachusetts, 90, 104–105, 125, 146
"(The) Boy in the Boat," 100, 182

Bradford, Perry, 34, 46, 166
"Brainstorm," 71
Brashear, George, 90
Brass bands: New Orleans, 20–21; Territory, 3–7, 52–54, 57, 59, 63, 106
Braud, Wellman, 125
Broadway, Danceland, 96
Broadway musicals, 20–22, 44, 84
Brooks, Shelton, 53
Brown, Bill, 124
Brown, Bobbie, 105
Brown, Lawrence, 115, 151
Brown, Milton, 153
Brown, Walter, 64
Brunswick record label, 76, 130
Brymn, J. Tim, 25–26, 43
"Bucktown Stomp," 74
Buffalo, New York, 54, 145
"Bull Blues," 89
Bunch, Frank, 106–107, 184; and his Fuzzy Wuzzies, 106–107
Burke, Ceele, 151
Bushell, Garvin, 18, 46
Butler, Billy, 88
Butterbeans and Susie, 106
Buxton, Iowa, 17
"By the Waters of Minnetonka," 91

Cabarets, 18–19, 21, 23–24, 37, 39–40, 41–42, 44–46, 57–59, 63, 69, 73–75, 81–85, 88–90, 98–101, 115, 123–126, 140–147, 151, 155
Calamese, Alex, 75
Calloway, Cab, 75, 97, 100, 125–127, 131–132, 135–136, 138, 140, 141–145, 147–148, 151, 153, 155; and His Orchestra, 100, 125, 141–142. See also Missourians, the
Camden, New Jersey, 138
Campbell, Edgar, 43, 53
Capitol Palace, 99, 110
Capone, Al, 68–69, 147
Carney, Harry, 86, 105, 125–126, 137
Carolina Cotton Pickers, 150
"Carolina Fox-Trot," 24
Carolina Stompers, 183
Carroll, Diahann, 131
Carruthers, Earl, 137
Carter, Benny, 86, 94–95, 97, 138
Carver, Wayman, 108
Casa Loma Orchestra, 133

Castle, Vernon and Irene, 31–32, 42
" 'Cause I Feel Lowdown," 75
CBS, 131
Celestin, Oscar, 21, 107
Central State University (Ohio), 110
Challis, Bill, 92–93, 115
Chambers, Elmer, 90
"Chant of the Weed," 138
Charleston, South Carolina, 17, 22, 51,
   53–54
Charleston, West Virginia, 17
"Charlie's Idea," 115
Charlotte, North Carolina, 149
Cheatham, Doc, 75, 95, 105, 146
Check and Double Check, 126
Chicago, Illinois, 16, 21–24, 29–30, 34,
   36–42, 46, 49, 53, 55, 57–59, 63–64,
   67–81, 83–84, 86–87, 91, 93, 95, 97,
   99, 102, 110, 114, 120, 125, 128–129,
   133, 141–142, 147–148, 152
"Chicago Breakdown," 75
Chicago Daily News, 73
Chicago Defender, the, 29–30, 67, 68, 69,
   73, 105, 109, 123, 125–126, 160
Chicago Footwarmers, 74
Chocolate Beau Brummels. *See* Whyte,
   Zach
Chocolate Dandies, 111, 134, 171, 178–179
Cicero, Illinois, 147
Cincinnati, Ohio, 29, 36, 112, 146
Circus bands, 17–18, 21, 51, 54–55, 57,
   100
Clark, June, 56, 96, 99, 124
Clark, Pete, 108
Clay, Sonny, 59–60, 114–115, 151, 186
Clayton, Buck, 86
Clef Club, 26, 84
"Clementine," 152
Cleveland, Ohio, 29, 54–56, 103, 110, 145
Clorindy, 25
Cloud, Bob, 108
Club Alabam, 72, 82–85, 87–90, 123–124,
   177
Club 'Bamville, 90
Club Richman, 99
Cobb, Oliver, 154
Cole, Bob, 25
Cole, June, 94
Coleman, Bill, 110–111
Coleridge Taylor School of Music, 23
Coliseum (Chicago), 67

Coliseum Ballroom (Minneapolis), 183
Collective ensemble jazz style, 20–21,
   43–49, 59–60, 64, 73–74, 76–80, 85,
   88–89, 96, 99, 106–107, 114–115, 120,
   143
Collier, James Lincoln, 39, 85, 125, 193
Collins, John, 141
Collins, Lee, 148
Collins, Siki, 119
Columbia record label, 34, 44, 76, 130
Columbia, South Carolina, 106
Columbus, Ohio, 17, 55, 58, 110
Condon, Eddie, 40
Congress Hotel, 133, 148
Connie's *Hot Chocolates*, 100, 140
Connie's Inn, 99–101, 124, 140, 146
Cook, Will Marion, 25–26, 30, 43, 50
Cooke, Charles "Doc," 36–37, 40–41, 55,
   71–73, 76, 81, 147
Cookie's Gingersnaps, 71, 76
Coon, Carlton, 86
Coon-Sanders Nighthawks, 71, 86
"Copenhagen," 92
Cosby, Bill, 131
Cotton Club, 75, 80, 85, 99, 100–101,
   124–126, 142, 145
Cotton Club (Los Angeles), 115, 141, 151
Cotton Club Orchestra Inc., 75, 100, 119.
   See also Missourians, the
Cottrell, Louis, 154
Coy, Gene, 63
Coycault, Ernest "Nenny," 35, 59–60, 114
Crackerjacks, 154
Crawfordsville, Indiana, 54, 100
Crawley, Wilton, 142–143
"Crazy Blues," 34, 46
"Crazy Rhythm," 75
Creagh, Gus, 43
Creath, Charlie, 62, 120
Creole Band, The, 30, 35, 37, 45, 56–59
"Creole Love Call," 126
"Creole Rhapsody," 126
Crooke, Gene, 63
Crump, "Mister" Ed, 51
"Cutie's Blues," 41

Dabney, Ford, 18, 26, 34, 43, 45, 48, 50, 84
Dallas, Texas, 29, 30, 63, 116–118, 152
"Dallas Blues," 197
Dance halls, 20–21, 24, 30–32, 37–38, 42–
   43, 50–53, 55–58, 63, 65, 71–73, 81,

83, 90, 92–94, 96–98, 104, 110–114, 115, 116, 118, 124–125, 128, 132–136, 141–156

Dark Clouds of Joy, 119, 134

Davis, Leonard "Ham," 62, 100, 119

Davis, Meyer, 50

Davis, Miles, 79–80

Dawson, William L., 117

Dayton, Ohio, 111

Dean, Demas, 97

Deas, Eddie, 146

Decca record label, 145

"Deep Henderson," 74

Della Robia Gardens, 108–109

Dent, LaForest, 117

DeParis, Sidney, 100

DePriest, Oscar, 68

Desdunes, Dan, 57

Des Moines, Iowa, 57

Detroit, Michigan, 19, 29, 36–37, 99, 110–111, 148

Dickenson, Vic, 111–112

Dickerson, Carroll, 72–73, 76, 78, 99, 128, 140, 147, 174; and his Symphonic Syncopators, 99

Dickerson, R. Q., 62, 119

"Dicty Blues," 89

"Dippermouth Blues." *See* "Sugarfoot Stomp"

Dixieland Jug Blowers, 106

Dixie Syncopators. *See* Oliver, Joe "King"

Dixon, Charlie, 90

Dixon, Ike, 97

Dodds, Johnny, 39, 68, 74, 76, 78, 81, 148, 164; Washboard Band, 74

Dodds, Warren "Baby," 38–39, 61–62, 76, 176

Dominique, Albert. *See* Albert, Don

Dominique, Natty, 35, 74

"Don't Be That Way," 145, 194

Dorsey, Will H., 22–24, 36

Dorsey Brothers Orchestra, 133

Douglas, Clifford "Boots," 135, 154; Boots and His Buddies, 154

Douglas, Tommy, 152

"Down Home Rag," 43, 165

"Down My Way," 79

Down South Music Company, 88

Drake, St. Clair, 22, 82, 160

Dreamland Ballroom, 71

"Dreamland Blues," 188

Dreamland Cafe, 75, 77

DuBois, W.E.B., 86

Dudley, Sherman H., 19, 30, 50

Dunbar, Paul Laurance, 25

Duncan, Hank, 96

Dunn, Johnny, 46, 57, 90

Durante, Jimmy, 34, 45

Durham, Eddie, 136, 138, 145–146, 153, 193

Dusen, Frankie, 39

Dutrey, Honore, 39

Dyett, Walter, 70

East St. Louis race riot, 45

"East St. Louis Toodle-Oo," 124

Edwards, Eddie, 44

Eighth Illinois National Guard, 17, 23, 57

Eldridge, Roy, 112, 133, 149

"Elephant's Wobble," 64

Elgar, Charles, 23–24, 36–38, 48, 57, 63, 68, 71–73, 76, 147

Elkins, Leon, 151

Ellington, Duke, 50, 75, 80, 82, 85, 90, 99–102, 105, 115, 119, 122–128, 130–137, 139, 140–142, 144–145, 147–148, 150–151, 155, 189–191; and his Orchestra, 122–126, 137, 189

Escudero, Rafael, 90

Europe, James Reese "Jim," 18, 26–27, 31–34, 42–45, 48, 50, 80, 85, 89, 95, 165; Society Orchestra, 27; 369th Infantry Band, 18, 95

European musical norms, 16, 21

Evans, Herschel, 117

Evans, Stump, 74

Evansville, Indiana, 54

Evergreen, Alabama, 17

Excelsior brass band, 20

Fagan, Jay, 96–97

"Fat Babes," 195

Fayetteville, North Carolina, 106

"Feelin' The Way I Do," 89

Fisk Jubilee Singers, 109

Fisk University, 83, 109, 137, 145

Fitzgerald, Ella, 145

Floyd, Troy, 116–117, 119, 151, 154

Fort Dodge, Iowa, 57

Foster, George "Pops," 51, 59, 61–62, 143

Freeman, Bud, 40

Fulbright, Dick, 108

Fuller, Earl's Famous Jazz Band, 45

Gaines, Charlie, 146
Gant, Willie, 27
Garland, Ed, 59
Garland, Joe, 96
Gennett record label, 76, 112, 130
Ghettoes, 15, 19, 22, 25, 28–31, 36, 41, 50, 67–70, 84–87, 115
Gillespie, Dizzy, 78, 107
Gilmore, Buddy, 52
Glaser, Joe, 127, 141
Glenn, Lloyd, 117, 154
Goldkette, Jean, 92–93, 111, 174; Victor Recording Orchestra, 92–93
"Go Long Mule," 92
"Good Feelin Blues," 185
Goodman, Benny, 31, 81, 133, 138, 145–146, 151, 156, 194
Gorham, Jimmy, 146
Grand Terrace, 80, 81, 148
Grand Theater, 23–24, 37
Great Day, 122, 137, 140, 146, 189–190
"Great Migration," 15, 21–22, 25, 28–30, 34–37, 41, 48–49, 51, 56–57, 59–60, 68, 85–86, 116, 156
Green, Abel, 124
Green, Charlie, 57, 90, 94
Greer, Sonny, 105, 123–124
Gregory, Herb, 105
Greystone Ballroom, 111
Gunn, Jimmy, 149
Gushee, Lawrence, 58, 163
"Gut Bucket Blues," 77

Hall, Edmond, 108, 144
Hall, Herb, 154
Hall, Philmore "Shorty," 107
Hallelujah (film), 115
Hammond, John, 146
Hampton, Lionel, 114–115, 151
Handy, W. C., 24, 32, 43–44, 46, 51–52, 54, 57, 89, 106
Hardin, Lil. *See* Armstrong, Lil Hardin
Hardwick, Otto, 123
Hardy, Marion, 141
Harlem, 41–42, 85, 94, 96–101
"Harlem Speaks," 127
Harmon, Paddy, 71, 73, 81
Harris, Arville, 190
Harris, Michael, 160
Harrison, Jimmy, 56, 94, 190
Harrison, Laurence, 75

Hawkins, Coleman, 46, 83, 90–94, 111, 136, 190
Hawkins, Erskine, 150; 'Bama State Collegians, 150
Hayes, Edgar, 137, 144
Hayes, Thamon, 92, 152
"Heebie Jeebies," 77
Hegamin, Lucille, 24
Helena, Arkansas, 63
Henderson, Fletcher, 30, 47–48, 57, 60–61, 63, 68, 72, 74–75, 77, 79, 81–97, 99, 101–102, 108, 111–113, 115, 119, 122–124, 128–129, 133, 135, 137–140, 143, 146, 149, 174–175, 177–180, 189–191, 193–194; and His Orchestra, 82–85, 87–95, 110, 122–124, 137–139, 146, 177–180, 189–190
Henderson, Horace, 137
Herbert, Melvin, 108
Hernandon, Guy, 116
Herriford, Leon, 115
Heywood, Eddie Sr., 106, 149, 181
Hickman, Art, 46
Higginbotham, J. C., 143
Hightower, Lottie, 72, 76
Hightower, Willie, 72
Hightower's Night Hawks, 72, 76
Hill, Alex, 78
Hines, Earl "Fatha," 73–74, 81, 128–129, 148, 150, 152, 195; and his Orchestra, 148
Hinton, Al, 117
Hite, Les, 114, 115, 135, 141, 151
Hite, Mattie, 24
Hodges, Johnny, 97, 104–105, 125–126
Hoefer, George, 166
Holder, Terence "T," 116, 119, 151, 153; Dark Clouds of Joy, 119, 153
Holiday, Billie, 133
Holiday, Clarence, 190
Holland, "Peanuts," 119
Hollywood Club, 123
Hopkins, Claude, 50, 96, 105, 137, 140, 143–144, 146
Horton, Bob, 97
"Hot and Anxious," 137–138
Hot Chocolates, 140
Hot Springs, Arkansas, 183
"Hot-Tempered Blues," 100
Houston, Texas, 30
Howard, Darnell, 76

INDEX

Howard, Paul, 59, 115, 187
Howard Theater, 50
Howard University, 83, 143
"How Come You Do Me Like You Do," 92
Hsio Wen Shih, 82–83, 86, 101, 137, 144
Humes, Helen, 52
Hunter, Lloyd, 113–114, 134, 150–151, 196
Hyder, Doc, 105, 146

"I Can't Get The One I Want," 89
"I Found A New Baby," 152, 188, 197
"I'll See You In My Dreams," 92
Immerman, George and Connie, 99
In Dahomy, 25
"In Dat Morning," 109
Indianapolis, Indiana, 55
"In My Dreams," 114–115
Irvis, Charlie, 125
Irwin, Cecil, 40, 148
"It Don't Mean a Thing If It Ain't Got That
    Swing," 126

"Jackass Blues," 112
Jackson, Alex, 112; Plantation Orchestra,
    112
Jackson, Dewey, 62, 120
Jackson, Quentin "Butter," 112
Jackson, Rudy, 125
Jackson, Tony, 24, 37
Jacksonville, Florida, 108, 147
James, David "Jelly," 96
The Jazz Singer, 128
Jefferson, Hilton, 97
Jenkins Orphanage, 17, 46, 53–54, 100,
    119, 150
Jetr-Pillars Orchestra, 154
Jim Love Orchestra, 183
Johnakins, Leslie, 149
Johnson, Bill, 35, 39, 58, 164
Johnson, Budd, 117–119, 152
Johnson, Charlie, 100, 105
Johnson C. Smith University, 149
Johnson, Deacon, 44
Johnson, Hall, 44
Johnson, Howard, 97, 105
Johnson, James P., 27, 46–47, 50, 56, 96
Johnson, James Weldon, 25
Johnson, J. Rosamond, 25–26, 56
Johnson, Keg, 117, 119, 150, 152
Johnson, Lem, 117
Johnson, Roy, 97, 109
Johnson, Walter, 190

Jones, Clarence, 40–41, 70, 75–76
Jones, Claude, 56, 94, 112, 190
Jones, Davey, 61
Jones, Isham, 40
Jones, Jonah, 52
Jones, Richard M., 35, 69, 77, 176
Jones, Shrimp, 90
Jones, Wardell, 137
Jones, Willie, 112
Joplin, Scott, 20
Jordan, Howard, 53
Jordan, Joe, 36

Kansas City, Missouri, 29, 60, 63–65, 86,
    103, 116, 119, 120, 138–139, 151–153,
    187
Kelly's Jazz Band, 183
Kelly's Stables, 74, 76
Kentucky Club, 84–85, 123–124
Kentucky Jazz Syncopators, 183
Keppard, Freddie, 33, 35–37, 45, 71, 74,
    173
King, Clifford, 73
"King Porter Stomp," 118
Kirby, John, 144
Kirk, Andy, 119, 130, 132, 134, 152–153;
    Dark Clouds of Joy, 119, 132, 134, 153
Kirkpatrick, Don, 97
Knights of Pythias, 17, 22
Krupa, Gene, 81, 133
KVOO, 152

Ladd's Black Aces, 34, 45, 88
Langston, Tony, 37
Lankford, P. B., 62
LaRocca, Nick, 44–45
Lawrence, Charlie, 115
Lee, Buddy, 52
Lee, George E., 64, 116–117, 130, 150
Lee, Julia, 64, 117
Leonard, Harlan, 152
"Let's Start Over," 183
Lewis, Ed, 117, 187
Lewis, Lockwood, 53–54, 97, 141
Lewis, Ted, 97, 142
Lincoln Gardens, 74
Lincoln, Nebraska, 116
"Linger Awhile," 88
Livingston, Fud, 174
Logansport, Indiana, 37
Lombardo, Guy, 133
Long Branch, New Jersey, 189

Los Angeles, California, 29, 35, 59–60, 103, 111, 114–115, 141
Louisville, Kentucky, 22, 36, 51–53
Love, Clarence, 152
Love, Preston, 135
"Low Down on the Bayou," 193
Lunceford, Jimmie, 75, 109, 133, 135–137, 140, 145–146, 152, 153, 194
Lynch, Willie, 183
Lynd, Robert and Helen, 104, 110

MCA. *See* Music Corporation of America
McCloud's Night Owls, 116–117
McKinney, Bill, 56, 110
McKinney, Nina Mae, 128
McKinney's Cotton Pickers, 56, 73, 110–111, 128–129, 132–135, 148–149, 174, 185
McLean, Albert, 19
McPartland, Jimmy, 40
"Madhouse," 195
Madison, Bingie, 96, 144
Mahara's Minstrels, 44, 57
"Mama. Don't Allow," 151
"Mandy, Make Up Your Mind," 61, 112
Manetta, Manuel, 39
Marable, Fate, 61, 63, 100
Marigold Gardens, 114
"Market St. Stomp," 183
Marshall, Kaiser, 90, 94, 189
Mason, Norm, 62
"Memphis Blues," 24, 52
Memphis Jug Band, 106
"Memphis Scronch," 106
Memphis, Tennessee, 19, 23, 30, 51–52, 145, 147
Metcalf, Louis, 62, 95, 119, 125
Metropolitan Theater, 70, 128
Miami, Florida, 108
"Michigan Stomp," 112
Midnight Frolics, 43
Mikell, Eugene, 43, 95
Miley, Bubber, 46, 124–126
Millender, Lucky, 128
Miller, Clarence, 24; Peerless Orchestra, 24
Mills, Irving, 122–127, 138, 141–142, 144, 145, 148, 155, 189–190
Mills Blue Rhythm Band, 138, 141, 144. *See also* Blue Rhythm Band
Mills Brothers, 131
Milwaukee, Wisconsin, 57–58, 113–114

Minneapolis, Minnesota, 57, 113–114, 135, 151
"Minnie The Moocher," 138, 142
"Missouri Squabble," 72
Missourians, the, 75, 100, 141–142, 182
Mitchell, George, 52, 76, 79
Mobile, Alabama, 26, 51, 107–108
Mole, Miff, 112
Monogram Theater, 23
Montgomery, J. Neal, 108–109, 149, 184
"The Mooche," 126
"Mood Indigo," 126, 194
Moore, Clarence "Cosperous," 71
Moore, Grant, 114, 135, 150–152, 196
Moore, Jack, 57
Morgan, Sam, 107
Morris, Thomas, 99
Morton, Benny, 94
Morton, Jelly Roll, 21, 24, 34–35, 37, 59, 68, 76–77, 79–82, 87–88, 90, 143, 147, 176; Red Hot Peppers, 76, 79–80, 87, 176
Morton, Norvel, 174
Mosby, Curtis, 59, 114–115, 151
Moten, Bennie, 63–65, 116–119, 130, 135, 137–139, 142, 153, 188, 193; Kansas City Orchestra, 138–139, 153
"Moten Swing," 193
Motion picture theaters, 18–19, 23–24, 30, 40–41, 49, 70–71, 81, 87, 103–104, 115, 128, 132, 138, 142, 146–147
Motts, Robert T., 23
Mundy, Jimmy, 195
Muncie, Indiana, 104
Music Corporation of America (MCA), 80, 127, 152
Music teachers, 17, 23, 53, 63, 101, 117
Myers, Duncan, 43

Nance, Ray, 148
Nanton, Joe, 125–126
Nashville, Tennessee, 22
Natchez, Mississippi, 129
Nesbitt, John, 111, 149, 185
Nest Club (Chicago), 74
New England Conservatory of Music, 94
New Orleans Rhythm Kings, 40
New Orleans, Louisiana, 16, 20–21, 23–24, 29–30, 34–42, 44–48, 51, 54, 57–63, 65, 68, 72–75, 77–79, 96, 107, 114, 143, 154

Newton, Frankie, 111
New York, New York, 16, 19–20, 24–27,
    29, 31, 34, 41–50, 52, 53, 55, 60, 63,
    68, 70, 72–75, 77, 79–102, 110, 119,
    120, 138–146, 148–149
New York *Age*, 93
Nicholas, Albert, 143
Nichols, Red, 112, 133
Nixon, Teddy, 90–91
Noone, Jimmie, 35, 71, 74, 81, 128, 148,
    175
North Carolina Ramblers, 183

Oberstein, Eli, 132
Okeh record label, 46, 67, 76–77
Oklahoma City, Oklahoma, 116, 124, 153
"Old Man Blues," 151
"Old Man River," 71, 194
Oliver, Joe "King," 34, 36–42, 45, 47–48,
    59–60, 64, 68–69, 73–77, 81–82, 85,
    88, 92, 97, 107, 125, 143, 147, 164,
    175; Creole Jazz Band, 38–41, 47–48,
    60, 64, 68, 73–77, 85, 87–88, 91, 107,
    175; Dixie Syncopators, 74–75, 175
Oliver, Paul, 105, 161
Oliver, Sy, 17, 112, 136–137, 145, 149,
    185, 194
Omaha, Nebraska, 17, 57–58, 103, 113,
    134–135, 150, 152
"(The) One I Love Belongs To Somebody
    Else," 71
101 Ranch Wild West Show, 17
Onward Brass Band, 20
Orendorf, George, 115
"Organ Grinder's Swing," 194
Original Dixieland Jazz Band (ODJB), 34,
    42, 44–45, 47, 56, 64
"Original Dixieland One-Step," 151
Ory, Kid, 35–36, 59–60, 68, 76–78, 170
"Ory's Creole Trombone," 59–60, 170
Ostransky, Leroy, 159
"Overnight Blues," 115
Owl Theater, 36, 128
Oxley, Harold, 127, 145

Pace, Harry H., 44, 47, 52
Pace-Handy Publishing, 44, 47, 52, 124
"Paducah," 111
Paducah, Kentucky, 61
Page, Oran "Hot Lips," 118, 153
Page, Walter, 68, 116–124, 138, 153; Blue
    Devils, 116, 118, 138, 153

Panico, Louis, 40
Pantages circuit, 57
Paramount record label, 76, 130
Parham, Tiny, 75, 81, 148
Paris, Gil, 97
Paris, Tennessee, 106
Parker, Charles, 55, 58
Parker, Charlie, 78
Parrish, Avery, 150
Pasquall, Jerome Don, 62, 73, 94, 119
Pearl Theater, 138, 146
Pekin Inn, 23
Perez, Manuel, 35–37, 48, 61
Perkins, Frank S. "Red," 18, 57, 113–
    114, 121, 134–135, 150–151; Dixie
    Ramblers, 121
Petit, Buddy, 35
Peyton, Dave, 23–24, 36, 68–70, 74–75,
    77, 81, 84, 87, 93, 128, 130, 137, 147,
    173
Perry, Doc, 50, 105
Petrillo, James Caesar, 69, 71, 147–148
Philadelphia, Pennsylvania, 16, 19, 29, 50,
    104–105, 122, 138, 146
Phonograph records, impact of, 28, 32–34,
    38–48, 56–60, 64–83, 86–89, 100,
    103–104, 106–109, 111–115, 117-123,
    130, 135–156
Piano rolls, 25, 33
Pickford Theater, 128
Pinkard, Maceo, 57
Piron, Armand, 21, 46–47
Pittman, Booker, 119
Pittman, Mrs. P. Washington, 63, 117
Pittsburgh, Pennsylvania, 29, 88
Plantation Cafe, 74–75
Plessy vs. Ferguson, 20
"Poet and Peasant" overture, 24
Portland, Oregon, 58
Port Washington, Wisconsin, 76
Poston, Joe "Doc," 74
Powell, Rudy, 86
Prather, Harry, 149
Preer, Andy, 100, 119–120; Cotton Club
    Orchestra, 75, 100, 119–120, 182
"Pretty Baby," 24
Primus, Eugene, 105
Procope, Russell, 94–96
Professionalization of music, 17–27, 84, 95,
    122–136, 155–156
Prohibition, 68, 74, 75, 98–101

"Put It There," 185

Radio, impact of, 68, 75, 86, 97, 103–104,
    108, 120–121, 126, 131–132, 152
"Radio Rhythm," 193
Ragas, Harry, 44
Ragtime, 18–20, 24, 27, 50, 63
Rainey, Gertrude, "Ma," 18
"The Ramble," 115
Ramsey, Fred, 18
Randolph, Irving "Mouse," 62, 119, 154
Randolph, Zilner, 141, 148
Reavey, James, 97
Redman, Don, 60, 64, 68, 71, 73, 78,
    82–83, 88–91, 93–95, 98, 102, 108,
    110–112, 118, 120, 131, 133, 136,
    138–139, 148–149, 174, 177
"Red Summer" (1919), 87
"The Reefer Man," 142
Reeves, George, 23
Reeves, Reuben, 174
Regal Theater, 70, 81, 97, 128, 142
"Reminiscing in Tempo," 127
"Respectables" v. "shadies," 22, 68–71,
    82–83, 160
Rhodes, Todd, 56, 111, 149
Rhone, Happy, 43, 96
Rhythm Club, 99
Rice, Eli, 113–114, 142, 150, 152
Rice, Sylvester, 150
Richmond, Indiana, 76, 112
Richmond, Virginia, 30, 109
Riff, the, 64, 100, 117–118, 137–138
Riis, Tom, 161
Ripley, Ohio, 54
Riverboat bands, 60–63, 120
Robbins, Everett "Happy," 58
Roberts, Luckey, 20, 27, 46, 50
Robichaux, John, 35
Robichaux, Joseph, 21
Robinson, George, 108
"Rock and Rye," 195
Rockford, Illinois, 41
Rockwell, Tommy, 141, 143
Rockwell-O'Keefe Agency, 127
Roseland Ballroom, 80, 83, 88, 91–95, 124,
    143, 190
Ross, Allie, 43, 99
Ross, Alonzo, 97, 108, 136; Deluxe
    Syncopators, 108, 136
Roulette, Vernon, 76

Royal, Marshall, 115
Royal Aces, 116–117
Royal Gardens cabaret, 37, 73
"Rudy Vallee's Fleishman Yeast Hour," 131
"Ruff Scufflin," 117, 187
Rushing, Jimmy, 40, 58, 117, 138, 153
Russell, Luis, 97, 140–141, 143–144, 194
Russell, Ross, 64

St. Cyr, Johnny, 39, 61
"St. James Infirmary," 117
St. Louis, Missouri, 17, 22, 34, 60–63, 65,
    75, 100, 116, 119–120, 125, 154
"St. Louis Blues," 55
St. Louis Merrymakers (Wichita Falls,
    Texas), 116, 117
St. Paul, Minnesota, 58, 61
Sampson, Edgar, 136, 144, 194
San Antonio, Texas, 116, 119, 135, 154
Sanders, Joe, 86
San Francisco, California, 58, 59
Savannah, Georgia, 17
Savoy Ballroom (Chicago), 73, 81, 128–129
Savoy Ballroom (New York), 93, 96–98,
    110, 141, 142, 144–145
Savoy Bearcats, 96–97
Sbarbaro, Tony, 44
"Scandinavian Stomp," 106
Schafer, William J., 20
Schenectady, New York, 97
Schuller, Gunther, 64, 78–79, 100, 124, 137
Scott, Cecil, 56, 97, 110–111, 149; and His
    Bright Boys, 56, 110–111
Scott, Howard, 90
Scott, James, 20
Scott, Lloyd, 56, 97, 110–111
Seattle, Washington, 59
Sebastian, Frank, 115, 141, 151
Sedric, Eugene "Gene," 17, 62, 119
Segregation, 17, 20–21, 29, 35, 51–52, 115,
    118–120, 131–134
Senior Milton, 56
"Sensational Mood," 150–151
"Shanghai Shuffle," 92
Shaw, Artie, 133
Sheet music, 18–21, 24–27, 33, 43, 46–47,
    52, 55, 61–62, 70–72, 88
Sherman, Texas, 116
Shields, Larry, 44
Shoffner, Bob, 58
Show Girl, 122, 190

Shribman, Charles, 124–125
Shuffle Along, 44, 84, 99
Shuffle Inn, 99
Simeon, Omer, 76, 96, 148
Simms, Art, 113
Simpson, Cassino, 148
Sioux Falls, South Dakota, 116
Sissle, Noble, 43–44, 84, 130
Six Brown Brothers, 43, 62, 64, 165
Skeets, Charlie, 96, 143
"Slidus Trombonus," 59, 170
"Slow Motion Blues," 114
"Sluefoot," 71
Smart Set troupe, 19, 50
Smith, Ada "Bricktop," 24
Smith, Buster, 63, 117–124, 136
Smith, Carl "Tatti," 116
Smith, Cricket, 42–43
Smith, Joe, 56, 90, 95, 111, 181
Smith, Leroy, 55, 99, 104, 140
Smith, Major N. Clark, 53
Smith, Mamie, 34, 46, 57–58, 76, 90, 128;
    and her Jazz Hounds, 58
Smith, Russell, 84, 94, 190
Smith, Stuff, 119
Smith, Willie, 137, 146, 194
Smith, Willie "The Lion," 27, 96
Snowden, Elmer, 99, 123–124
"Society Blues," 60, 170
Sodero's Military Band, 170
"Solitude," 127
"Someday Sweetheart," 41
"Sophisticated Lady," 127
"So This Is Venice," 41
Souchon, Edmond, 38
Sousa, John Phillip, 24, 43
Southard, Henry, 59
Spikes, Johnny and Reb, 59–60, 65,
    114–115, 151
Spikes Seven Pods of Pepper, 170
Spivey, Victoria, 63, 183
Sporting houses, 18–19, 21, 24, 31, 50, 65
Springfield, Ohio, 54, 56, 97, 110–111
"Springfield Stomp," 110
"Squabblin'," 118, 188
"The Stampede," 94
"Stardust," 111
Stark, Bobby, 94–95, 190
"Starvation Blues," 117, 187
States Theater, 36
Stecker brothers, 113, 124

Steele, Joe, 97
Stein, Jules, 127
Steiner, John, 174
Stevens Hotel, 73
Stewart, Rex, 92, 94–95, 105, 181, 190
Stewart, Sammy, 55, 68, 70–71, 147, 174
Stewart, "Smiling" Billy, 109, 130, 149
Still, William Grant, 44
"Stompin' At The Savoy," 145, 194
"Stomp If Off," 194
"Stomp Off, Let's Go," 70–71
Stone, Jesse, 64, 116–117, 119, 151; Blue
    Serenaders, 117
"Stop Kidding," 185
Storer College, 88
"Stratosphere," 194
Streckfus brothers, 60–63, 100
Stride piano, 27, 46, 50
"Sugar," 57
"Sugarfoot Stomp" ("Dippermouth Blues"),
    88, 92
Sweatman, Wilbur, 23–24, 36, 42, 45, 50,
    57, 64, 99, 123, 142
"Sweet Georgia Brown," 57
Swift, Hugh, 75
Synco Jazz Band, 56. *See also* McKinney's
    Cotton Pickers

Tall, Sam, 64
Tate, Buddy, 117
Tate, Cicero, 174
Tate, Erskine, 23, 36, 40–41, 52, 70–71,
    75–76, 87, 147, 173–174
Tate, James, 174
Taylor's Dixie Serenaders, 149
Tent shows, 17–19, 21, 51, 106
Terre Haute, Indiana, 108
Teschemacher, Frank, 40, 133
Theater Owner's Booking Association
    (TOBA), 19, 30, 54, 104, 106
Thomas, George "Fathead," 111
Thomas, Joe, 62, 150, 154
Thomas, Walter "Foots," 62, 119
Thompkins, Eddie, 137, 150
Thompson, "Big Bill," 68
Thompson, Creighton, 43
"Tiger Rag," 115
"Tiger Stomp," 115
Tio, Lorenzo, Jr., 40
Tirro, Frank, 89–90
"T.N.T.," 94

"Toby," 193
Tolbert, Skeets, 149
Toledo, Ohio, 55–56
Towles, Nat, 150, 152
Trent, Alphonso, 63, 116, 118–119, 129, 151–152, 188, 197
Triangle Harmony Boys, 106–107
"Trombone Moanin' Blues," 106
Trueheart, John, 97, 105
Trumbauer, Frank, 33, 62, 92, 113, 115
Tucker, Mark, 124–125
Tulsa, Oklahoma, 152
Tuskegee Institute, 17, 53, 107
Tynes, George, 105, 146

University of Illinois, 137
University of Iowa, 137

Vaudeville, 18–19, 21, 23–25, 28, 30, 34–37, 40–43, 45, 48–50, 54–55, 57–59, 64–65, 70–71, 73, 74, 76, 78, 104, 106
Vendome Theater, 52, 101
Vicksburg, Mississippi, 106, 147
Victor record label, 33–34, 42, 44–45, 76, 79–80, 97, 108, 126, 130, 132, 145
Vinson, Ed, 58
Vocalion record label, 76, 130
Vodery, Will, 24, 43, 84

Wade, Jimmie, 40–41, 72, 147
Waifs' Home of New Orleans, 5
Walder, Woodie, 64
Waller, Thomas "Fats," 96, 111, 128, 140
Walker, George, 25
"Wang Wang Blues," 47
Warmack, George, 105
Washburn College, 90
Washington, D.C., 16, 49–50, 97, 104–105, 123, 142
Washington, Jack, 137
Waters, Ethel, 47, 128, 133
WDAF (Kansas City), 86
Weatherford, Teddy, 70
Weaver, George, 57
Webb, Chick, 97–98, 136, 140, 144–145, 194
Webb, Speed, 111–112, 114, 149
Webster, Ben, 117, 153
Wells, Dickie, 52, 110–111
"West End Blues," 112, 185

Western Vaudeville Manager's Association (WVMA), 57
Wetherington, Crawford, 137
Whaley, Wade, 35
Whately, John "Fess," 53–54, 107, 136, 150
Wheeler, Doc, 146
Whetsol, Art, 123
White, Harry "Father," 138, 142, 144
Whiteman, Paul, 46, 55, 71, 88, 93, 132–133, 153
Whyte, Zach, 97, 112, 134–135, 149, 185; Chocolate Beau Brummels, 112, 134
Wichita, Kansas, 116
Wichita Falls, Texas, 116
Wickliffe, John, 53, 57–58
Wiedoeft, Rudy, 33, 62
Wilberforce, Ohio, 56
Wilberforce University, 56, 83, 110, 137
Wilcox, Ed, 137, 145–146
"Wild Waves," 130, 144
William Morris Agency, 127
Williams, Bert, 25–26
Williams, Clarence, 46–47
Williams, Cootie, 108, 126
Williams, Mary Lou, 153
Williams-Piron Music Company, 46–47
Williams, Stanley R. "Fess," 53–54, 96–97, 128, 130, 136, 140, 142, 147; Royal Flush Orchestra, 136
Williams v. Mississippi, 29
Williamson, Charlie, 106, 149, 183
"William Tell" overture, 24
Wills, Bob, 152–153
Wilson, Garfield, 22, 24
Wilson, Teddy, 111–112, 133, 149
Winston-Salem, North Carolina, 19
Wisconsin Music Circuit, 113, 124
Woode, Henri, 150–151
Wooding, Sam, 72, 75, 180
Wright, Lamar, 64, 117

Xenia, Ohio, 54, 56

"Yes, I'm in the Barrel," 77
Youmans, Vincent, 122, 189
Young, Bernie, 113, 141, 148
Young, Lee, 117
Young, Lester, 117, 135–136
Ysaguirre, Bob, 190

Zanesville, Ohio, 145
Ziegfeld, Florenz, 43, 122